A CENTURY OF
BIBLICAL ARCHAEOLOGY

A CENTURY OF
BIBLICAL ARCHAEOLOGY

by
P.R.S. Moorey

The Lutterworth Press
Cambridge

The Lutterworth Press
P.O. Box 60
Cambridge
CB1 2NT

British Library Cataloguing in Publication Data
Moorey, Roger
  A century of biblical archaeology.
  I. Title
  220.93

  ISBN 0 7188 2825 9

Printed in Great Britain by
WBC Print Ltd., Bridgend, Mid Glamorgan.

Contents

Abbreviations

A.A.S.O.R. *Annual of the American Schools of Oriental Research*

A.D.A.J. *Annual of the Department of Antiquities of Jordan*

A.S.O.R. *American Schools of Oriental Research*

B.A. *Biblical Archaeologist*

B.A.R. *Biblical Archaeology Review*

B.A.S.O.R. *Bulletin of the American Schools of Oriental Research*

H.U.C.A. *Hebrew Union College Annual*

I.E.J. *Israel Exploration Journal*

J.S.O.T. *Journal for the Study of the Old Testament*

P.E.F. *Palestine Exploration Fund*

P.E.Q. *Palestine Exploration Quarterly*

P.J. *Palästina-Jahrbuch*

Q.D.A.P. *Quarterly of the Department of Antiquities in Palestine*

Z.A.W. *Zeitschrift für die Alttestamentliche Wissenschaft*

Z.D.P.V. *Zeitschrift des Deutschen Palästina-Vereins*

Acknowledgement

I am most grateful to Dr. Graham Davies for a careful reading of the manuscript. For the final version I am wholly responsible.

Chronological Table

Egypt		Palestine		Mesopotamia
Egypt		*Palestine*		*Mesopotamia*
	AD		AD	
Roman Empire		Roman Empire		Parthians
	BC		BC	
	30		140	
Hellenistic Period (Ptolemaic Dynasty)		Hellenistic Period (Seleucid and Hasmonean dynasties)		Hellenistic Period (Seleucids)
	330		330	
← (Intermittently)		Achaemenid Persian Empire		→
	500		500	
		Babylonian Captivity Iron Age IIB-C (Divided Monarchy)		Neo-Babylonian Period
The Late Period				Neo-Assyrian Period
		Iron Age IIA		Middle Assyrian Period
	1000	(United Monarchy) Iron Age I	1000	Middle Babylonian Period
The New Kingdom		Late Bronze Age II		The Kassite Period
	1500	Late Bronze Age I	1500	
The Second Intermediate The Middle Kingdom		Middle Bronze Age II (IIB-C)		The Old Babylonian Period
		Middle Bronze Age I (IIA)		The Isin-Larsa Period
	2000		2000	
The First Intermediate		Intermediate Period (Early Bronze IV- Middle Bronze I)		The Ur III Period
				The Akkadian Period
The Old Kingdom		Early Bronze Age III		Early Dynasty
	2500		2500	III
		Early Bronze Age II		Early Dynastic II Early Dynastic I
Proto-Dynastic	3000		3000	
		Early Bronze Age I		The Jamdat Nasr Period
		Proto-Urban Period		
				The Uruk Period
Pre-Dynastic		The Chalcolithic Period		
	4000		4000	The Ubaid Period

Maps

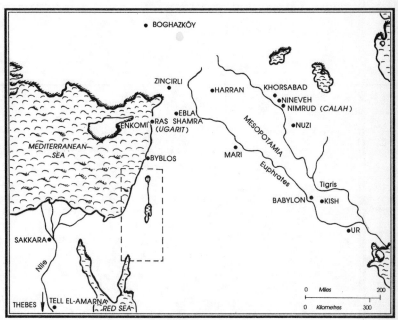

Key Sites outside Palestine

Map II

Hazor

Tell Abu Hawam

Megido

Taanach

Beth-Shan

Dothan

Samaria

Tell el-Farah (North)

Shechem

Tel Qasile

Shiloh

Bethel

Tell en-Nasbeh

Ai

Jericho

Gezer

Gibeon

Tell el-Ful

Beth-Shemesh

Jerusalem

Ramat-Rahel

Dibon

Tell el-Hesi

Tell ed-Duweir (Lachish)

Tell el-Ajjul

Tell Jemmeh

Tell el-Farah (South)

Tell el-Kheleifeh

Key Excavations before 1960

Map III

Dan

Tell Keisan

Dor

Megiddo

Tel Mevorakh

Jezreel

Taanach

Pella

Tell es-Saidiyeh

Tel Michal

Tell Deir Alla

Tel Qasile

Shiloh

Izbet-Sartah

Tell el Umeiri

Aphek

Ai

Tell el-Ful

Sahab

Gezer

Jerusalem

Tel Batash

Heshbon

Ashdod

Tel Miqne

Ashkelon

Tell ed-Duweir (Lachish)

Tell el-Hesi

Deir el-Balah

Tel Masos

Beersheba

Arad

Bab edh-Dhra

Buseirah

Timna

Kuntillet-Ajrud

Key Excavations after 1960

Introduction

This concise historical survey of the relationship between Near Eastern archaeology and Biblical Studies, conventionally termed biblical archaeology, belongs to a series addressed in the first instance to students of theology rather than to archaeologists. But, since it is written by an archaeologist not by a biblical scholar, it inevitably has the bias of that particular side of the relationship. Any book seeking to trace the development of an interdisciplinary subject always runs the risk of over emphasizing one partner at the expense of the other; but with 'archaeology' as the substantive and 'biblical' as the adjective the matter is to some extent prejudged from the outset. This is, moreover, predominantly an historical study of archaeology in relation to the Old Testament rather than the New, for reasons that will become apparent as the survey proceeds. Throughout, it has been necessary to take for granted some knowledge of the course of Old Testament Studies, since 1800, and a general understanding of the procedures of archaeology, as this is an *essay* rather than an exhaustive study of the subject.[1]

In the last thirty years archaeologists have spent much time in seeking to define the special character of their discipline, but relatively little attention has been given in that time to the particular complexities of archaeological research in historic (text-aided) as distinct from prehistoric (textless) periods. This might surprise the layman since one of the sharper tests of the many explanatory models prevalent in the literature of the so-called 'new' archaeology is provided by the confrontation of contemporary texts and mute material evidence. This particular challenge may have been avoided for two main reasons. First, the cautious know that it is impossible to be in firm control both of the textual data and of the evidence of 'dirt' archaeology, whilst the bold prefer to operate in prehistory, where the formulation and testing of models or hypotheses would appear to suffer from fewer restraints. Second, and more relevant here, there has traditionally been a deep-seated mutual suspicion between those who deal mainly, if not exclusively, with the written word, however exiguous that may be in certain periods, and those whose chief concern is with material culture, especially now that recovery and interpretation of it owe so much to the procedures of natural and social scientists. Even in an earlier generation, when archaeologists strove to write historical or cultural rather than anthropological or sociological studies of antiquity, relations were often distant, if not openly hostile.

It is not a coincidence that the most contentious relationships archaeology has had with famous texts have been with two of the world's greatest literary achievements, the Bible and the Homeric Poems: 'biblical archaeology' and 'Homeric archaeology', each with roots deep in nineteenth-century scholarship. In both cases the texts as they stand are not primary historical sources, though they may incorporate them. The problem of authenticity or historicity is fundamental whenever the evidence of these texts is confronted with the evidence of archaeology. But there is a sharp distinction of overwhelming significance for the subject of this survey. The Old Testament is not only central to one major religion, Judaism, and in varying degrees relevant to two others, Christianity and Islam; but it is also unique among religious works of this status in describing a deity who acts in history. To a greater or lesser extent its historicity may be theologically held to be crucial to its message. Thus many of those involved with Near Eastern archaeology since the middle of the last century have come to it, and continue to come to it, through a deep religious involvement with the Bible.

In the last fifty years, archaeologists, and others, not so motivated have come to regard biblical archaeology as a byword for prejudice and unscientific procedures. In this respect it has all too often been assessed rather more than is just from its popular idiocies and blatant shortcomings. These have recurrently obscured its primary achievement in restoring the Bible to the world whence it came after centuries isolated in a cultural vacuum. There has been, as there will continue to be, good, bad and indifferent research and scholarship in biblical archaeology, as in any academic discipline; but it will remain unusually vulnerable to prejudice. It may never avoid the value judgements of those, on the one hand, for whom specific religious beliefs and scholarship are inseparable and, on the other, those for whom such conjunctions are anathema. Nor is it likely that it will for long avoid one of those sporadic bursts of popular enthusiasm for sensational and speculative 'discoveries', which have marked its history.

Biblical archaeology developed primarily as a Christian, indeed it might be said a Protestant, academic discipline. It was pursued by men and women from the western world, predominantly Anglo-Saxon or Teutonic in their attitudes and education, whose research interests had little or no relevance to the indigenous communities of the Near East. The momentum of archaeological investigation for about a century after the first biblical reference was recognized in an extra-biblical text was sustained in the Near East by foreign Christians, some devout, some barely observant, but all from childhood steeped in a literal reading of the Bible to which they turned naturally for analogies and illustrations, if not for direct inspiration. With the end of formal European domination of the region in the middle of this century and most particularly after the creation of the State of Israel, circumstances radically changed, with profound implications for the development of biblical archaeology as an academic discipline.

The vast majority of the Near East's population sees no reason to study the subject at all. Indeed, they positively reject it, as implying support for the modern state of Israel, where, in extreme and understandable contrast, the quest for the biblical past has been pursued with great intensity from the foundation of the State through archaeological investigation. The status of biblical archaeology has been held to be self-evident and beyond question; recent religious and academic challenges have done little to modify this view. In the long run it is these confrontations, rather than academic debates among expatriate archaeologists and biblical scholars, which are likely to determine the fortunes of biblical archaeology well into the next century.

Ashmolean Museum, Oxford, 1990   P.R.S. Moorey

1. See, for example: R.E. Clements, *A Century of Old Testament Study* (revised edition), The Lutterworth Press, 1983; H.D. Lance, *The Old Testament and the Archaeologist*, Philadelphia, 1981; P.R.S. Moorey, *Excavation in Palestine*, The Lutterworth Press, 1983; J.R. Bartlett, *The Bible: Faith and Evidence*, British Museum Publications, 1990.

1

The Birth of Biblical Archaeology (1800-1890)

> In the Near East and neighbouring Egypt everything from the ancient times appears to us as ruins or as a dream which has disappeared ... The archives of Babylon, Phoenicia and Carthage are no more; Egypt had withered practically before the Greeks saw its interior; thus, everything shrinks to a few faded leaves which contain stories about stories, fragments of history, a dream of the world before us (Herder, 1784-91).[1]

In 1800 the Bible stood virtually unchallenged at the centre of the intellectual and religious life of the western world, a unique self-contained legacy from the ancient Near East. The Pentateuch was commonly regarded as the work of Moses and attempts were very seldom made to analyse the composition of the Old Testament historically: 'the criticism of the Old Testament, the dates of the several books, their origin etc., all seem to me undecided, and what Wolf and Niebuhr have done for Greece and Rome seems sadly wanted for Judaea'.[2] Judaea's neighbours were little more than phantoms even to the most learned, seen dimly through the text of the Old Testament, the writings of Josephus and of the more readily accessible Graeco-Roman authors. The inscribed monuments of Near Eastern antiquity, where they survived above ground, were largely unknown or misunderstood; their languages dead. Artists who sought to portray scenes from the Bible, as so many still did, used either a wholly western idiom for costume and setting or else a vaguely oriental imagery blending fantasy with travellers' tales. It was to be one of the greatest triumphs of western scholarship in the nineteenth century to take the Bible out of this isolation, where it had been held for the better part of two thousand years. Systematic fieldwork in Egypt and Western Asia, including pioneer excavations, and brilliant philological scholarship combined to demonstrate how it related to other literatures and religions of the region, which had until then been largely forgotten.

By 1890, when the century of this survey formally opens with Petrie's pioneer excavations at Tell el-Hesi (p. 27) in Palestine, archaeologists and philologists had revealed two distinctive and very early civilizations, one in Mesopotamia (Assyria and Babylonia) and one in Egypt, and shown that their inscriptions might not only be recovered through surface exploration and excavation, but also read. When read they rapidly transformed contemporary understanding of the biblical world. Peoples more akin to the ancient Hebrews, with parallel histories and related customs, suddenly emerged with their own voice. Even more sensationally, historical figures known from the Old Testament appeared in extra-biblical texts. It was no longer possible to accept without question that the origins, religion and society of the peoples of ancient Israel had necessarily been different in kind from those of their neighbours.

Towards a definition of Biblical Archaeology

The earliest archaeological discoveries in Egypt and the Near East coincided with a time when ordinary men and women in the more literate societies of the Christian world were unusually concerned with the authority and integrity of Holy Scriptures. The diffusion of recent scientific discoveries in a Bible-bound generation among the educated and of an older eighteenth-century rationalism among the largely illiterate masses presented all thinking men and women, not only theologians and churchmen, with unprecedented choices. A revolution in the biological and geological sciences in the middle of the nineteenth century, associated above all with the names of Darwin and Lyell, had established the immensity of geological time and the high antiquity of man; concepts as liberating to archaeologists as they were challenging to the authority of Genesis.

At a time when explorers and scholars were seriously engaged for the first time in rediscovery of the ancient Near East, the most vigorous intellectual controversies of the day touched them very closely, whether they liked it or not. At a time when catastrophe and creation were being challenged in favour of evolution and gradualism, when already in some quarters biblical scholarship was beginning to expose inconsistencies and anachronisms in the Old Testament text, both sides in these intellectual controversies looked to the new archaeological discoveries for support. From the outset the freshly revealed and recently deciphered

2

inscriptions of Egypt and Assyria were as likely to be enlisted by the Evangelicals and Traditionalists to authenticate fundamental scriptural truth as by Christian sceptics, by agnostics or by secularists to justify application of the new science of historical source criticism to biblical narratives. The scale and intensity of public interest in Western Europe and North America were consequently remarkable and have rarely been repeated.

It is not easy in such circumstances to distinguish the relative roles of piety and disinterested scholarship among the pioneers. Some, like Edward Robinson, were explicit about their motivation (p. 15), inaugurating a long tradition of active American investigators trained in biblical studies and theology. To others, primarily in England and France, the biblical relevance of their discoveries was largely a matter of indifference or fortunate accident, which brought financial support and academic interest otherwise unlikely to be available. As one of Layard's (p. 8) more cynical friends pointed out to him in 1846:

> The interest about your stones is very great, I hear - and if you can as I before said attach a biblical importance to your discoveries you will come the complete dodge over this world of fools and dreamers; you can get some religious fellow to inspire you with the necessary cant, for which I won't think a bit the worse of you.[3]

The critical importance of this connection in raising public support for field work is reflected in the terms of reference of many of the early societies created to promote and sustain research in Palestine and adjacent regions. Birch's suggestion in 1870 that the first society anywhere created specifically to 'investigate and systematize the Antiquities of the ancient and mighty empires and primeval peoples whose records are centred around the venerable pages of the Bible' should be known as The Society of Biblical Archaeology was 'a stroke of genius, for it appealed not only to philologists, but to theologians of all shades of thought'.[4]

Birch's inaugural lecture to this Society, delivered in London early in 1871, provided an enduring paradigm for the subject:

> [Its] scope is Archaeology, not Theology; but to Theology it will prove an important aid. To all those it must be attractive who are interested in the primitive and early history of mankind; that history which is not written in books nor on paper, but upon rocks and stones, deep in the soil, far away in the desert; that history which is not found in the library or the mart, but which must be dug up in the valley of the Nile, or exhumed from the plains of Mesopotamia.[5]

This definition is as significant for what it does not say as for what it does. This is apparent when it is contrasted with the terms of reference of the short-lived Palestine Exploration Society founded in New York in 1870:

> the work proposed . . . appeals to the religious sentiment alike of the Christian and the Jew . . . Its supreme importance is for the illustration and defense of the Bible. Modern scepticism assails the Bible at the point of reality, the question of fact. Hence whatever goes to verify the Bible history as real, in time, in place and circumstances, is a refutation of unbelief.[6]

This comparison focuses from the start a prevailing dichotomy between the enduring religious, often sectarian, commitment of so many American scholars involved with archaeology in the lands of the Bible and the secular training and disposition of British practitioners, whose more detached attitude is equally evident in the declared aims of the Palestine Exploration Fund established in London in 1865 (p. 19).

Inevitably, in view of the finds then being made and the methods used, archaeology for Birch in 1871 was seen primarily as a matter of the recovery and study of ancient inscriptions, 'the monuments'. Its range in relation to the Bible was as widely defined as might then be imagined, embracing current research in Egypt, in Assyria and Babylonia, in Palestine and in Sinai, as well as in Arabia. Although it has become customary to give priority in histories of biblical archaeology to the pioneers of the systematic study of biblical topography in Palestine (p. 14), they initially contributed more directly to Biblical Studies than to any relationship between archaeology and the Bible. Birch's inaugural lecture to The Society of Biblical Archaeology portrays more accurately the manner in which the subject was conceived by those who participated directly in its most formative years. It is no accident that it was the paradigm to which Albright returned two generations later (p. 67).

The rediscovery of ancient Egypt

It is hard to dispute conventional wisdom which places Napoleon at the head of those who opened the eyes of the western world to the antiquities of the biblical lands. Through his personal initiative scholars accompanied his ill-fated Egyptian Expedition of 1799 to compile the first modern survey of the land and its standing monuments, superbly published in Paris between 1802-25 in the multi-volumed *Description de l'Egypte*. Even more significant was their recovery of the renowned Rosetta Stone, which passed with the spoils of war to the British

Museum. Its bilingual Greek and Egyptian inscription was to provide the key to the decipherment of ancient Egyptian within a generation of its discovery. 'In the success which attended the efforts of the first inquirers to interpret the hitherto occult monuments of Egypt', declared Birch in 1871, 'lay the failure or success of determining the chronology and history; the struggle was over the hieroglyphy, the spoil was the solution of the historical problem. It was then discovered that the Egyptians were not only a highly civilised and most ancient people, but that their history was of the highest importance for the study of Biblical Archaeology'.[7]

Egyptology developed rapidly. Within a decade of Champollion's death in 1829, only years after his brilliant decipherment of Egyptian hieroglyphs, Gardner Wilkinson's superbly illustrated *Manners and Customs of the Ancient Egyptians* (1840), revised for the following generation by Birch in 1878, had made the art and history, beliefs and daily life of ancient Egypt widely known. Meanwhile Lepsius (1810-84), by general consent the greatest Egyptologist after Champollion, had led a Prussian expedition to Egypt and Nubia (1842-45), which retrieved a wealth of fundamental information published between 1845 and 1859 in the twelve monumental volumes of the *Denkmäler aus Aegypten und Aethiopien*. This supplemented the important publications of monuments by Champollion and Rosellini with accurate, if conventionalized, copies of scenes and texts of all periods. Although Lepsius had conducted excavations at the site of the Labyrinth in the Faiyum, and precociously included stratified drawings of sections across the site in his records, it was the Frenchman Mariette (1821-81) who laid the foundations of the Egyptian Antiquities Service, created a National Museum of Antiquities in Cairo, strove to control the wholesale expropriation of antiquities, and excavated many new monuments.

Birch was in no doubt about the significance of this revolution in scholarship.

> So important have been those studies of the synchronistic history of the two nations [i.e. Egypt and Israel], that it will be impossible hereafter to adequately illustrate the history of the Old Testament without referring to the contemporaneous monuments of Egypt; and not alone the history, but the laws, institutions, and even turns of thought and expression, have many points of resemblance in the two nations.[8]

Birch singled out for special notice Champollion's study of Shishak's topographical list of cities at Karnak (Thebes), detailing his campaign into Palestine at the end of the tenth century BC (cf. 2 Chronicles 12:3) and the identification of 'Hebrews' in Egyptian records of the Ramesside period, taken to be relevant to the Exodus narrative.

In 1882 the stated aims of the Egypt Exploration Society at its foundation in London recognized the critical importance of the biblical connection in sustaining the new discipline. The Society was 'to organize expeditions in Egypt, with a view to the elucidation of the History and Arts of Ancient Egypt and the illustration of the Old Testament narrative, so far as it has to do with Egypt and the Egyptians'. Plans for initial fieldwork turned upon hopes of recovering records of the Hebrews' presence in Egypt from mounds in the Delta, identified as the site of the capital of the Land of Goshen. Public interest in the news that Naville (1844-1926) had found the walls upon which the Israelites had laboured for pharaoh at Tell el-Maskhuta (Pithom), served powerfully to promote biblical archaeology in 1883, however, intensely specialists might dispute the identification.

Although he was internationally renowned as an Egyptologist, Naville's interest in fieldwork was confined to the recovery of texts, the longer and more monumental the better, through the use of contractors and engineers to remove the surrounding debris. Petrie (1853-1942), his immediate successor in the service of the Egypt Exploration Society, provided a marked contrast:

> to such a man (Petrie) every potsherd and every brick was pregnant with archaeological significance . . . The aristocratic Naville was willing to spend time on raising historical questions by copying and interpreting inscriptions, but to him the less said about the base work of digging the better, and as to collecting observations on pottery and the like, it might be fitting for the mere scientist, but it was no work for a man trained in the humanities.[9]

The emergence of Petrie in Egypt, as later in Palestine (p. 27), was to mark the beginning of scientific procedures on excavations and in their publication.

However, it was a chance find in 1887 that gave the site of Tell el-Amarna, about 190 miles south of Cairo on the right bank of the Nile, a place of particular significance in the development of biblical archaeology. Peasants digging there for nitrous earth to use as fertilizer revealed the foreign office archives of the pharaohs Amenophis III and IV, of the fourteenth century BC, written in Akkadian, the language of international diplomacy, in the cuneiform script on clay tablets. Disregarded at first even by experts, many were lost before museums in Berlin and London realized their significance and saved between three and four hundred of them. They were to offer a unique record of Egypt's relations with rulers in the Levant and remain unmatched in the archaeological record (p. 41).

The inscriptions of Assyria

It was, however, not so much in the development of Egyptology as of Assyriology that the potential role of archaeology in biblical scholarship first began to be fully apparent, not always in circumstances beneficial in the long run to either discipline. Before 1800, European travellers to Mesopotamia had published observations of lasting value on its distinctive ancient inscriptions and in rare cases had accurately determined the character and location of early sites; but none had the stimulating influence on his immediate successors exercised by Rich (1787-1821) through his researches at the outset of the nineteenth century. He was, and still largely is, most renowned for his pioneer surveys of Babylon and his primitive excavations there. They were celebrated in a verse by Byron, published in 1820, which is the earliest popular recognition of the importance of fieldwork for biblical topography:

'But to resume, - should there be (what may
not
Be in these days?) some infidels, who
don't
Because they can't, find out the very spot
of that same Babel, or because they won't
(Though Claudius Rich, Esquire, some bricks has got,
And written lately two memoirs upon't)'

(*Don Juan*: 5th Canto: *LXII*)

Even more influential was Rich's subsequent study of the site of ancient Nineveh, adjacent to modern Mosul, marked out by the mounds of Nebi Yunus and Kuyunjik, and his copies of the stonecut cuneiform inscriptions at Persepolis in Iran, all published by his widow after his early death. They inspired epoch-making excavations in northern Mesopotamia, a little over a decade after their appearance in print.

Mohl (1806-76), one of the secretaries of the Société Asiatique in Paris, an Arabist with a strong interest in cuneiform inscriptions recovered from Mesopotamia, was convinced by Rich's reports that the time had come not merely to describe and plan the ancient mounds of that region, but also to dig into them. At his instigation a vice-consulate was created at Mosul by the French Government in 1842 to which Botta (1802-70), a French citizen of Italian extraction, was appointed with direct encouragement to undertake excavations in local mounds. Botta had taught himself Arabic when still a schoolboy and had been formally trained in medicine and the natural sciences. He had served early in his career as a ship's doctor, then as a physician in Egypt under Mohammed

7

Ali, before acting as a travelling naturalist for the Louvre in the Red Sea area. In his late thirties, when seeking more permanent, financially rewarding employment, he had entered the French consular service.

After abortive excavations on the mounds of Nebi Yunus and Kuyunjik, those most accessible from Mosul, Botta's attention was diverted to Khorsabad, some ten miles away, where he uncovered the ruins of the palace of the Assyrian king Sargon II (c. 721-705 BC). In 1845 he returned to France with a fine collection of stone sculptures and inscriptions from this palace for the Louvre. Botta first described his excavations in published letters to Mohl; but the French Government then sponsored a fine series of volumes of drawings of the reliefs between 1846 and 1850, which introduced the ancient Assyrians to the modern world in their own imagery. Botta's career soon passed into eclipse. Unlike his British counterparts, he never seems to have been enthralled by his discoveries nor to have profited from the public recognition they brought him.

Close study of the still undeciphered cuneiform inscriptions Botta had brought back to Paris allowed Longperrier to read the name *Sar-gin* in one of them and to identify him with the 'Sargon, King of Assyria' mentioned in Isaiah 20:1 in a paper published in the *Revue Archéologique* in 1848; the first name of an Assyrian King to be correctly read by a modern scholar in an extra-biblical text. Longperrier also read the word *Ashur* and translated correctly about half the title 'Glorious Sargon, King, Great King, King of Kings, King of the country of Ashur'.

In the meanwhile the other great pioneer of archaeological excavation in Assyria, the Englishman Henry Layard (1817-94), had established his reputation. Layard, who had been trained in London as a lawyer, found art and antiquities more to his taste. He abandoned the legal profession in 1839 and set out overland to seek his fortune through family connections in Ceylon, but was diverted into adventurous travels in Iran before being enlisted in 1842 by Sir Stratford Canning, British Ambassador to the Ottoman court at Istanbul for what amounted to secret service work in Mesopotamia, Iran and Turkey. Long familiar with Rich's publications, and fully informed about Botta's discoveries, Layard eventually succeeded in 1846 in persuading Canning to support him, both diplomatically and financially, in his ambition to excavate Nimrud and Nineveh. Layard is representative of many of the pioneer excavators in the Near East, well-educated but not a specialist, courageous and enterprising, widely experienced in dealing with Arabs and Turks. Like Botta before him and many after him, Layard dug as

8

inclination directed, wholly ignorant of the complex structure of ancient mounds, always seeking stone monuments and only recovering the most obvious and spectacular of smallfinds. Where stone sculptures lined mudbrick walls he was able to plan structures, when only mudbrick and mudbrick debris survived he was baffled.

The primary impact of Layard's discoveries was made in London, as Botta's had been in Paris, by Assyrian sculptures shipped home for public exhibition. They captured the nation's imagination through the press and fired the Bible-reading public with an interest that Layard's best-selling *Nineveh and its Remains* (1849) vividly served to reinforce. This lucid, at times dramatically written, book described the ruined Assyrian palaces with their bas-reliefs, monumental lion and bull colossi, paintings and inscriptions, which were still unread at the time of publication. The reliefs brought to life a people who had been the notorious scourge of Israel in the Old Testament. Not the least enthusiastic among Layard's readers were the Evangelicals, who saw the fate of Nimrud and Nineveh proclaimed by the prophets now remarkably confirmed by excavation. Only later would it become apparent that obliteration and abandonment were so common a fate for ancient Near Eastern cities that their modern condition was neither proof of divine retribution against the Assyrian oppressor nor of prophetic wisdom.

In the later 1840s confusion existed over the proper identification of Nineveh on the ground, though Rich had been right a generation earlier. Botta, in his publications of excavations at Khorsabad, consistently referred to it as Nineveh. In 1849 Layard entitled his popular account of work at Nimrud as if it were Nineveh, whilst as late as 1850 Rawlinson concluded that all three formed 'a group of cities which in the time of the Prophet Jonah were known by the common name of Nineveh'.[10] Soon after this it became clear that the twin mounds of Kuyunjik and Nebi Yunus (traditional site of Jonah's grave) concealed the ruins of ancient Nineveh; that Nimrud was ancient Kalah; and that Khorsabad was ancient Dur-Sharrukin: royal city of Sargon.

In the years between 1845 and 1850, as archaeological discovery produced more and more cuneiform inscriptions, and improved copies of those long known became available, success with decipherment of the texts accelerated in England, France and Germany. It was the royal inscriptions of Assyria, generally referred to for a generation or more as 'the monuments', though some were on small baked-clay cylinders, prisms and tablets, which were to provide key information for linking the infant science of Assyriology with Old Testament studies, at least in the more liberal centres of learning. The Books of Kings and the historical chapters of Isaiah held crucial bilingual clues, since they preserved in Hebrew the names of Assyrian kings like Tiglath-Pileser and Esarhaddon, and of major cities like Nineveh and Nimrud (Kalah), now appearing for the first time in the ancient Assyrian language (Akkadian). Longperrier's perspicacity has already been noted (p. 8); but already in 1846 Hincks, an Irish clergyman whose role in the decipherment is too easily overlooked, had read the names of Nebuchadnezzar (II) and his father on inscribed clay building bricks recovered from Babylon by earlier travellers.[11]

In 1849 Layard published *The Monuments of Nineveh* (First Series) and in 1851 *Inscriptions in the Cuneiform Characters* at the same time as Botta's great volumes appeared (p. 8). In 1850 the British scholar Rawlinson (1810-95), generally acknowledged to be the 'Father of Assyriology', published his translation of the inscription on the Black Obelisk of Shalmaneser III of Assyria (c. 859-24 BC) excavated by Layard at Nimrud in 1846 and then brought to the British Museum. Although he deciphered many of the proper names of cities and countries correctly, he read the crucial Assyrian royal name as *Te-men-bar*, dating him to the thirteenth or twelfth century BC, and did not read correctly the names of Hazael of Damascus or Jehu 'son of Omri'. But within a year this epoch-making link with the Old Testament had been established.

Grotefend (1775-1853), who had been the first to decipher the Old Persian cuneiform script a generation earlier, now suggested in a German learned journal dated in August 1850 that the Assyrian king's name should be read as Shalmaneser, as in 2 Kings 17:13, the ruler now known as Shalmaneser V (c. 726-22 BC). Then in England, in *The Athenaeum* of 27 December in the same year, Hincks argued that 'Yua, son of Humri' was to be identified with Jehu of Israel, which meant that the Shalmaneser of the Black Obelisk must have reigned a century before the ruler of the same name who, in the Old Testament, was credited with the sack of Samaria. It is now generally agreed that the phrase 'son of Omri' in the Assyrian text, which is incorrect if read literally, should be taken to mean simply 'son of the house of Omri' or 'Israelite'.

Historical links between the newly discovered Assyrian monuments and the Old Testament now began to emerge one after the other as more and more texts were translated. In the course of 1851 Rawlinson found the names of Hezekiah, Jerusalem and Judah in an inscription of King Sennacherib (c. 704-681 BC) on a colossal, stone, human-headed bull recovered by Layard from Nineveh (cf. 2 Kings 18-19; Isaiah 36-37), though in his publication of it in 1853 Layard used a translation of Sennacherib's annals independently prepared by Hincks. It was again Hincks who in 1852 read the names of Menahem of Samaria on carved stone slabs from the North-West Palace at Nimrud, proving that they had been commissioned by the Assyrian king 'Pul' of 2 Kings 15-19, though Hincks thought this was Sargon II rather than Tiglath-Pileser (cf. 2 Kings 15:29), whose coronation name as King of Babylon was 'Pulu'.

Thus it was that, within a decade, Assyriology had developed to the point where Layard, toward the end of his second great popular description of his researches, *Discoveries in the Ruins of Nineveh and Babylon* (1853), was able to list in Assyrian and Hebrew some fifty-five rulers, cities and countries appearing both in the Old Testament and in the newly discovered Assyrian texts. It was as much a tribute to his own enterprise as to the linguistic skills of Hincks and Rawlinson. Four years later the appearance in London of *Inscription of Tiglat Pileser I, King of Assyria* as translated by Sir Henry Rawlinson, Fox Talbot Esq., Dr Hincks and Dr Oppert, four independent and almost identically deciphered translations of the same text, established Assyriology internationally as a reputable academic discipline.

If Layard and Rawlinson had come to dominate the first stage in the history of the relationship between archaeology and the Bible, the full impact of this new interdisciplinary study was realised in the next generation in the remarkable, but sadly brief, career of George Smith (1840-76). Today he is best remembered for a lecture he delivered to the recently founded Society of Biblical Archaeology in London during December 1872, when he announced his discovery of an inscribed clay tablet from Nineveh (Kuyunjik) in the collections of the British Museum containing an account of a flood roughly parallel to the biblical story of Noah and the Ark.

Smith's career to this point had been hardly less memorable than his discovery. He had been apprenticed at the age of fourteen to be trained as an engraver of bank notes, at which he proved a master. Meanwhile he developed a passion for the study of the historical books of the Old Testament by reading accounts of the new discoveries in Assyria and of the decipherment of cuneiform. He haunted the galleries of the British Museum, where the relevant finds were exhibited and came to the attention of the Keeper, Samuel Birch, and his colleagues who soon realized that this young man was astonishingly well-informed about their collections. Late in 1866 Smith was appointed as an assistant in the Museum to be employed as a 'repairer', charged with searching the tablet collections for joins between fragments.

In his own account Smith particularly emphasized his biblical interests: 'in 1866 seeing the unsatisfactory state of our knowledge of those parts of Assyrian history which bore upon the history of the Bible, I felt anxious to do something towards settling a few of the questions involved.'[12] Smith was probably the first to appreciate fully the complexity of the problems presented by any attempt to provide a detailed correlation of the chronological information offered by Assyro-Babylonian sources and the historical books of the Old Testament. He admitted his own bewilderment in his publication of one of the fundament texts, *The Assyrian Eponym Canon* (1875): 'I must confess that the view held by the two Rawlinsons and the German professors is more consistent with the literal statements of the Assyrian inscriptions than my own, but I am utterly unable to see how the biblical chronology can be so far astray here as the inscriptions lead one to suppose'.[13]

The public, however, would not leave Smith to such academic debates. So compelling was their interest in his apparent proof of the veracity of the Old Testament Flood story, always a touch-stone amongst biblical fundamentalists, that a London newspaper, *The Daily Telegraph*, paid his expenses for renewed excavations at Nineveh in quest of the missing fragments of the Babylonian Flood Legend. Remarkably, in two seasons of work there in 1873-74, he succeeded in recovering an almost complete version, but at the cost of his life. He died of dysentery on an aborted trip in 1876. It is for ever to be regretted that enthusiasm rather than judgement led someone of his nervous temperament, without knowledge of Arabic or experience of excavation in the Near East, to be cast in a role for which he was so ill-equipped when, in a museum among tablets, he has had so few peers. He was, in Sayce's merited tribute, 'a genius with the heaven-born gift of divining the meaning of a forgotten language . . . '

Assyriology and Old Testament Studies

By co-incidence Smith's renowned discovery of the 'Flood Tablet' brought into focus for the first time the potential relevance of the new discoveries to the Pentateuch at just the moment when Wellhausen (1844-1918), in Germany, was challenging conventional views of its authorship and historicity as they had never been challenged before. Although this is not the place to enter into any detail about Wellhausen's profound and enduring impact on Biblical Studies,[14] it is necessary to define its relation to biblical archaeology in the 1880s. Speculations about the prehistory of the Hebrews and their religion were not then new to German biblical scholarship, but Wellhausen, as in so much he wrote, gave coherence and a fresh intellectual cutting edge to the subject. He fortified doubts about the historical context of the Patriarchs and Moses not only, as is well known, through literary and historical source-critical analysis ('Higher Criticism') of the Pentateuch, but also through conjectures about primitive religion based upon the assumption that pre-Islamic bedouin traditions were the best available comparative source for understanding the earliest stages of Hebrew religion.

It has sometimes been held against him that his only resort to external sources was to anthropological analogies of such dubious validity, when the new archaeological discoveries were so much more to the point. But this distorts the historical perspective, for at the time his ideas were being developed, in the earlier 1870s, virtually nothing was known of the archaeology of Palestine and little of the new information coming from Assyro-Babylonian and Egyptian texts bore directly upon the problems with which he was primarily concerned. It was not until some decades later, when Wellhausen's 'Documentary Hypothesis' had largely triumphed in academic circles in Europe, that information from the new discoveries came to play an important role in the comparative studies of ancient Near Eastern literature and mythology which were to have a seminal effect in Old Testament studies (p. 46). Biblical archaeology was initially involved neither in the genesis nor in the sustenance of Wellhausen's hypothesis, but in attempts to counteract it. His powerful challenge to orthodoxy and tradition gave added impetus to the quest for inscriptions which might be cited in favour of the historicity of the Patriarchal narratives and the authorship of Moses (see p. 40).

At the time when Wellhausen's views were still filtering through academic circles in Germany, the evidence of 'the monuments' was still used cautiously by biblical scholars more to elucidate than to authenticate the scriptures. This trend is well-illustrated by a single major work written and revised through the later 1870s and earlier 1880s: Schrader's *Die Keilinschriften und das Alte Testament*. Schrader (1836-1908), Professor of Theology at Jena and then of Oriental Languages in Berlin, was the father of Assyriology in Germany. He had long been a student of cuneiform and was well read in the works of the pioneers of decipherment. His authority at this stage was enhanced by his own substantial contributions to Old Testament criticism in which he took a cautious, but highly informed, stance.

His book is a model of nineteenth century German scholarship. Its range of reference and argument make it an epitome of the relationship at the time of publication between the results of archaeological research and the Old Testament text. It is arranged as a commentary on those passages in the Old Testament, book by book, most illuminated by the new discoveries. As its English translator remarked, 'not a stray article in any magazine or journal, English or continental, appears to have escaped the unslumbering attention of the author and every scrap of evidence on the subject in hand is cautiously sifted and its significance duly estimated'.[15] Although the emphasis of the book was naturally controlled by texts available to him, Schrader presented for the first time an agenda as relevant today as it was over a century ago. He had most to say of foreign relations under the Divided Monarchy and of regnal chronology at that time; of the relation of Assyro-Babylonian literature to the earlier chapters of Genesis; of historical topography; of Hebrew lexicography and Assyriology. Indeed, the consistency of the primary lines of inquiry from Schrader in the 1880s to Albright in the 1930s is striking. Schrader, however, does not enter into the already emerging controversies over the historicity of the Patriarchal and Conquest narratives for which, as has already been noted, neither 'the monuments' nor yet 'dirt' archaeology offered sufficiently relevant information. Progress in that direction was to come from research in the biblical homeland, not on its periphery.

The quest for Biblical Palestine

In Assyria the pioneers were engaged upon an exciting enterprise of discovery which fired the public imagination from the start. In Palestine they were recovering a lost landscape, well-known to a Bible-reading generation on the printed page, but divorced by almost two thousand years from a real world. Fundamental as their research was to be for scientific study of ancient Palestine, it lacked the glamour of buried monuments and rediscovered languages. In the first decade of the nineteenth century two discoveries in particular, both in Transjordan, anticipated the golden age of biblical topography. In 1802 Seetzen rediscovered Gerasa and Philadelphia-Amman and in 1809 Burckhardt put Petra back upon the map, a quarter of a century before Burgon's (1813-88) couplet fixed this remarkable site in the popular consciousness:

> Match me such marvel save in Eastern clime,
> A rose-red city half as old as time (*Petra*:132).

By common consent the American Edward Robinson (1794-1863) is the founding father of modern study of biblical topography. He was a professional scholar, reared in the puritan tradition in a family of farmers and preachers.

> As in the case of most of my countrymen, especially in New England, the scenes of the Bible had made a deep impression upon my mind from the earliest childhood; and afterwards in riper years this feeling had grown into a strong desire to visit in person the places so remarkable in the history of the human race. Indeed in no country of the world, perhaps, is such a feeling more widely diffused than in New England.[16]

Robinson's training and academic experience before he went to Palestine had been varied. He started academic life as a tutor in mathematics and Greek, before studying at Andover Theological School in Massachusetts, a centre of conservative biblical scholarship, under Moses Stuart, a brilliant Hebraist, whom he later assisted as an instructor in Hebrew and biblical literature. From 1826 to 1830 he studied in Germany, where at Berlin, Göttingen and Halle he became acquainted with the best of contemporary German research then little known in America. In the following decade as the foremost American biblical scholar of the day he translated *A Hebrew and English Lexicon of the Old Testament* by Gesenius, with whom he had studied in Germany, and wrote his own *A Greek and English Lexicon of the New Testament*. In 1837 he accepted the professorship of Biblical Literature in the Union Theological Seminary at Boston on condition he might travel to the Holy Land before starting work. 'I had long meditated the preparation of a work on biblical geography, and wished to satisfy myself by personal observation as to points on which I could find no information in the books of travellers.'[17]

Although, when he departed for a stay of two and a half months in Palestine in 1838, Robinson had with him the works of two outstanding recent travellers, Burckhardt and Laborde, his main academic guides epitomized an older tradition. In Latin he had the Dutchman Adrian Reland's *Palestine illustrated by Ancient Monuments* (1714), 'which next to the Bible is the most important book for travellers in the Holy Land'. This monumental handbook, critically digesting all relevant information from earlier sources, had been much neglected until his use of it. The other book, von Raumer's *Palästina*, was of a similar kind, but published at Leipzig in 1835. For his second journey, again of just over two months, in 1852, Robinson had a new masterpiece of German scholarship, still partly in proofsheets. It was by his former teacher Carl Ritter, who had made full use of Robinson's own report on his first journey, published in 1841, for his multi-volumed comparative geography of Palestine and the Sinaitic Peninsula: *Vergleichende Erdkunde der Sinai-Halbinsel von Palästina u. Syrien* (Berlin, 1848-55).

It was Robinson's distinction in 1838 to be the first fully equipped scholar to pursue the historical geography of the Bible on the ground. As he freely acknowledged, he was greatly indebted to his travelling companion Eli Smith, one of his former pupils who had become a missionary in the Levant. Smith's experience of the area and most particularly his fluency in Arabic allowed the kind of interrogation of the local population that was best designed to establish the extent to which the old nomenclature had clung to the landscape of Palestine, since an exact record of modern Arabic place-names was vital to a proper study of ancient topography. Fortunately tradition proved to have been singularly tenacious. Two principles guided their research:

> The *first* was, to avoid as far as possible all contact with the convents and the authority of the monks; to examine everywhere for ourselves with the Scriptures in our hands; and to apply for information solely to the native Arab population. The *second* was, to leave as much as possible the beaten track, and direct our journies and researches to those portions of the country which had been least visited.[18]

The combination of Robinson's biblical knowledge and Smith's local expertise revolutionised knowledge of the biblical landscape. Although neither man was an epigrapher nor yet an archaeologist, indeed both were ignorant of the significance of *tells*, their contribution to the foundations of biblical archaeology was fundamental. Robinson's study of biblical topography and criticism of tradition was remarkably successful. Nearly all his identifications of biblical sites and his topographical notes have stood the test of time. His correct identification of over a hundred sites was significant as much for the critical method it successfully demonstrated as for its direct contribution to knowledge. As Alt later remarked, 'in Robinson's footnotes are buried the errors of generations'. He was less successful in his treatment of the Holy Places in Jerusalem, where his tendency to denigrate everything 'monkish' prejudiced his views.

In any attempt not only to unravel, but to interrelate, the various strands in nineteenth century intellectual life that contributed most directly to the genesis of biblical archaeology it is of some interest to recall that Birch, in his inaugural lecture to the Society of Biblical Archaeology in 1871, did not mention Robinson, for Robinson had not discovered any 'monuments'. After considering the recently deciphered Assyrian and Egyptian texts, Birch next went on to consider Phoenician: 'the precision attained by the researchers into the inscriptions of that country and the philology of the Phoenicians have played by no means an unimportant part in the study of Biblical Archaeology.'[19] Already in the middle of the eighteenth century Swinton and Barthélemy, notably the latter, had used recently discovered Graeco-Phoenician bilingual inscriptions in Cyprus and Malta to attempt a decipherment of Phoenician. It was not, however, until the appearance in 1837 of *Scriptura linguaeque Phoeniciae monumenta quotquot supersunt* (Leipzig) by Gesenius that all accessible documents were presented in accurate copies and deciphered with outstanding skill and fine judgement. This pioneering phase of Phoenician studies culminated in Movers's multi-volumed *Das phonizische Altertum* (1841-56), an encyclopaedic summary of the available information on the Phoenicians and their colonies.

It was not only the recovery and study of inscriptions that gave Phoenicia a primary role in these formative years. It was in Phoenicia that the first excavations in Syro-Palestine were conducted, albeit very primitive in technique. In 1860 Renan (1823-92), who already enjoyed a European reputation as a man of letters and an expert on Semitic languages and Near Eastern archaeology, arrived in Beirut as archaeological envoy of Napoleon III at a time when French military occupation of the Lebanon followed Druse massacres of local Christians. Not for the first time, nor the last, soldiers provided labour for excavations, whilst the French navy offered transport for men, up and down the Phoenician coast, and for antiquities back to France. In a year of intense activity, Renan directed four campaigns, each based on a single centre: Aradus, Byblos, Tyre and Sidon. He also travelled into Galilee and southern Palestine. He gathered a vast amount of information on standing monuments, rock-cut tombs and surviving visible inscriptions, rapidly published in a book which remains the foundation stone of Phoenician archaeology, *Mission de Phénicie* (Paris, 1864). A more famous, indeed at the time notorious, by-product of this trip was Renan's *Vie de Jésus* (1863), the first life of Christ to present a vivid and accurate picture of the land in which he had lived.

In the generation between Robinson's first journey in 1838 and the creation of the Palestine Exploration Fund in London in 1865 numerous other travellers pursued points he had raised, but only Tobler and Guérin worked systematically and professionally on the same scale. Tobler was a Swiss doctor, a scientist and sometime politician, who became involved by chance in the exploration of Palestine after a pleasure trip there in 1835. Although Robinson's work has largely come to overshadow Tobler's achievement in the English-speaking world, he found ways to accomplish much, particularly where Robinson had been restricted by the relative brevity of his visits or his Protestant prejudice against the Holy Places of Jerusalem and its surroundings. As a result of his extended visit in 1845-46 and briefer ones in 1857 and 1865, Tobler produced numerous fundamental works on the topography of this area, whilst later in life he brought his unique, firsthand knowledge to bear in pioneer editions of the early pilgrims' records of their travels.

Guérin's first visit to Palestine in 1852 coincided with Robinson's second. By the time of his last, in 1875, sponsored teamwork was already beginning to supersede the enterprise of even the most industrious individuals, short of time and money as they so often were. Guérin visited Palestine five times, in 1852 and 1854 when he concentrated mainly on welltrod ground, then in 1863, 1870 and 1875 on special missions supported by the French Government that produced his many volumed study of the *Geography of Palestine* (1868-75). In retrospect this may be seen to have complemented to a remarkable degree the contemporary survey initiated by the Palestine Exploration Fund. However, he made relatively few identifications which have survived subsequent scrutiny, as his critical method was markedly inferior to Robinson's.

By now the first excavations had been undertaken in Palestine. In 1850-51 a French explorer de Saulcy, had investigated the so-called Tombs of the Kings in northern Jerusalem. In 1863 he returned with a permit from the Ottoman government for excavation, which in the event was little more than earth clearance. He mistakenly attributed these tombs to the Davidic Dynasty. They are now accepted as being the tombs described by Josephus (*Antiq.* XX.17-96, 101; *War* V.147) with three pyramids built about AD 50 by Queen Helena of Adiabene, a convert to Judaism from a petty kingdom in the northeast of modern Iraq.

When the Palestine Exploration Fund was founded in London in 1865 it preceded the Society for Hellenic Studies by some fourteen years, the Egypt Exploration Society by twenty. Public demand for its establishment drew strength from various sources, among them excitement over the discoveries in Mesopotamia, concern at the desperate state of the Holy Places first called to public attention by the Crimean War (1853-56), and the vigorous controversy arising from the publication of Darwin's *On the Origin of Species* in 1859. This, particularly, accelerated a demand for scientific reaffirmation of the authority of the Bible and a close examination of the origins of the Christian faith. At this stage the tradition of scholarly exploration in Palestine had had little impact on the public at large, since it had produced neither trophies for public museums nor yet inscriptions of immediate biblical relevance.

The way forward was opened up in 1864 when Baroness Burdett Coutts, wishing to provide Jerusalem with a good water supply, arranged for Captain Wilson of the Royal Engineers to draw up an accurate survey of the city and its neighbourhood.

The Palestine Exploration Fund was not a religious society, though inevitably created under the patronage of the established Church of England. It was intended to provide 'for the accurate and systematic investigation of the archaeology, topography, geology and physical geography, natural history, manners and customs of the Holy Land, for biblical illustration'. As an early prospectus pointed out, the researches of previous explorers

> have been partial and isolated, and their results in too many cases discrepant with each other. What is now proposed is an expedition of thoroughly competent persons in each branch of research, with perfect command of funds and time, who should produce a report on Palestine which might be accepted by all parties as a trustworthy and thoroughly satisfactory document.[20]

The Fund's initial programme of research was twofold, to produce a modern map of the entire country and to begin the systematic investigation of Jerusalem through excavation, not least since Robinson had neglected its topography. A preliminary survey by Wilson led eventually to the outstanding Survey of Western Palestine by Stewart, Condor, Kitchener and others between 1871 and 1878. Their great map, scaled one inch to the mile, published in 1880, covers 6000 square miles, from a point near Tyre to the Egyptian desert, from the Jordan to the Mediterranean. Some 9000 Arabic place names were recorded, though not always accurately, and the map was followed by a series of complementary *Memoirs*. These included the earliest archaeological site by site reconnaissance of the region, compromised by an imperfect understanding of the significance of *tells*, many of which were omitted. Debatable as some of the new biblical identifications would prove to be, and unsatisfactory as the archaeology might be without any means of dating sites, there has never been any doubt that in the long run this enterprise contributed more to the right understanding of the archaeology and ancient history of Palestine than any other single undertaking in the nineteenth century. Later surveys of eastern Palestine, Sinai and the Arabah were less comprehensive, but no less important for future research.

The excavations in Jerusalem sponsored by the Fund were to have a more equivocal legacy. In 1867 Captain Charles Warren, an officer of the Royal Engineers like Wilson, was sent to investigate a whole series of problems relating to the ancient topography of the Holy City. His task, was far more formidable than his sponsors in England could possibly have appreciated. The local religious authorities were deeply suspicious and the accumulation of debris adjacent to the Temple Platform, which had to be investigated, was some eighty to a hundred feet deep in places. Warren proceeded in the only way he knew: 'the system adopted in excavating at Jerusalem was that ordinarily used in military mining; therefore it is unnecessary to describe the details, as these can be obtained in any book of reference.'[21] Even if his methods had been more careful, without any means for dating the masonry or the pottery sherds his digging revealed, Warren stood little chance of resolving the topographical questions to which he had been directed. The inadequacy of his means, conceptual as much as technical, were further demonstrated by his conclusion after soundings that Tell es-Sultan (Jericho) (p. 34) was a natural formation and his assumption that Tell el-Ful (p. 69) was a Crusader structure.

Two scholars who at times worked under the auspices of the Palestine Exploration Fund were soon to make special contributions to its growing reputation. Gottlieb Schumacher was a resident of Haifa, officially recognized as an engineer surveying for a proposed railway. He was principally sponsored by the German Society for the Exploration of Palestine *(Deutscher Palästina-Verein)* founded by the Lutherans in 1877. Schumacher pioneered the archaeological mapping of Transjordan and was later to have a conspicuous place amongst the pioneer excavators in Palestine (p. 33).

More remarkable was Clermont-Ganneau (1846-1923), a pupil of Renan, who was appointed French Consul in Jerusalem in 1867. He was a scholar of Robinson's calibre, unusual among his generation in Palestine for the number of famous inscriptions ('monuments') with which he came to be associated. In 1870 he was largely responsible for rescuing the black basalt 'Moabite Stone', an inscription of King Mesha of Moab (cf. 2 Kings 1:1; 3:4-27) found by chance at Dibon in Jordan in 1868. He first obtained a squeeze of the inscription and then later rescued the fragments, after the local inhabitants had broken it up. This is the most important historical inscription ever found in the region. At the time it was taken as evidence that the Greeks had added nothing to the alphabet they received from the East.

Clermont-Ganneau was involved in early studies of the rock-cut inscription in the channel leading to the Pool of Siloam accidentally discovered by a schoolboy in 1880. First properly cleaned by Guthe, head of the German Palestine Exploration Society in 1881, then squeezed by a number of scholars, it was cut out of the rock in 1891 by private individuals before being seized for the Ottoman Museum in Istanbul. The inscription, which contains no royal name in the surviving part, was attributed to Hezekiah on the basis of 2 Chronicles 32:4, 30. Clermont-Ganneau also located a Greek inscription reused in the walls of a school near the Haram esh-Sharif, site of the Temple in Jerusalem, that warned Gentiles against entering the inner courts of the Temple (cf. Acts 21:28) and important Greek and Aramaic rock-cut inscriptions, 'of Alkios. Boundary of Gezer', which established the site of ancient Gezer (p. 32).

As will be a recurrent pattern in this survey, biblical archaeology in its first generation was concerned overwhelmingly with the Old Testament. New Testament Studies have generally been more concerned in the past century with manuscripts and textual theories than with material culture and extra-biblical inscriptions. When, in 1881, the Revised Version of the New Testament was prepared, the earliest available manuscripts were on vellum dating to the fourth century AD. At that stage no papyri bearing directly on the textual history of the Bible were yet available, though Egypt was already beginning to yield the first of an apparently endless stream of literary and non-literary papyri of the Graeco-Roman Period, which were to be vital for a fuller understanding of the cultural background of the New Testament.

Discoveries among papyri concentrated attention largely upon the Gospels. Acts was to be more directly illuminated by monuments and inscriptions, since the writer incorporated much local colour into his narrative that might be checked by reference to the archaeology of Turkey in the appropriate period. From the 1880s through to the 1920s, Ramsay (1851-1939), a classicist by training who was Regius Professor of Humanities at Aberdeen University from 1886-1911, was almost alone in sustaining the necessary fieldwork. His long series of journeys through Turkey, using Paul's travels as the basis for his explorations, were marked by unusual physical energy and scholarly insight. Many inscriptions were recorded fundamental to modern understanding of the historical topography and cultural setting of the Pauline narratives and the epistles, even if they did not always throw direct light on them. The results of his work were not only published in the usual learned journals, but reached a much wider public through a remarkable sequence of books subsequently unmatched in the popular literature of New Testament archaeology (p. 48).

It is appropriate that a cursory survey of the first half century of biblical archaeology should close with direct reference to the literature of the subject. Never again were there to be so many popular books that conveyed both the excitement of discovery in the field and in the study. The pioneers, predominantly writing in English or French, had published their work either in expensive portfolios for the libraries of the rich or the learned, or in volumes exactly like those of contemporary travellers, which depended on skill with words to convey atmosphere as much as information. They were usually written as a narrative, vivid but episodic, impressionistic rather than exact; biblical quotations were frequent and expected. Illustration was generally in vignettes, again evocative rather than precise. It was in this genre that the first excavators in Jerusalem wrote their accounts, for they were not professional scholars and their audience was not primarily academic. Even when, like Renan, they were academics they aspired to create works of literature rather than to provide scientific reports for their colleagues.

In the German-speaking world, by contrast, the new discoveries were very selectively absorbed into the general studies of ancient Hebrew culture which had been an academic tradition since at least as early as de Wette's *Lehrbuch der hebräisch-judischen Archäologie nebst einem Grundrisse der hebräisch-judischen Geschichte* (Leipzig, 1814). In such handbooks antiquities had long been integrated into encyclopaedic studies of the conditions of life, of the customs, and of the civil and religious institutions of the ancient Hebrews, based upon documentary sources, since 'archaeology' was used in the original Greek sense. As when Josephus wrote his *Jewish Archaeology*, it was synonymous with ancient history. Although these manuals gradually changed character to accommodate the new information emerging from topographical studies in Palestine, from excavations in Palestine and Phoenicia, and from Assyriology and Egyptology, they long retained their restricted view of field archaeology as a source of *relia*, of aspects of material culture, to be used merely for illustration of an ancient text. They followed a pattern not significantly modified until Watzinger and Albright wrote general studies of the archaeology of Palestine, a generation after the first scientific excavations had been conducted on a *tell* there. For Hilprecht's popular and enduringly useful *Explorations in Bible Lands during the 19th Century* (1903), Benzinger, whose *Hebräische Archäologie* (1894) was a standard German handbook with the barest reference to fieldwork, produced a concise survey of 'Researches in Palestine', to which Hilprecht had only allocated about forty pages in a volume of nearly eight hundred. Significantly, Mesopotamia was given five hundred pages, which (allowing that it was Hilprecht's own topic) offers some indication of the low status in which the archaeology of Palestine itself was held at this stage, a decade after Petrie's pioneer excavation at Tell el-Hesi had opened up its archaeology in an enduring way.

1 Cited by M. Larsen in 'Orientalism and the Ancient Near East', *Culture and History* 2 (1987), p. 96.

2 A.P. Stanley, *Life of Thomas Arnold D.D. Headmaster of Rugby*, London: Popular Edition, 1904, p. 351: Thomas Arnold writing to Baron Bunsen in 1835.

3 Cited by H.W.F. Saggs in *Assyriology and the Study of the Old Testament*, University of Wales Press, 1969, p. 11.

4 E.A. Wallis Budge, *The Rise and Progress of Assyriology*, London, 1925, p. 262.

5 S. Birch, 'The Progress of Biblical Archaeology: an address', *Transactions of the Society of Biblical Archaeology* I (1872), p. 12.

6 Cited by Roland de Vaux, 'On Right and Wrong Uses of Archaeology', in J.A. Sanders (ed.), *Near Eastern Archaeology in the Twentieth Century*, New York, 1970, p. 67.

7 S. Birch, op. cit., p. 2.

8 S. Birch, op. cit., p. 3.

9 F.L. Griffith cited by M.S. Drower in T.G.H. James (ed.), *Excavating in Egypt: The Egyptian Exploration Society 1882-1982*, British Museum Publications, 1982, p. 28.

10 H.C. Rawlinson, 'On the Inscriptions of Assyria and Babylonia', *Journal of the Royal Asiatic Society* 12 (1850), p. 417.

11 A.H. Layard, *Discoveries in the Ruins of Nineveh and Babylon*, London, 1853, p. 139, note.

12 G. Smith, *Assyrian Discoveries: an account of explorations and discoveries on the site of Nineveh, during 1873 and 1874*, London, 1875, p. 9.

13 G. Smith, *The Assyrian Eponym Canon*, London, 1875, p. 182.

14 Cf. R.E. Clements, *A Century of Old Testament Study*, Lutterworth Press, 2nd revised edition, 1983, pp. 7ff.

15 E. Schrader, *The Cuneiform Inscriptions and the Old Testament*, London, 1885-88, translated by O.C. Whitehouse.

16 E. Robinson, *Biblical Researches in Palestine, Mount Sinai and Arabia Petraea in 1838*, London, 1841, p. 46.

17 E. Robinson, *Biblical Researches in Palestine and the adjacent regions: a Journal of Travels in the Years 1838 and 1852*, London, 2nd edition, 1856, vol. I, p. 36.

18 E. Robinson, op. cit., n. 16, p. 377.

19 S. Birch, op. cit., p. 7.

20 Cited by F.J. Bliss, *The Development of Palestine Exploration*, London, 1906, p. 256.

21 C. Warren in W. Morrison (ed.), *The Recovery of Jerusalem*, London, 1871, p. 56.

2

Excavations and Texts: early confrontations (1890-1925)

From a Theological Lecture-room to the Digger's camp seems to be a far cry, but in reality it is not so. All knowledge is correlated (Bliss, 1906).[1]

The widely accepted view that it takes a generation for any worthwhile idea to achieve public recognition is particularly evident in relationships between diverse academic disciplines. In any one subject the foremost achievers and thinkers will recurrently be out of step with the conventional mainstream, whilst interested laymen may often still be concerned with issues long since eclipsed in academia. Within academic circles themselves there is usually a significant lapse of time before scholars in one discipline are fully aware of the most recent achievements or procedures in another, even a closely related one. Thus, for more than a generation after widespread controversy broke out over Wellhausen's 'Documentary Hypothesis' and the claims of the Higher Criticism in the last quarter of the nineteenth century, it was more often the archaeological discoveries and interpretations of the decades before 1890 rather than those current at the time that were commonly cited, both by biblical scholars and by the writers of popular biblical commentaries and handbooks. Albright, whose exceptionally well-read youth had been passed at the time (p. 68), was in no doubt of the disparity.

The successful decipherment of Egyptian and cuneiform was rejected by some of the foremost Orientalists of the nineteenth century, and few ranking biblical scholars paid any attention to either until after the century had begun ... and the discovery that pottery was an indispensable chronological tool of the serious historian was summarily rejected by many academic experts between 1890 and 1910.[2]

Throughout the middle years of the nineteenth century, as the modern landscape and the historical topography of Palestine were systematically explored and recorded for the first time, the pioneers remained ignorant of the true significance of the many mounds (*tells*), which they surveyed and marked on their maps. They seem to have regarded them either as natural formations or as the bases or platforms for buildings. When they observed no standing ruins, they dismissed them. It was Schliemann's excavations in north-west Turkey at Hissarlik, which he identified with Homeric Troy, that first demonstrated the structure and significance of a Near Eastern *tell* in the years between the opening of excavations there in 1871 and their final closure at his death, in 1890, after four seasons of digging.

Schliemann was assiduous in rapid, readable publication of his work, which captured the popular imagination in a way even the Assyrian discoveries had not. His readers were fascinated by the enthusiasm of an amateur archaeologist who had been lucky enough, or so it seemed at the time, to find exactly what he had sought: Homeric Troy and its treasures. In doing so, and this was his most enduring technical legacy, he had revealed a long series of pre-Homeric settlements, the ruins of which, superimposed one upon the other, had formed a *tell*. He showed how by cutting trenches into such a mound the sequence of remains could be revealed and recorded. Stratigraphy - observing changes in a mound's growth - enabled changes in material culture to be placed in order of time with the earliest at the bottom, the most recent at the top. It was not, of course, as simple as that, but his demonstration of the basic fact was the foundation of modern archaeology in the Near East.

The first generation of excavators in Palestine

The father of systematic excavation in Palestine, Flinders Petrie (1853-1942), knew Schliemann, who visited his excavations in Egypt; but his real inspiration was the British archaeologist General Pitt Rivers, whose excavations on his estates in Wiltshire and Dorset in England, which he had inherited in 1880, opened the era of modern fieldwork, distinguished by its greater precision and detail. Pitt Rivers' prescription for good excavation is as memorable as it is challenging:

> Excavators as a rule, record only those things which appear to them important at the time, but fresh problems in Archaeology and Anthropology are constantly arising, and it can hardly fail to have escaped the notice of anthropologists . . . that, on turning back to the old accounts in search of evidence, the points which would have been most valuable have been passed over from being thought uninteresting at the time. Every detail should, therefore, be recorded . . . [3]

It was a goal to which even Petrie could not attain. In 1954 Mortimer Wheeler, who knew Petrie and much admired his work in other respects, was to castigate him for not insisting on constant supervision of his workmen and precision recording of finds in their three-dimensional context.

> It is abundantly apparent that, between the technical standards of Petrie and those of his older contemporary Pitt Rivers there yawned a gulf into which two generations of Near Eastern archaeologists have in fact plunged to destruction . . . There is still no real understanding of the primary principle of all excavation, that no shovelful of earth shall be cut save under direct and skilled supervision.[4]

The great tradition that descends from Pitt Rivers through Petrie to Wheeler and Kenyon will be further examined in due course (p. 94). Here it need only be said that no-one, not even Wheeler, has achieved, and then successfully published, excavations to the standards Pitt Rivers envisaged, least of all on a Near Eastern *tell* where the complexities of stratigraphy and the sheer quantity of evidence recovered for processing dwarfs anything Pitt Rivers ever encountered in England.

Petrie had no formal schooling nor university training. He learned surveying and drawing from his father, inherited a taste for collecting coins, fossils and minerals from his mother, and always attributed to his maternal grandfather, Matthew Flinders of Australian fame, his talent for exploration. In archaeology he was self-taught, receiving neither training nor constructive criticism from the Egypt Exploration Fund in his early years. Instinctively he devised a few fundamental principles from which he never departed: care in excavation; proper preservation and documentation of even the most trivial objects; accurate planning; and, above all, prompt publication. It is a method commonly termed 'scientific', a favourite adjective in this context, used to mean that he was systematic and precise in a way unknown among excavators before him in the Near East and very rare for decades after he had shown the way.

Petrie's pioneer excavation in Palestine, at Tell el-Hesi in 1890, was epoch-making, but its faults were to be as influential as its achievements. His rapid return to work in Egypt meant that they went uncorrected in the Palestinian tradition for over a generation. His recording system, devised primarily for cemeteries and one-period settlement sites in Egypt in the 1880s, was inadequate for the demands of a major Palestinian *tell*. His method of digging in arbitrary levels, rather than with the natural bed lines of debris (p. 95), was too easily abused when used by the inexpert. Moreover, Petrie never really abandoned the view, drawn from his early experience in Egypt, that it was possible to equate the rate of accumulation of debris with a specific time-scale, a misconception widely held among pioneer excavators.

The Palestine Exploration Fund had first approached Petrie as early as July 1889, since they had no-one with the necessary expertise to begin the excavations they planned once their great mapping projects were ended (p. 19). Petrie agreed in principle and consulted Sayce (p. 41) about possible sites to dig. Sayce suggested 'Ajlan and Tell ez-Zeita, thought then to be ancient Lachish. When the excavation permit from the Ottoman authorities finally came, Petrie undertook his own reconnaissance in the Spring of 1890. He found neither Umm Lakis, which he had thought might be Lachish, nor 'Ajlan suitable. He preferred Tell el-Hesi, where the east side of the mound had already been eroded to reveal the superimposed levels of ancient occupation. This, as he well appreciated, would greatly facilitate his work. Petrie and Bliss, his successor at the site, believed this *tell* to be ancient Lachish, whereas today it is more generally held to be ancient Eglon, the name preserved in nearby Khirbet 'Ajlan.

In a subsequent lecture to the Palestine Exploration Fund, Petrie presented the key problems and his procedures in an account that remains fundamental to the history of excavation in Palestine. It reveals how well he had grasped the formation of a *tell* and the means for dating different occupations, combining a precocious, if crude, appreciation of stratigraphy with his natural gift for typology (the systematic classification of objects), the cornerstones of modern archaeological procedure in the field. He also pinpoints the crucial contrast between text-aided and textless archaeology in this region.

> The first difficulty that we meet with is that there are no coins and no inscriptions to serve to date any of the levels. How then can we read history in a place if there is not a single written document? How can we settle here what the date of anything is, if not a single name or date remains? This is the business of archaeology. Everything is a document to the archaeologist. His business is to know all the varieties of the products of past ages, and the date of each of them. When our knowledge is thus developed, everything teems with information. Nothing is so poor or so trivial as not to have a story to tell us. The tools, the potsherds, the very stones and bricks of the wall cry out, if we have the power of understanding them.
>
> But how are we to proceed in a country where we know nothing as yet of the age of its products? It is like an inscription in an unknown language: for that we have to wait for a bilingual tablet, and so begin to

read the unknown from the known. Thus in the same way we must wait till we find objects from other countries of known age, intermixed with those as yet unclassified, in order to spell out the archaeology of a fresh country. This interpretation of the archaeology of Palestine was the special attraction to me for working there. The materials of known age proved but scanty in my work; a few pieces of pottery were all I had to rely on. To anyone unfamiliar with such evidences this might seem a slender basis for the mapping out of a history; yet I had full confidence in it.[5]

Crucially it was Petrie's knowledge of Egyptian dynastic chronology, and the objects distinctive of each period which allowed him to use the Egyptian antiquities found in Tell el-Hesi to establish an absolute dating for the associated Palestinian pottery. 'And once settle the pottery of a country, and the key is in our own hands for all future explorations. A single glance at the mound of ruins, even without dismounting, will show as much to anyone who knows the styles of the pottery, as weeks of work may reveal to a beginner.'[6] Although Petrie's view might now seem unduly optimistic, the critical breakthrough had been made. Whereas previously Robinson, Warren and numerous others had been unable to date the sites they recorded or dug for want of an ubiquitous indicator of date, Petrie had shown how pottery sherds might be just that. It is this analytical tool, constantly refined, which underpins all the archaeology of Palestine from the Pottery Neolithic onwards. Petrie's pottery terminology 'Amorite' (Early and Middle Bronze Age) and 'Phoenician' (Late Bronze Age) might now seem simplistic, but in some ways it is better than that used by Macalister (p. 32) a few years later.

With his excavation published as *Tell el Hesy (Lachish)* by 1891, Petrie returned to Egypt, leaving future work there in the hands of Bliss, an American who had first worked briefly with him at Maydum in Egypt. Bliss, the son of a Presbyterian missionary, had been raised in the Lebanon where he had learned Arabic. Petrie's work at Tell el-Hesi had been restricted to trenches on the slopes, as the summit was under cultivation. In 1891-93 Bliss concentrated on the north-east quarter of the acropolis, excavating a great wedge-shaped trench ('Bliss's Cut'), which removed almost a third of the mound and long remained the most distinctive feature of the site. He excavated in 'layers', treating them arbitrarily as absolute horizontal bands regardless of their structural eccentricities.

In his four seasons of excavation, published in 1894 as *A Mound of Many Cities*, Bliss grouped the occupation levels into eight strata of 'cities' extending in date from the third millennium BC to the Roman period. Fatally he failed to integrate Petrie's ceramic method into his analysis, leaving his publication without sufficient detail to advance the subject significantly. Although the Petrie-Bliss pioneer archaeological chronology was remarkably accurate back until about 1500 BC, the inadequacies of the published reports were largely responsible for German disregard for the potential of ceramic chronology. This was fatal to its contemporary status in serious Biblical scholarship.[7] Biblical Studies more rapidly absorbed the single clay tablet Bliss found in 1892 in his level III, contemporary with those from Tell el-Amarna. Since it was written about Lachish, it seemed at the time to confirm Tell el-Hesi's ancient identity. 'Suleiman, who found it, called it a 'saboony' - that is, a bit of soap. The men were told to look sharp after more of the same brand.'[8]

Bliss, continuing in the service of the Palestine Exploration Fund, next excavated in Jerusalem with a British architect, Dickie, from 1894-97 in continuance of Warren's formidable programme of research (p. 20). At the southern end of the eastern ridge (Ophel) he encountered the perennial obstacles to excavation in the Holy City. Land rights and standing crops forced him to tunnel; tunnels raised the suspicions of the religious authorities and were archaeologically inappropriate; and tourists hounded him. In the face of such obstacles and in the absence of stratigraphical controls he achieved remarkable results; 'in the history of the exploration of Jerusalem, nothing was on the scale, or of the importance, of the work of Bliss and his predecessor Warren. The achievements of both were heroic.'[9]

In 1898, in collaboration with the Irish archaeologist Macalister, who was working for the first time in Palestine, Bliss was required to turn his attention to the Shephelah, generally in quest of the Philistines, specifically to locate ancient Gath. Nine sites were listed in his brief from the Palestine Exploration Fund, but Tell es-Safi was the one preferred. Macalister's reflections upon this directive, over a quarter of a century later, are very much to the point:

> We learned from experience; and experience in the campaign thus inaugurated has taught us the undesirability of this kind of roving commission. It was another illustration of the old mistake of embarking on excavation work with a fixed programme. The programme set before the excavator was, 'Find Gath'. It would have been better to have said, 'Excavate Tell es-Safi, and see what it has to tell us, whether you succeed in discovering its ancient name or not ... ' in so brief a space (two or three years) nothing could be done but to make a number of soundings on some of the selected sites. Excavation by soundings is only a degree less

unsatisfactory than excavation by tunnelling. It gives us a little more direct information as to the chronological stratification of the debris; but not so completely as a larger clearance.[10]

Cogent as Macalister's retrospective judgement was, all was not wasted. The excavations at Tell es-Safi (not confirmed as Gath), at Tell Zakariyeh, at Tell el-Judeideh, which gave a broad stratigraphic sequence of Pre-Israelite, Jewish (Iron II) and Hellenistic-Roman remains, and Tell Sandahanna, where a major Hellenistic city (Marissa) was revealed, were decisive steps forward in the range of material culture they uncovered. The ensuing report, *Excavations in Palestine during the years 1898-1900*, remains among the best of the early archaeological publications for the region. In it the stratification of the *tells* was properly, if roughly, determined and a good sample of correctly dated pottery was published in four groups; 'Early Pre-Israelite' (Early and Middle Bronze Age); 'Late Pre-Israelite' (from Middle Bronze to Early Iron Age), 'Jewish' (Iron Age II) and 'Seleucid'. It was to be a generation before this broad framework was substantially improved.

One of the most interesting accounts of the earliest stages of Palestinian archaeology is that provided by Bliss in the published version of his 1903 Ely Lectures at the Union Theological Seminary, not least the sections devoted to the years when he was directly involved. They offer the first attempt by a field archaeologist to assess the role of survey and excavation in the study of biblical topography. Following Petrie, he laid great emphasis on the evidence of pottery: 'every ruin is covered with potsherds and much may be learnt without excavation.'[11] By extension, he argued, this dumb chronological evidence allowed for traditional biblical identifications to be tested archaeologically and, if rejected, for new ones to be proposed, though he was well aware of the limitations of pottery evidence, particularly in cases where names might have moved from an old settlement to a new one:

> . . . in attempting a precise identification based on onomastic and topographical grounds, it is necessary to bear in mind that the remains must be commensurate in extent with what may be gathered from the historical references regarding the size of the ancient town to be identified; that these remains must show a depth of accumulation sufficient to account for its historical range, and that the indications of age furnished by the pottery must agree with the notices.[12]

The Palestine Exploration Fund's concern with the Philistines was sustained between 1902 and 1908 by Macalister's major excavation at Tell el-Jazar, conclusively identified by Clermont-Ganneau as ancient Gezer a generation earlier (p. 21). It had the marked advantage of belonging to expatriate bankers who not only put the site freely at the disposal of the Fund, but also provided Macalister with the services of a local agent who was to prove indispensable. These excavations, when some three-fifths of the total mound were excavated, have given Macalister's career in Palestinian archaeology, briefly renewed in Jerusalem in 1923-25, a considerably more mixed reputation than his subsequent distinction as the first holder of a professorship of Celtic Archaeology in University College, Dublin, from which he did not retire until 1943. Ironically, by fulfilling his duty to publish his work in a final report, Macalister provided the prime witness for the prosecution. With all their faults, the three volumes of *Excavations at Gezer* (1912) endure as one of the major contributions of the pioneer phase of excavation in Palestine.

The Gezer excavations suffered from the worst practices of the time. Macalister worked alone, supervising some two hundred untrained labourers, through an Egyptian foreman, who first dug a single trench, forty feet wide, the whole breadth of the mound from the eastern end. They then dug a similar trench alongside and filled the first with debris from the second. Thus, with further trenches and the same procedure, Macalister worked his way across the mound of Gezer, each cutting penetrating to bedrock at a depth of forty-two feet in some places. There was no control over stratigraphy, as he realised and seems to have accepted; the interrelation of objects and debris was ignored: 'the exact spot in the mound where any ordinary object chanced to lie is not generally of great importance'; and recording was wholly inadequate even by the standards of the day as, for example, they were exemplified by Petrie in Egypt or Arthur Evans and his assistants at Knossos in Crete, where photography was already a key aspect of recording in the field. Macalister, determined 'to turn over the whole mound' in the hopes of finding a royal archive, was overwhelmed by the scale of the work and crippled by the inadequacies of his technique and the absence of any expatriate support staff.

The published architectural plans for eight 'strata' in the history of Gezer are in reality composite, each made up of buildings from different levels of occupation, since his levelling and surveying were inadequate for the purpose. No record is given to permit the identification of which area, let alone which trench, any published object came from. Artefacts were simply classified by arbitrarily named phases, covering centuries in some cases. Consequently, his most famous single find, the so-called 'Gezer Calendar', a short early alphabetic inscription scratched on a piece of limestone, may not be closely dated from its archaeological context. When a gap in occupation for much of the Iron Age was overlooked, an erroneous correction was introduced into the pottery chronology established by Macalister in his earlier work with Bliss. However, it was at Gezer that the first proper separation of Middle ('Second Semitic') and Late Bronze Age pottery was made.

In one thing it would be hard to fault Macalister. His publications for scholars and general readers alike were prompt and informative. His seasonal reports for the *Palestine Exploration Fund's Quarterly Statement* remain admirable reviews for the informed general reader. He was, moreover, the first excavator in Palestine to write a popular, if idiosyncratic, account of his excavations, as early as 1906, specifically to meet the charge that 'however interesting the researches of the Society [i.e. the Palestine Exploration Fund] maybe to geographers and anthropologists, the plain Bible student, who is not concerned with abstract science, derives little or no benefit from them; and they do not help him to an explanation of any difficulties that may meet him in his reading'. *Bible Side-lights from the Mound of Gezer* now reads as a naive attempt to refer aspects of the material culture of Gezer, as Macalister had recovered it, to specific biblical passages, but in the case of the 'High Place' and other major discoveries it did something to meet the needs of the ordinary Bible reader as responsibly as possible.

By the time Macalister was well established at Gezer, the Fund was no longer alone in sponsoring excavations. Sellin's work at Tell Taanach from 1902-04 is sometimes taken to stand at the head of the German contribution to field archaeology in Palestine, though at the time of gaining a permit Sellin, who was a distinguished biblical scholar in the conservative tradition, held an academic position in Vienna and was sponsored by the Austrians. This was also the first excavation in the ancient kingdom of Israel. Despite almost immediate publication by Sellin, few of his finds have passed permanently into the record. In the first season Sellin, who then had Schumacher (p.20) working with him, found one of the finest Bronze Age houses yet explored and a famous decorated baked-clay incense stand; in 1903 he recovered four cuneiform tablets dating to about 1450 BC, a century before those from Tell el-Amarna. In 1904 he found more, making his seven tablets and five fragments the largest group of tablets written in the Akkadian language yet to be found on a single Palestinian site. Sellin followed Petrie in characterizing by types of pottery the four periods into which he divided Taanach's history, though even by the standards of the time his field methods were primitive.

Until this time the German Society for the Study of Palestine (Deutsche Palästina-Verein), founded in 1877 by the Lutherans, had sponsored many studies of Palestine as well as Guthe's unsuccessful excavations on the south-east hill in Jerusalem in 1881, but it had not become involved in a *tell* excavation. In 1903, when German excavations in Egypt and Mesopotamia enjoyed a high political profile in Europe, where the *Babel und Bibel* controversy was also raging (p. 46), they decided to start work at Tell el-Mutesellim, ancient Megiddo, with the direct financial support and patronage of the Kaiser. There may be little doubt that the choice of this outstanding northern site, mentioned in various extra-Biblical sources, was largely governed by its potential contribution to issues raised by the *Babel und Bibel* debate, not least the hope of finding relevant inscriptions. The excavations were directed by Schumacher, by far the most experienced German available, with Benzinger, who had published a volume entitled *Hebräische Archäologie* in 1894 (p. 23), serving as his deputy when needed.

The main excavation at Megiddo was a massive trench cut from the northern edge of the mound southwards across the top. At first twenty metres wide it was extended to thirty as work proceeded in the years from 1903 and 1905. There were no stratigraphical controls and, though Schumacher, who was a trained draughtsman, produced fine looking plans he did not avoid surveying errors. He set out to produce an exclusively architectural publication, but abandoned this plan halfway through to accommodate associated objects in the report published in 1908. Thereafter his notes and drawings were lost. When a further volume appeared it was written much later by Watzinger, a classical archaeologist by training with no first-hand knowledge of the excavations and nothing save the detailed first volume, *Tell el-Mutesellim* to assist him. Yet, over twenty years after Schumacher's report, he provided a very necessary and distinguished companion volume drawing upon his experience of excavation at Jericho (p. 35) and his general knowledge of fieldwork in Palestine. The equivocal nature of material evidence accounts for his two most significant errors of interpretation. Preconceptions about types of masonry bedevilled his quest for Solomonic buildings and a gap in occupation in the area excavated distorted his view of the transition from the Late Bronze to Early Iron Ages.

In 1907 and 1909 and again in 1911 Sellin, who by then had returned to an academic post in Germany, undertook the first of the well known series of excavations at Tell es-Sultan, ancient Jericho, in collaboration with Watzinger. Technically this work has stood the test of time better than Sellin's earlier excavations since it was properly staffed with architects. *Jericho* (1913) is the first really adequate excavation report on a Palestinian site, with good plans, fine photographs and instructive observations on stratigraphy, but it is compromised by Watzinger's misguided ceramic chronology: 'Canaanite' (really Early Bronze Age), 'Late Canaanite' (Middle Bronze I) and 'Israelite' (Middle Bronze II). Sound fieldwork had been compromised by an erroneous chronological interpretation based, not on established pottery chronologies, but on Sellin's arbitrary identification of the wall destroyed by Joshua (in fact Middle Bronze Age in date) and another of the same early period attributed to Hiel the Bethelite in the ninth century BC on the strength of 1 Kings 16:34.

For innovative fieldwork at this time, it is necessary to turn to the excavations at Samaria directed by Reisner, Fisher and Lyon from 1908-10, after a brief initial season under Schumacher in 1908. This work was sponsored by the American School for Oriental Study and Research in Palestine which, after some years of planning, had finally become a reality in 1900: 'to prosecute Biblical, linguistic, archaeological, historical, and other kindred studies and researches under more favourable conditions than can be secured at a distance from the Holy Land.'[13] The excavations were amply funded by an American banker.

Reisner (1867-1942), like Petrie, was an Egyptologist by training and lifelong persuasion, who went briefly to Palestine, set outstanding standards, but then withdrew before they had been properly developed and passed on to the next generation. His emphasis on adequate training and staffing, on the close supervision of work in progress, and on detailed and accurate recording of finds, including a systematic use of photography, was epoch-making in relation to the activities of his generation of excavators in Palestine, but they alone would not have transformed archaeology as an investigative discipline.

It was Reisner's exceptionally clear insight into the structure of a *tell*, and by chance he was committed to digging an exceptionally complex one, and his intelligent appraisal of how it should be interpreted that prepared the way for critical changes in the next generation. He immediately realised that, although his German colleagues might show exemplary skill as surveyors and architects, they could never hope to phase and date the construction of buildings correctly, or for that matter objects found in association with them, without careful recognition and separation of the layers of debris in and around the structures.

The hill (i.e. of Samaria), as we approached it, presented a mass of broken horizontal and vertical strata, and some time elapsed before we recognized the significance of all its features. When it became clear that regular horizontal strata were not to be expected, the plan was adopted of clearing . . . until we found a floor-level either actually existing or indicated by the foot of a superstructure wall on the surface of a different kind of debris. Then we cleared along this level. At first, puzzled by the filled holes . . . these filled holes were completely cleared in connection with higher stratum from which the filling had come. Finally, with a knowledge of our deposits which made it possible to recognize almost instantly the character and age of the debris, we were able to proceed with greater consistency.'[14]

Reisner's work at Samaria, or more precisely his account of it from which this extract was taken, has been widely accepted as marking a watershed in the development of field archaeology in Palestine. But the extent to which Reisner actually followed the precepts so ably expounded in his publication of 1924, when digging over a decade earlier, has been much debated in view of the fact that his main collaborator Fisher (p. 54) was later to use more archaic methods, reminiscent of Petrie's procedures at Tell el-Hesi, when excavating at Megiddo (p. 51). Undoubtedly Reisner's published analysis of the stratigraphy of a *tell* goes much further than anything described by Petrie and, in many places, anticipates methods now attributed more commonly to the 'Wheeler-Kenyon' school (p. 94). Yet Reisner's legacy was more in what he wrote than what he actually did in Palestine or was able to convince his immediate colleagues was worth emulation. The limitations of Reisner's stratigraphical recording in particular and of archaeological dating in general are well illustrated by continuing debate over the Samaria Ostraca, which constitute perhaps his single most important discovery for biblical archaeology.[15]

Mackenzie, who had worked with Arthur Evans at Knossos in Crete, sharpened investigations into the Philistines when he excavated at Ain esh-Shems (Beth-Shemesh) in 1911-13 for the Palestine Exploration Fund. His earlier experience in Aegean archaeology proved most appropriate at this site, since it enabled him to recognize the painted 'Philistine' pottery (so named by Thiersch four years earlier), which was abundant there. He was also able to reverse Macalister's tendency at Gezer to date 'Jewish' (Iron Age II) pottery too late.

In these early days, as thereafter, significant information from time to time emerged from enterprises that were not always what they seemed. The Parker excavations of 1911 in Jerusalem were little more than a treasure hunt sponsored by an English syndicate, but fortunately Père Vincent was on hand to recognize the importance of their finds. By chance rather than by intention their investigation of the water supply from the Virgin's Fountain on Ophel had shown that Jebusite Jerusalem had been on the south-eastern, not on the western, hill and that there had been a town there early in the Bronze Age.

No less remarkable was Lawrence and Woolley's survey of the Wilderness of Zin sponsored by the Palestine Exploration Fund on the eve of the First World War. They produced a report unique in being published first in 1914-15 as a scientific monograph and then, in 1936 after Lawrence's early death, as a work of literature by a commercial publisher. Neither revealed explicitly that the whole enterprise was more of an exercise in military intelligence than archaeology. 'Mr. Woolley and I are not Semitic specialists, and our hurried flight (six weeks in January - February 1914) across the country did not give us either time or opportunity to collect place names. We therefore deal simply with the archaeological remains in the desert.' Both men concluded that it was the routes from Aqaba to the Mediterranean, not from Suez to Pelusium, that had been used for Solomon's trading enterprises.

To judge by the rates of more recent times, excavators in Palestine before 1914 were commendably prompt in making their results accessible to the reader, but usually in a manner that failed to capture the attention of serious students of the Bible. The indifference of biblical scholars to Palestinian archaeology at this stage may be explained in part by the paucity of inscriptions recovered at a time when ancient documents particularly dominated biblical archaeology, in part by the uncertain and often confused character of the conclusions the archaeologists themselves drew from their results. Albright's summing up of the position as it was in 1914 is sharp, but hardly unfair, for this was the point at which he entered the subject and he was particularly sensitive at the time, as a student of Assyriology and of the Bible, to the shortcomings of the contemporary archaeological situation:

> The dates given by Sellin and Watzinger for Jericho, those given by Bliss and Macalister for the mounds of the Shephelah, by Macalister for Gezer, and by Mackenzie for Beth-Shemesh do not agree at all, and the attempt to base a synthesis on their chronology resulted, of course, in chaos. Moreover, most of the excavators failed to define the stratigraphy of their site, and thus left its archaeological history hazy and indefinite, with a chronology which was usually nebulous where correct and often clear-cut where it has since been proved wrong.[16]

From the outset archaeology in Palestine had (as it continued to have) a communication problem. Comprehensive, readily intelligible publication of the raw data of the subject has consistently lagged behind progress in other technical aspects of the discipline, compromising even competent attempts to convey the most important results of archaeological excavation and interpretation to the public. When Petrie came to write up his excavation report on Tell el-Hesi he had already created a workmanlike format, congenial to his laconic style, in reporting his earlier work in the Egyptian Delta. These books mark the transition from the literature of travel modified for the purposes of archaeological reporting by Layard and others to the full-blown archaeological reports evolved in the twentieth century in all their bewildering variety. Petrie's reports still have rather more in common with Layard's writings than they do with Reisner's. The style is lax, illustration is minimal and not particularly well executed, and only pottery receives proper appraisal. There is no way in which the reader might hope to reconstruct the process of excavation from the report.

In the decade before 1914 it was German excavators who did most to improve the presentation of archaeological reports, assisted by lavish royal patronage. The approved style had been established by the excavators of Zincirli in Turkey (1888-92); a format that was to control the appearance of German excavation reports for the Near East until the middle of the next century. Architectural units controlled the reporting, as they had the excavation, and the horizontal plans of structures, often with meticulous details of layout and construction in words and illustrations, took precedence in the account. Typological study and systematic illustration of everyday objects, as advocated by Petrie, was largely absent. Where pottery and other small finds were reported it was either select items from within a specific building complex, where their precise find spot was rarely given, or a concise review of a random sample, usually only of pottery or seals. It is the standard of illustration whether of ground plans, simple archaeological sections or objects, which raises these reports to a higher level than most contemporary publications. Photography was used to particular effect.

Informed and lucid syntheses that would assist the specialist as much as they would involve the general public were rare from the beginning. The first to have endured in the literature of biblical archaeology is Vincent's *Canaan*, published in 1907. It follows the model of contemporary German manuals, but is distinguished by the author's first-hand knowledge of the primary material then increasingly available to him from excavations in Palestine. Vincent, who had arrived there in 1891, spent most of his adult life as a member of the French Dominican Ecole Biblique in Jerusalem, founded a year earlier by Lagrange (1855-1938). Although it was not recognized as the official French Archaeological

School until 1921, it had already come to play a vital role among permanent religious institutions in the development of biblical archaeology, though not involved in any major excavations. The liberal character of its biblical studies and its sceptical approach to 'sacred sites' were then unique in Catholic scholarship. Some of its members were to combine these attitudes with direct and intimate knowledge of the land and its antiquities, of archaeology and archaeologists, to become the local lifeline of the subject for generations. Its learned journal, the *Revue Biblique*, created in 1892, carried their attitudes and their scholarship far and wide.

Vincent's *Canaan* is an encyclopaedic review of the available evidence for the material culture of that region passing from towns, to cult, to funerary evidence, to pottery and to prehistoric archaeology before closing with a general review of Canaan's place in history. In its later chapters it embraces material later than the eclipse of historic Canaan. This book appeared soon enough to avoid the worst confusions of the day, but not too soon to inject a more sure archaeological sense and dimension into the Germanic tradition of manuals of biblical archaeology. The author's range of reference and intimate knowledge of the evidence ensure its enduring value as a guide to the achievements of the formative years in Palestinian field archaeology.

The same may not be said of its closest equivalent in English, Handcock's *The Archaeology of the Holy Land* (1916). Handcock pays due tribute to Vincent's work, from which he borrowed his typological framework, but he entirely lacked Vincent's first-hand experience and judgement. Albright, who had known the book from his student days, rapidly dismissed it, since it

> only yielded greater confusion [than the excavators' published chronologies], since each chapter included material really belonging to several different archaeological phases; he even covered a thousand years in one chapter where he should have covered three centuries, and then covered much of the same ground in the next chapter under the impression that he was dealing with a new period![17]

Material remains of the Iron Age were mixed with those of the Bronze Age so that 'Israelite' objects were as often as not cited as Canaanite and 'post-exilic' was as likely as not to refer to pre-exilic evidence. When the excavators were so much at odds, it was hardly likely that their reports could be amalgamated to make sense, least of all by someone with no direct experience of the excavations or objects in question.

Near Eastern Archaeology and the Bible: confrontation and controversy

Although the rapid development of field archaeology in Palestine in the years between 1890 and 1914 did not modify the paradigm for biblical archaeology provided by Birch a generation earlier, there was a marked shift in emphasis. Inscriptions still dominated any connection between archaeology and biblical studies but, whereas attention had previously been directed to the relationship between extra-biblical sources and Kings and Chronicles, it was now increasingly focused on those inscriptions which might resolve the vigorous controversy over the authorship and history of the Pentateuch stirred up by the views of Wellhausen and his followers. A great many people, theologians and laymen alike, were keenly interested to know whether the archaeological discoveries supported the new views or whether they refuted them. For the first time in fifty years there was debate as much about the content of the inscriptions in relation to the Old Testament narratives as about the more fundamental question of the appropriate methods to be used in employing extra-biblical sources to resolve literary and textual problems.

In a typically forthright passage, written a generation later, Wallis Budge, a contemporary Keeper in the British Museum, drew a vivid, if biased, picture of the situation:

> The particular mistakes that the early Assyriologists made arose from a bias in their minds. Assyriology was for them not so much a science as a weapon in controversies about the Bible. The facts of Assyriology were used as arguments for or against what is called the 'Higher Criticism of the Old Testament'. This resulted in certain details being given a significance that they did not possess . . . This atmosphere was especially noticeable in England; and many worthy men were of the opinion that a large number of Biblical parallels could be found if sought for in the cuneiform inscriptions . . . And Mr. Basil Cooper, a Press correspondent, used to visit the [British] Museum every week to obtain for his paper information of any Biblical parallel that had been discovered since his last visit.[18]

As early as 1896 an American scholar, Francis Brown, in an address given as President of the Society of Biblical Literature, challenged the increasingly popular view that the archaeological discoveries destroyed the case of the critics:

> But one of the crudest mistakes in using Archaeology as a conservative ally is made when it is employed to win a battle in literary criticism. It is not equipped for that kind of fighting. It has its proper place in the

determination of historical facts, but a very subordinate place, or none at all, in the determination of literary facts. To attempt to prove by Archaeology that Moses wrote the Pentateuch, is simply grotesque. The question is not whether Moses could write, it is whether he did write certain books which there is strong internal and historical ground for holding he did not write; and on this point Archaeology has nothing to say, nor is it likely she will have anything to say.[19]

This position was most vigorously contested for over thirty years by Sayce in a long series of books written as much for the general reader as for the scholar or the biblical student, notably *The Higher Criticism and the Verdict of the Monuments* (1894). Sayce (1845-1933) was an Anglican clergyman with an informed and expert knowledge of the recently deciphered languages, who was Professor of Assyriology at Oxford from 1891-1919 and is best remembered today for his contributions to Hittite Studies. As late as 1923, in his lively and still readable *Reminiscences*, Sayce was still provocatively arguing that:

> Subjective fantasies must make way for the solid facts of science which were at last being recovered. One after another the foundations upon which such theories [i.e. of Wellhausen and the Higher Critics] had been built had been shown to be baseless; first came the Tell el-Amarna tablets and their revelation of the use of writing in the pre-Mosaic age, then that of the legal code of Khammurabi, the contemporary of Abraham, and finally that of the Aramaic papyri of Elephantine. With hardly an exception the archaeological discoveries of the last thirty-five years in the Nearer East have been dead against the conclusions of the self-appointed critic and on the side of ancient tradition.[20]

Before examining the nature of Sayce's arguments, something must be said of the evidence upon which they were based. As has already been noted (p. 6), the Tell el-Amarna Letters had been a chance find in the 1880s which it took sometime for the academic world to appreciate at its true value. In 1896 all the known tablets in museums and private collections were copied and translated by the German Assyriologist Winckler, who included the 'Lachish tablet' (p. 30). Subsequently Petrie, who had found a few more tablets in his excavations at Tell el-Amarna in 1891-92, wrote a popular account based closely on Winckler's study. Entitled *Syria and Egypt from the Tell el-Amarna Letters* (1898), it made their contents equally well known in the English-speaking world. By 1907, when the Norwegian Assyriologist Knudtzon produced the first volume of his classic *Die El-Amarna Tafeln*, he was able to include 358 tablets. A companion volume of commentaries and glossaries, with which he was assisted by Ebeling and Weber, appeared in 1915.

No single group of inscriptions has played such a central role in attempts to elucidate the protohistory of ancient Israel.[21] They were the most significant extra-biblical documents to be published since the earliest days of Assyriology. They revealed for the first time the use of Akkadian as a diplomatic language throughout Western Asia and into Egypt in the second half of the second millennium BC, the archaeological Late Bronze Age in Palestine. This identified a possible means of transmission of Assyro-Babylonian culture to Palestine and established the antiquity of writing and letters there. As many of the Tell el-Amarna texts are letters from minor rulers in Palestine and the Lebanon to the Egyptian pharaoh, they offer unique glimpses of political and social life in Canaan in the fourteenth century BC. Above all, for those concerned with their implications for the earliest history of Israel, they include references to a group of people known as the *Habiru*, whose recorded activities were rapidly equated with the biblical Hebrews and incidents in the biblical narratives about Joshua. The debate over this group, albeit in different terms, continues a century later.

During his excavations at Thebes in Egypt in 1896, Petrie[22] discovered a black granite stela of Amenophis III re-used in the time of Merneptah (c. 1224-14 BC) for a hymn in the Pharaoh's honour to go in his mortuary temple. A fragmentary duplicate is known from neighbouring Karnak. Spiegelberg, who was studying Ramesside graffiti at the time in Thebes, was invited by Petrie to publish the hymn in a 'plain' English translation in Petrie's excavation report and at the same time in a learned journal in Germany, so both the academic world and the public rapidly heard of the discovery of what remains the earliest certain mention of 'Israel' (*I.si.ri.ar*?) in an extra-Biblical text. The 'Israel Stela' is a landmark in biblical archaeology, recurrently discussed, since the enigmatic character of the text, where Israel is given as a people not as a region, leaves their precise location in Canaan at this time uncertain.

In 1901-02 the French excavators at Susa in south-west Iran recovered a large stela of diorite, over seven feet high, inscribed with the law code of King Hammurabi of Babylon (c. 1792-50 BC), which had been taken from some Babylonian city to Susa as the spoils of war by the Elamites. This remarkable text rapidly became the focus of comparative study, not only as the oldest law code then known from the Near East, but for its correspondences to the Hebrew codes preserved in the Pentateuch. At the time of discovery and for sometime afterwards the recognition of similarities between Hammurabi's Laws and those of the early Hebrews were seen as a powerful challenge to attempts to date the Mosaic Law well into the first millennium BC.

The contribution of papyri found in Egypt to the development of Biblical Studies is a subject in itself. It is only possible here to call attention from time to time to examples that played a critical role in the relationship between biblical scholarship and archaeology. In 1907 Sachau published a collection of Aramaic papyri, from the German excavations at Elephantine in southern Egypt, which had been written locally by Jews settled there in the fifth century BC. More publications on them followed over the next twenty years, not least Albright's first learned paper in the *Upper Iowa Academician* in 1911. They provided fresh impetus for the study of the Diaspora and of Ezra and Nehemiah in particular[23] and were responsible for the important place the post-exilic period took in the literature of biblical archaeology in the first half of this century. They were supplemented to some degree from 1919 by the gradual publication of the Zeno Archives, discovered by local peasants in the Faiyum, which throw light on Palestine in the third century BC and on the Tobiad Dynasty of Ammon.

It was these newly discovered or freshly published documents, from Egypt and Mesopotamia, that largely sustained the campaign waged by the conservatives, Sayce conspicuous amongst them, in the name of archaeology against the Higher Criticism and its advocates. The most learned and judicious of their opponents from within the field of Biblical Studies was S.R. Driver, the Regius Professor of Hebrew at Oxford, whose contribution on 'Hebrew Authority' to a volume edited by Hogarth in 1899 on *Authority and Archaeology: Sacred and Profane* and whose inaugural Schweich Lectures of 1908, *Modern Research as Illustrating the Bible* (1909), 'did far more good by warning students against the dangers of 'archaeology' than . . . did harm by discouraging those biblical scholars who were inclined to leap too hastily into the archaeological arena'.[24] They remain required reading for anyone who sets out to understand the equivocal and delicate relationship that archaeology has had from the outset both with its champions and its detractors in Biblical Studies. Even Albright never bettered the closing remarks in Driver's third Schweich Lecture:

> To understand properly an ancient literature such as that of the Bible we need all the help and light that we can get from whatever quarter - from philology, from criticism both documentary and historical, from many special studies, such as geography, geology, botany, zoology, from the observation of customs in Bible Lands, and also from archaeology. The special value of archaeology consists in the fact that it affords us, in most

cases, contemporary evidence; and hence in a most welcome manner, as the case may be, illustrates, supplements, confirms or corrects, statements or representations contained in the Bible. It co-operates with documentary - otherwise, though not very clearly, called 'higher' - criticism, in helping us to distinguish narratives in the Bible which are contemporary with the events recorded from those which are of a later date, thereby assisting us to place its different parts in their true historical perspective. We must, however, be on our guard against confusing, as is sometimes done, the *facts* of archaeology with the ingenious but precarious, inferences or hypotheses sometimes founded upon them.[25]

At the heart of Driver's criticism of Sayce's numerous attacks upon the Higher Criticism lay the difference between the direct and the indirect testimony of archaeology, which at this time meant exclusively the witness of extra-biblical inscriptions ('the monuments'). As Driver recurrently pointed out, although it may be legitimate for those who accept the historical character of the Old Testament narratives on independent grounds to combine them with archaeological information to present a composite picture, it is not legitimate to regard this, as Sayce and those of his persuasion so often did, as *proof* of historicity. In any such demonstration a sharp distinction must always be drawn between statements which rest only upon the authority of the Old Testament and those which depend upon the testimony of extra-biblical texts. Without this careful separation confusions and misunderstandings are inevitable, proliferating particularly in popular and avowedly polemical works. 'Professor Sayce, unfortunately, often neglects this distinction; and confuses the illustration of a narrative, known, or reasonably supposed, to be authentic, with the confirmation of a narrative, the historical character of which is in dispute.'[26]

The situation was rather different in Germany, where the heart of progressive Old Testament scholarship was long to remain. British, American and other European scholars might excel in textual criticism and in Hebrew philology, but the most creative biblical scholars were still those active in Germany. After 1885 the most original had to contend with the dominance of the Wellhausen School in academic circles. Two scholars in particular, Gunkel and Kittel, in different ways, brought external sources to bear upon Old Testament scholarship and, in doing so, introduced German-speaking biblical scholars to the potential of recent archaeological discoveries in regions adjacent to the Holy Land. Both men were compelled to wait a long time by their academic colleagues before they obtained recognition for work of marked originality. Before setting their publications rather more precisely into their contemporary context, passing attention must be paid to the relevant archaeological research in the Near East in which Germans were then particularly engaged.

Between 1890 and 1914 the pace of archaeological investigation in Mesopotamia gathered momentum with the first revelation of Sumerian archives and artefacts in major excavations by the Americans at Nippur from 1888/9 and the French at Telloh, ancient Girsu, from 1877. At Babylon, from 1899, the Deutsche Orient-Gesellschaft sponsored excavations, directed by Koldewey, which were only to come to an end with the British occupation of the region in 1917. These excavations yielded spectacular architectural remains and numerous tablets particularly of the Neo-Babylonian period (c. 625-539 BC). Among the buildings Koldewey thought he had identified was the substructure of the famous 'Hanging Gardens'. Within these subterranean rooms he discovered some two hundred tablets dating from the tenth to the thirty-fifth years of the Babylonian king Nebuchadnezzar II (c. 604-562 BC), dealing with the issue of rations in corn and oil to captives, amongst them *Ia' u-kinu* of *Iāhudu* (and variant spellings); Jehoiachin of Judah (2 Kings 25:29). The vaulted chambers were not dungeons for the captives, as has sometimes been suggested, but repositories for standard administrative archives. The contemporary German excavations at Assur, directed by Andrae (1903-13), produced no finds with such a direct bearing upon the Biblical narrative, but they recovered basic information about Assyria before its government was centred on Nimrud and Nineveh, as well as the burial chambers of the Assyrian Kings.

The world of the Old Testament was more substantially illuminated by the work of the German Assyriologist Winckler (p. 41) in 1906-07, 1911-13 at Boghazköy, site of the Hittite capital Hattusa, some one hundred miles east of Ankara in Turkey. These excavations, which still continue, revealed over 10,000 tablet fragments inscribed in the cuneiform script. Those written in Akkadian immediately revealed that these were the Hittite royal archives of the fourteenth and thirteenth centuries BC, when the Hittites were a major power in Western Asia. The local Indo-European Hittite language, in which most of the texts were written, was first deciphered in 1915, by the Czech scholar Hrozny. This allowed modern scholars to read legal, mythological and religious texts that provided a whole new range of background information for Old Testament scholars. The Old Testament writers knew best the peoples of Syria who inherited the Hittite legacy in states in and around Carchemish ('Land of Hatti') in the early first millennium BC. These are the peoples known to ancient historians today as the 'Neo-Hittites', whose culture was revealed during these years by the German excavations directed by von Luschan and others at Zincirli (1888-1902) and the British at Carchemish (1911-14) under the direction successively of Hogarth and Woolley with T.E. Lawrence as their assistant.

German involvement with Assyriology, and the Kaiser's active interest in all that concerned the Near East, had a marked impact on contemporary Biblical scholarship in Germany. By insisting upon the Old Testament's debt to the literary and religious traditions of the ancient Near East as a whole Gunkel, with his associate Gressmann, brought external influences into the mainstream of critical study as Wellhausen had not. In his first major published study, *Creation and Chaos and the Beginning and End of Time (Schöpfung und Chaos in Urzeit und Endzeit*, Göttingen, 1895), Gunkel explicitly refuted aspects of Wellhausen's case for the late dating of Genesis 1 by demonstrating close parallels in the recently revealed mythology of Assyro-Babylonia. Wellhausen responded swiftly. Nor were the younger man's academic prospects enhanced by the contemporary excesses of those German Assyriologists who were advocating an almost total dependence of the Bible upon the rediscovered religion of Babylonia, thereby compromising those scholars more responsibly advocating study of the Old Testament in the light of its wider Near Eastern context. Although the so-called *Babel und Bibel* controversy in particular and related pan-Babylonian trends in general[27] are more properly treated as an aspect of the intellectual history of Assyriology than of biblical archaeology, in the long run their influence on the relationship between the new discoveries and biblical scholarship in Germany was not entirely propitious and partly accounts for the enduring scepticism with which the best biblical scholars there treated the results of archaeological investigation (cf. p. 104).

Although Kittel's name is most often heard today in connection with his edition of the Hebrew Bible, his *History of Israel* has good claim to be the earliest landmark in the assimilation of archaeological evidence by a major biblical historian still worthy of serious attention. This history first appeared in two volumes in 1888 and in 1892 (with an English translation in 1895), about a decade after Wellhausen's with which it took issue. Kittel challenged his predecessor from a more conservative position and suffered academically for being out-of-step. There was no new edition of his second volume until 1909 and not until 1912 of the first, in which Wellhausen had been particularly criticized. Thereafter, as the world of biblical scholarship in Germany broadened its horizons, the book's fortunes were transformed. From the third edition of the first volume in 1916 this became the first history of Israel in which nearly a century of study of ancient inscriptions and other information from excavations was systematically worked into the narrative to reinforce the arguments Kittel had first developed as a young scholar. Thereafter, successive editions through to a sixth in 1923 epitomized the changing character of the subject as critical analysis of documents, central to the earliest editions, gave way increasingly to a balanced appraisal of the real world in which the Old Testament was set. By 1921 Kittel felt confident enough to affirm that 'the structure [of the Wellhausen School] lacked a foundation and the builders were without measuring rods'.[28]

By the time that Kittel's history was into its final edition, German biblical scholarship was passing to a no less gifted generation, among whom Alt (1883-1956), a pupil of Kittel who was eventually to succeed him in his professorial chair, was to play a significant role in the forthcoming debate over the proper relationship between Palestinian field archaeology and Biblical Studies. Alt was the son of a clergyman, who had reacted to the *Babel und Bibel* controversy by writing a *Habilitationsschrift* which investigated the important historical rela- tionships existing in antiquity between Israel and Egypt as a response to excessive concentration on the Babylonian legacy among the older generation. From 1922, for a year and a half, he was Director of the German Evangelical Church's Institut für Altertumswissenschaft des Heiligen Landes (founded in 1902) in Jerusalem in succession to its inaugural director, Dalman. For several years he acted as leader of its renowned study courses. The knowledge of the land and its archaeology he gained then was to be used to distinct advantage in his studies of the early history of Israel, which revitalized the subject with their now legendary accuracy and thoroughness. Like Robinson he combined great skill in historical topography with sound biblical learning. In his historico-geographical studies of the entry of Israel into Canaan Alt mentioned archaeology rarely, not out of disinterest or ignorance, but because he found the results of contemporary excavations in Palestine unsatisfactory for his purposes at an early stage[29] and saw no reason to change his mind through the 1930s (p. 104).

Dalman, whose name is now more often remembered for his remarkable studies of ethnography in Palestine, was one of the few scholars of his time who used their intimate knowledge of the land to elucidate the topography of the Gospels. Otherwise, even though it was an American New Testament scholar, Thayer, who did so much between 1895 and 1900 to ensure the foundation of the American School of

Oriental Research in Jerusalem, New Testament Archaeology remains ill-defined, overshadowed by discoveries relevant to the Old Testament on the one hand, by Early Christian archaeology, which lies outside the scope of his survey, on the other. Virtually all New Testament scholars not only pursued their research without reference to the world outside it, but were often openly hostile to those who sought to bring evidence from the rapidly developing archaeology of the Roman World in the first century AD to bear on it. Among biblical scholars and theologians there was a marked suspicion of classical archaeologists whose research touched them too closely, even one so able and enterprising as Ramsay (p. 21). He, with a uniquely extensive first-hand knowledge of classical sites in Turkey published his best work on topography and history, Roman law and life, in studies which significantly challenged traditional approaches to Paul and the epistles. He wrote a series of popular and widely read books, whose titles clearly mark out the range of his contribution between the 1890s and 1910: *The Church in the Roman Empire* (1893); *St. Paul, the Traveller and Roman Citizen* (1895); *A Historical Commentary on St. Paul's Epistles to the Galatians* (1900); *The Letters to the Seven Churches of Asia* (1905); and *The Cities of St. Paul* (1907).

Towards the 'Golden Age' of Biblical Archaeology

The First World War, which inevitably interrupted fieldwork, transformed the political complexion of the Near East, opening it up to expatriate archaeologists to a degree unknown under the Ottoman Empire. Professional archaeologists did not at once replace the gentleman-scholars who had been so prominent for a century, but their increasing role subtly changed attitudes and priorities, even in such august representatives of the old order as the Palestine Exploration Fund. Everywhere rising costs, now to be an enduring phenomenon, constrained private and public enterprise. Higher standards of excavation and survey required more staff and more equipment, both of which were increasingly expensive. Although intensified road-building and the widespread introduction of motorized transport opened up new areas and greatly eased the life of field archaeologists, this was the last generation for whom both the region and its peoples, at least in rural areas and isolated towns, retained much of their traditional character.

In the British and French Mandate Territories, which replaced the Ottoman administration in Syro-Palestine and Mesopotamia, new laws and properly constituted local departments of antiquities did much to inaugurate a period rich in archaeological discoveries. In 1920 the British administration in Palestine created a Department of Antiquities under Garstang (1876-1956), director of the recently established British School of Archaeology in Jerusalem (1919). Garstang was initially trained as a mathematician, but love of archaeology had taken him early to Egypt to work with Petrie (1899-1900) and then on to establish his reputation as an archaeologist there and in Turkey, with which his name is now particularly associated. Although he left the post in 1926 he achieved much in a short time, not least in establishing the amicable personal relationships between expatriate scholars engaged in research in Palestine that were to be so valuable in the development of archaeology between the two World Wars. His enterprising, if brief, excavations at Ashkelon (1920-21), in association with Phythian-Adams, had to be abandoned for political reasons, but not before significant discoveries had been made about the Herodian city there and, at some eight metres lower down, the Philistine occupation. Only recently has this magnificent, yet formidable, site begun to reveal its full potential (p. 165).

Under Garstang, and his immediate successors, a properly equipped Antiquities Department with liberal new legislation was entrusted with surveying, recording and preserving ancient monuments (over 2500 were scheduled), with facilitating legitimate research and with checking illegal digging for commercial profit. The foreign schools and institutes of archaeology in Jerusalem received every encouragement to revive their field research programmes. The permanent residents, notably Père Vincent at the Ecole Biblique, promoted continuity of method and offered a ready source of up-to-date information for all newcomers and periodic visitors. A proper museum, the Palestine Museum of Antiquities, was established in Jerusalem for new finds and for those from old excavations not sent to Istanbul before 1917.

The fraternity of scholars was reinforced in 1920 through the creation of The Palestine Oriental Society, with Lagrange (p. 38) as its first president, uniting Catholic and Protestant, Arab and Jew, in the same learned society whose journal was to give it an international voice until the Second World War. The American School was reopened in 1919 with the first issues of its *Bulletin* appearing in the same year. Bliss was appointed 'Adviser on Excavation' in 1920 and soon expressed his envy of the opportunities now open to excavators compared to the frustrations and restrictions of an archaeologist's life under Ottoman rule. At this time Albright arrived in Jerusalem to begin the remarkable career that is at the heart of the next two chapters (p. 55ff.).

American excavations reopened with Fisher's (p. 56) return to dig at Tell el-Husn (Beth-Shan) from 1921 to 1923 on behalf of the University Museum, Philadelphia; he handed over to two men whom he had trained, first Rowe (1925-28) and then Fitzgerald (1930-33). Although errors of method, compounded by a changing directorship, and long delayed publication, were to compromise this major excavation on a key site, two primary results were soon well known. A deep sounding, of some seventy feet, to virgin soil, passed through eighteen main occupation levels reaching well back into the fourth millennium BC, whilst Egyptian occupation at this strategically vital town was richly represented in the Late Bronze Age by distinctive domestic and religious architecture, hieroglyphic inscriptions, and important small finds.

In Jerusalem Macalister returned briefly in 1923 to excavate on Ophel under the auspices of the British School of Archaeology, followed by Duncan (1924-25) and Crowfoot (1927-28). Their united efforts seemed to confirm the view that pre-Maccabean Jerusalem had been confined to the eastern ridge. Meanwhile the Jewish Exploration Society, founded in 1914, had opened its first excavations at Hammat Tiberias under Slouschz in 1921. Most of the research undertaken by this Society during the British Mandate, and on behalf of the Hebrew University from its foundation in 1929, was concerned with Jewish subjects. Synagogues, Jewish burial sites, and post-biblical Jewish settlements were the primary targets for investigation. Work by Stekelis on prehistory and by Mayer on Islamic subjects were the exception.

However, research upon sites of Old Testament interest remained by far the most common under the new administration, though prehistory was not entirely neglected. Although the English scholars involved, unlike their American colleagues, were not usually in religious orders nor trained in Biblical Studies, they had been through an education system in which both Testaments still played a central role, so that those who had been trained in English grammar and public schools and in the older universities were as familiar with the Old as with the New Testament from earliest childhood, and some had combined study of biblical Hebrew with Latin and Greek at university. It is no accident that Jericho is, after Jerusalem, the most excavated site in Palestine nor that Herodian Samaria-Sebaste was excavated long before Caesarea, since it lay over the capital of the ancient kingdom of Israel. As Assyriologists began to free themselves from the charge that they were always primarily students of the Old Testament, most field archaeologists in Palestine remained faithful to the agenda of a Bible-bound generation.

There was, however, one remarkable exception, whose dynamism and vision placed him in advance of his time.

Breasted (1865-1935), an American Egyptologist of distinction, conceived and put into effect with remarkable resourcefulness a rather differently conceived programme of research into ancient Egypt and Western Asia. In 1919 his foundation of the Oriental Institute in the University of Chicago, with the indispensable financial support of John Rockefeller, Jr., had been justified in terms that were to inspire the most ambitious series of excavations ever undertaken in the region:

> How did man become what he is? That is really the question which the Oriental Institute has been organized to study. The Institute is therefore a research laboratory for the investigation of the early human career. It endeavours to trace the course of human development from the merely physical man disclosed by the palaeontologist to the rise and early advance of civilized societies, the product of a social and material evolution culminating in social idealism.
>
> A generation of archaeological research has dispelled all doubts as to the scene of this evolution, which is now recognized as having been the ancient Near East ... The ancient lands of this region today constitute an almost inexhaustible storehouse filled with perishing and still unsalvaged evidence disclosing early human development ....[30]

As befitted a historian of ancient Egypt, Breasted launched his carefully conceived programme of fieldwork there, but by the mid 1920s, like Egypt's most ambitious pharaohs long before, he was preparing to move north-eastwards:

> Meantime it had become highly desirable that the Institute should establish itself at some strategic point in Asia. The new railway connection between Egypt and Palestine made it practicable to expand activities in that part of Asia. The selection of a Palestinian site was determined by ancient international connections also. The powerful fortress city of Megiddo (Armageddon) had been held both by Egypt and by Asiatic powers for many generations.[31]

In 1925 a five year programme of research was inaugurated at Megiddo, with Fisher as the first field director from 1923 to 1927. The project was on a scale unprecedented in the archaeology of Palestine. The expedition was well housed and equipped with the most modern scientific instruments, including cameras suspended from anchored balloons. Excavation was conceived on a grandiose scale. It was planned to clear the mound, enormous as it is, level by level. After a trial dig the whole mound was purchased, opening a new phase in the history of archaeology in Palestine.

1 F.J. Bliss, *The Development of Palestine Exploration*, London, 1906, p. VIII.

2 W.F. Albright in *New Directions in Biblical Archaeology*, ed. D.N. Freedman and J.C. Greenfield, New York, 1969, p. 8.

3 A.L.E. Pitt-Rivers, *Excavations in Cranborne Chase near Rushmore, on the borders of Dorset and Wiltshire*, London, 1887-1905, I, p. XVIII.

4 R.E.M. Wheeler, *Archaeology from the Earth*, Penguin Books, 1956, pp. 30-32.

5 W.M.F. Petrie, *The Story of a "Tell" : a lecture*, Palestine Exploration Fund, London, 1892, pp. 5-6.

6 W.M.F. Petrie, *Tell el Hesy, Lachish*, London, 1891, p. 40.

7 Cf. W. Nowack, *Lehrbuch der Hebräischen Archäologie*, Freiburg, 1894, I, p. 265.

8 F.J. Bliss, *A Mound of Many Cities*, London, 1894, p. 153.

9 K.M. Kenyon, *Digging up Jerusalem*, London, 1974, pp. 29-30.

10 R.A.S. Macalister, *A Century of Excavation in Palestine*, London, 1925, p. 52.

11 F.J. Bliss, op. cit. n. 1, p. 293.

12 Ibid., pp. 292-293.

13 Cf. P.J. King, *American Archaeology in the Mideast: a History of the American Schools of Oriental Research*, Winona Lake, Indiana, 1983, p. 27.

14 G.A. Reisner, *Harvard Excavations at Samaria I*, Cambridge, Mass., 1924, p. 42.

15 Cf. G.E. Wright, 'Archaeological Method in Palestine - an American Interpretation', *Eretz-Israel* 9, 1969, pp. 124-125.

16 W.F. Albright, *The Archaeology of Palestine and the Bible*, New York, 1935, pp. 35-36.

17 W.F. Albright, 'The Old Testament and the Archaeology of Palestine', in *The Old Testament and Modern Study: a Generation of Discovery and Research* (ed. H.H. Rowley), Oxford, 1951, p. 1.

18 E.A. Wallis Budge, *The Rise and Progress of Assyriology*, London, 1925, pp. 270-271.

19 Cited by P.J. King, op. cit. n. 13, pp. 16-17; cf. C.F. Burney, *Israel's Settlement in Canaan: the Biblical Tradition and its Historical Background* (The Schweich Lectures, 1917), British Academy, London, 1918, pp. 1-2.

20 A.H. Sayce, *Reminiscences*, London, 1923, pp. 303-304.

21 Cf. recently W.L. Moran, *Les Lettres d'el-Amarna*, Paris, 1987.

22 W.M.F. Petrie, *Six Temples at Thebes, 1896*, London, 1897, pp. 13, 26-28, pl. XIII-XIV.

23 Cf. P. Grelot, *Documents araméens d'Egypte*, Paris, 1972.

24 W.F. Albright, op. cit. n. 17, p. 2.

25 S.R. Driver, *Modern Research as Illustrating the Bible*, London, 1909, p. 89.

26 S.R. Driver in D.G. Hogarth (ed.), *Authority and Archaeology: Sacred and Profane*, London, 1899, p. 150.

27 Cf. M.T. Larsen, 'Orientalism and the Ancient Near East', in *Culture and History* 2, 1987, pp. 96ff.

28 R. Kittel, 'Die Zukunft der alttestamentlichen Wissenschaft', *Zeitschrift für die alttestamentliche Wissenschaft* (Z.A.W) 39, 1921, p. 86; cf. H. Gressmann, 'Die Aufgaben der alttestamentlichen Forschung' *Z.A.W* 42 (1924), pp. 1-33 (especially pp. 8ff.).

29 See A. Alt, *Die Landnahme der Israeliten in Palästina*, 1925, p. 92.

30 J.H. Breasted, *The Oriental Institute: The University of Chicago Survey*, volume XIII, Chicago, 1933, pp. 2-3.

31 Ibid., pp. 74-75; cf. G.I. Davies, *Megiddo*, Lutterworth Press, 1986; A. Kempinski, *Megiddo: A City-State and Royal Centre in North Israel* (Münich, 1989).

3

The Golden Age of Biblical Archaeology
(1925-1948)

> . . . Palestine (where more sins have probably been committed in the name of archaeology than on any commensurate portion of the earth's surface) . . . (Mortimer Wheeler)[1]

For almost half a century after his first visit to Palestine in 1919, through a remarkable series of books, lectures and articles, Albright (1891-1971) redefined the relationship between archaeology and biblical scholarship. Before the advent of Albright the archaeology of Palestine had played little or no part in the controversies provoked by Wellhausen and his School. Albright rapidly drew it into the debate alongside a steady flow of new information, primarily from texts, recovered through continuing excavation in other Near Eastern countries. From first to last he assumed the widest possible definition for biblical archaeology, arguing that it 'is a much wider term than Palestinian archaeology . . . Biblical Archaeology covers all the lands mentioned in the Bible, and is thus coextensive with the cradle of civilization . . . Excavations in every part of this extensive area throw some light, directly or indirectly on the Bible.'[2]

By the time Albright was first actively involved in Palestine the two most influential points of departure for progressive Old Testament scholarship were Wellhausen's 'Documentary Hypothesis', analysing the development of the written tradition, and Gunkel's 'Form Criticism', which sought to understand the oral traditions believed to have preceded the written Pentateuch analysed by Wellhausen. Albright, and through him all those in the English-speaking world concerned with biblical archaeology, were soon to be primarily interested in the role of archaeology in authenticating Israel's earliest traditions, in explaining how Israel established herself in Canaan, and in assessing Israel's proper place in the ideological history of the ancient Near East.

However, German biblical scholars, now represented above all by Alt and Noth, sought to identify the 'originating' historical events which gave rise to the Old Testament narratives primarily through the internal evidence of the text. Albright was also engaged in this quest, but through external evidence provided by archaeology in Palestine and beyond, not through the history of tradition. He was moreover much concerned with placing Israel and its traditions within those of the ancient Near East through comparative studies of texts and material culture. In this his primary interest was historical. It was not until the next generation that this preoccupation was strongly influenced by the 'Biblical Theology' movement in the writings of his students, notably Wright (p. 77).

In retrospect the years between the World Wars have come to be seen as the time when biblical archaeology, particularly through men like Albright and Glueck, had an academic status and a self-confidence that it had not enjoyed before and was rarely to achieve again. As often in the infancy of a new branch of study, the advocates and optimists proposed simple archaeological answers to complex Biblical questions. It may now be seen that premature or immature conclusions were drawn from the necessarily restricted range of information offered by the new fieldwork. There was (as from time to time there continues to be) a tendency to jump to conclusions when new discoveries were announced, often in the most preliminary way. Ingenious hypotheses based upon a minimal sample of the archaeological evidence all too easily appeared to be persuasive solutions to long debated biblical issues. It was to take another generation before accumulating data tempered claims that the historicity of literary traditions might readily be established through a few excavations or through widely ranging surface surveys. It also took time for those involved to distinguish the questions which might reasonably be answered by archaeology from those which might not. Nor was it immediately apparent that archaeology was already posing problems and introducing questions which the literary traditions did not even suggest.

Archaeology in Palestine: Albright's colleagues and contemporaries

Although Albright has rightly come to dominate accounts of the American contribution to the archaeology of Palestine in the inter-war years, Fisher (1876-1941) was better known at the time and far more experienced in fieldwork. He was not, however, a scholar in the strict sense nor did he have the remarkable ability to date sites from their pottery which Albright acquired from the earliest years of his stay in Palestine. Fisher had started his archaeological career when a member of the Department of Architecture at the University of Pennsylvania. In 1898-1900 he joined the fourth season of excavations at Nippur in Iraq as unsalaried architect. There he was involved with mud-brick buildings and their debris. After World War I he took the initiative for American research in Palestine by opening excavations at Beth-Shan in 1921 (p. 50), then served in turn at Megiddo, Jerash and Beth-Shemesh. From 1925 until his death in 1941, as professor of archaeology at the American School in Jerusalem, he was at the heart of the subject in Palestine.

Fisher was a man greatly respected in his time for his broad conception of archaeology's role in Palestine and the blueprint he drew up for it, for his practical skills as a digger and instructor, and for his unfinished, unpublished magnum opus, *Corpus of Palestinian Pottery*. Glueck's tribute was resounding: 'his name will always be linked with the names of Schliemann, Petrie, Reisner and Vincent as among the most original of Near Eastern archaeologists.'[3]

Although Fisher's name is increasingly linked with Reisner's in descriptions of the best field methods used in Palestine before the introduction of the so-called Wheeler-Kenyon Method (p. 95), there is little evidence that Fisher, in practice, departed much from the methods he had learnt early in his career. He was pre-eminently an architect, who allowed his team of diggers to work in arbitrary 30cm levels, taking no rigorous, recorded account of the actual bedlines of debris which alone allow for the proper recognition of intrusive pits and graves. Even with the acute chronological controls which Albright was to bring to Fisher's field methods in the later 1920s and 1930s, his procedures were seriously flawed, leading him and others into many chronological confusions and uncertainties.

When he took command of the renewed Megiddo excavations in 1925 (p. 51), Fisher, to whom only part of the mound was accessible for excavation, made a fresh survey of it, excavated many graves cut into the south-eastern slopes (intended to take debris from later work in the summit) and reopened investigation of Schumacher's 'temple-fortress', where he separated a later fortress from an earlier temple, which was assigned to the goddess Astarte on account of the limestone altars and cult furniture found there. This erroneous conclusion survived into the volume by May in which these objects, earlier than the 'temple' and thus not indicative of its function, were fully published.[4]

Guy (1885-1952), the man chosen to succeed Fisher at Megiddo in 1927, spent most of his working life in the Near East, after serving both in the French and the British armies in the First World War. Under Woolley's direction he had participated both in the excavations at Carchemish (1920) and at Tell el-Amarna (1921-22), before being appointed Chief Inspector of Antiquities to the Mandatory Government. He excavated an Iron Age cemetery on Mt Carmel and surveyed prehistoric sites in the Huleh region before serving as director of the Megiddo excavations. After his departure in 1934 he became Director of the British School of Archaeology in 1938. The Second World War intervened and his last years were spent as a founder member of the Department of Antiquities in Israel.

At Megiddo Guy continued work on the summit, soon identifying what he believed to be the stables of King Solomon. He persuaded the authorities to purchase the whole mound for the Government of Palestine, thus making it available for the ambitious overall, layer-by-layer clearances envisaged by Fisher. As time went on more architectural remains, including a solid city wall and a gateway, were ascribed to the time of Solomon, as was the impressive rock-cut shaft and tunnel giving access to the local spring. Guy improved control over excavation and recording by assigning locus numbers to rooms or well-defined areas in a stratum and by pioneering aerial photography with a camera attached to a tethered balloon. However, the scale of his operation and his increasing care combined to slow work down to a point where it seems the controlling authorities in Chicago decided to replace him in 1934. In a brief interregnum junior staff helped prepare the now famous and indispensable reports on the previous decade of excavation. Of the main reports, *Megiddo Tombs* appeared in1938, *Megiddo* I, on the Iron Age and later levels (I-V), a year later, with important subsidiary volumes on the cult objects and the water-system.

Guy was eventually replaced by Loud, fresh from excavating Sargon's famous palace at Khorsabad in Assyria, first explored long before by Botta (p. 8). This excavation, also large scale, had however, taught him to proceed less ambitiously than had Fisher and Guy if he wished to satisfy his masters in the Oriental Institute in Chicago. At Megiddo he sunk a test trench to bedrock to establish a profile of the mound's history and laid out others to identify areas which would yield the best returns fastest, selecting the sites of a Late Bronze Age palace and temple, which were to prove rich in finds, notably carved ivories and precious objects in the palace and cult objects in the temple. A planned final season was aborted by the outbreak of World War Two in 1939. His report, completed by 1942 but not published until after the War (1948), suffers from the restrictions under which it was produced and from technical inadequacies. Loud's work at Khorsabad had been largely room clearance and he was not versed in stratigraphic *tell* digging. At Megiddo the strata were crudely defined and the finds attributed in his publication to a particular stratum combine what genuinely belongs to that level with material from other periods brought down into it by graves and pits dug from higher, later levels. Such distinctions may only be recognized by careful and continuous observation (p. 180). Yet *Megiddo* II (1948) marks a landmark in archaeological publication with its inclusion of a complete set of plans, area by area, stratum by stratum, with heights of walls and floors marked on them.

With the possible exception of the Tell ed-Duweir (Lachish) excavation reports (p. 62) no other publications have held such a central place in the archaeological literature of Palestine as the *Megiddo* volumes. The method of publication may have been far from perfect, but the range and organization of the text, the quality of illustration and tabulation, and the sheer wealth of published information has placed these books at the core of any study of the archaeology of Palestine in the Bronze and Iron Ages. The strategic importance of the site and its consequent historical significance, not least in the time of Solomon, has also given Megiddo a central role in biblical archaeology. Few aspects of the subject have been so recurrently discussed in the last fifty years as the 'buildings of Solomon' at Megiddo (p. 109).

One of the more remarkable figures now involved in fieldwork was Badè (1871-1936), who came late to archaeology after many years as a professor of Semitic languages and Old Testament literature, to the study of which he brought an unusual linguistic talent. Before undertaking the excavation of Tell en-Nasbeh (Mizpah) in 1926 he had studied archaeological field methods, as they had been developed in the American Southwest, at the University of New Mexico. He was subsequently to repay the debt by teaching courses there that brought back to New Mexico the techniques he had evolved in Palestine under the influence of Albright and Fisher, described in a pioneering textbook, *A Manual of Excavation in the Near East* (1934).

At the time of the excavations at Tell en-Nasbeh, Badè was Dean of the Pacific School of Religion at Berkeley, California, and worked under their sponsorship from 1926 to 1934, virtually clearing the whole of an eight acre mound, which had been considerably eroded in the centre. The hard work and tenacity of his team commands respect and the final reports by McCown (1947) are rich in small objects of the Iron Age; but the whole enterprise was vitiated by a failure to relate finds to their context as excavated and by an inadequate understanding of ceramic chronology. The most outstanding finds were clay seal impressions illustrating royal administration in Judah and a seal inscribed 'Jaazaniah, servant of the king', with a fighting cock device. Badè identified its owner with one of the four army captains who came to Mizpah after the Babylonian army left in 585 BC (2 Kings 25:23; cf. Jeremiah 40:8).

No less equivocal has been the reputation of the Haverfield College excavations, directed by Grant assisted by Fisher, at Tell er-Rumeileh or Ain Shems (Beth-Shemesh) from 1928-33. This site had originally been dug by Mackenzie for the Palestine Exploration Fund in 1911-12. It was in an important strategic position on the frontier between Judah and Philistia with a settlement history from at least the Middle Bronze Age to the Byzantine Period. The incoherence of the data recovered by Grant was to some degree clarified in the process of publication by Wright (1909-74), then a young student of Albright's, who assisted Grant, though he had not been a member of the excavation team. He applied his teacher's methods in a study that not only rescued important information on the early Israelite settlement at Beth-Shemesh, but also laid the foundations for his own distinguished career (p. 35).

Although the American excavations at Samaria (p. 36) had opened up the highlands of Palestine to excavation, it was not until 1922 that an earlier site was investigated there. Khirbet Seilun, identified as ancient Shiloh by Robinson in 1838, was then tested in a series of soundings by Schmidt, a Danish scholar. Albright identified the pottery for him, concluding that 'again we have archaeological confirmation of the statements of the Bible',[5] since the range of pottery he recognized coincided exactly with biblical indications of the periods when the town at Shiloh had flourished. Encouraged by these results work was continued in 1926, and again in 1929 and 1932, under the direction of Kjaer, Deputy Keeper of Prehistoric Antiquities in the National Museum in Copenhagen, 'an excellent archaeologist of the conscientious Danish type, working slowly and carefully never neglecting the smallest details',[6] but without experience of the archaeology of Palestine. Kjaer's sudden death from dysentry only a month after starting his third season of excavation brought work at Shiloh to a premature end, despite an attempt by Glueck to sustain it, and left the results to be rescued a generation later, from rough field notes, plans, photographs and objects held in Denmark, in a volume that does not do real justice either to Kjaer's work or to the importance of the site (cf. p. 63).[7]

Although remains of the later Middle Bronze Age were located in one cutting, the character of the occupation at that stage remained obscure, as did the extent of occupation at Shiloh in the Late Bronze Age. The most significant finds were made on the west side of the mound to which Albright, acting as archaeological adviser, had directed Kjaer's attention. Collared-rim storage jars were found there adjacent to a wall in a destruction level which Albright and Kjaer attributed to the Philistines after their victory over Israel at the battle of Ebenezer (1 Samuel 4:1-11; 5:1). Inadequate methods and the restricted area of excavation failed to reveal more at this stage about a major early Iron Age site.

From 1927 the Department of Antiquities of Palestine had an independent staff who inaugurated their own publication, the *Quarterly*, in 1931. Richmond was director from 1927 to 1937 with Hamilton as chief inspector, 1931-38, and then director until 1948. Excavation was not their prime concern. Yet Hamilton's work from 1932-33 at Tell Abu Hawam, an important site near the mouth of the river Kishon, which was probably on the coast in antiquity, was significant both for the quality of his rapid publication in the *Quarterly* (1935) and for his acute recognition of the importance and limitations of stratigraphical excavation at a time when few others even recognized the problems involved.

From the later 1920s through the 1930s the British contribution to field archaeology was sustained by Petrie and his students, by Crowfoot and Garstang, and by a remarkable new talent, the young Kathleen Kenyon. In 1926 Petrie returned to excavate in Palestine after years in Egypt, over seventy years of age and out-of-touch with the transformation in the region's archaeology that had been stimulated by his own excavations at Tell el-Hesi a generation earlier (p. 28). His lifelong independence of mind and action compounded this ignorance. He went to work in the Gaza region, exactly as he had in 1890, as necessity had then required but no longer did. Unmindful of the work of others since then, he established chronological inferences on the basis of typological comparisions between local objects and similar artefacts long familiar to him from his many excavations in Egypt. But such links were not numerous enough to compensate for his neglect of information locally accumulated by others between 1890 and 1925. His chronological system for Tell el-Ajjul (1930-34), for instance, was disastrously extended with material dated to the mid third when it should have been the mid second millennium BC. Nor did his appreciation of *tell* stratigraphy, very rare in Egypt, bear close examination, as Mortimer

Wheeler was mercilessly to expose in a notorious survey of Palestinian archaeology written thirty years later:

> These sections through the mound at Ajjul . . . represent a long and hard-worn tradition which dies hard. They were drawn in 1938 and published in 1952. Nevertheless, they belong technically to the infancy of archaeology and were, in fact, obsolete more than a century ago. Regard the absence of associated strata, the omission even of symbolical levels, so that the walls are suspended in section as if in a vacuum.[8]

In other words, Petrie's conception of stratigraphy was schematic and formal, paying little or no attention to the realities.

In just over ten years Petrie excavated at Tell Jemmeh (1926-27), Tell Farah (South) (1928-30) and at Tell el-Ajjul (1930-34), and in a more minor way at Anthedon and Petra (1935-37). It was an amazing, sustained achievement for a man of his age, as Wheeler and his other critics were the first to admit. Despite faults of method and lax supervision, the range of information he retrieved, and above all rapidly published, combined with his unusual care in investigating other sites within range of the mound he was excavating, provided an almost complete and enduringly valuable sequence of material culture for the Gaza region from later prehistory through into Islamic Period. Albright, by turns critical and complimentary in his final verdict on the 'revered Nestor of archaeologists', concluded that 'in spite of the haste and frequent lack of care with which Sir Flinders Petrie published his results, his promptness was always a great asset. As the Latin proverb has it, *Bis dat qui cito dat*'.[9]

Not the least of Petrie's virtues was the quality of the assistants he trained during a career-long dedication to the younger generation. As field archaeology recurrently demonstrates, no text book of method is an adequate substitute for the best practitioners of one generation training the best of the next in the field. Equally it is in the nature of the most able and enterprising of pupils to wish to go their way in due course.

When he began work at Tell Jemmeh Petrie had been joined by Starkey (1895-1938), who had already dug with him on his own account in Egypt. He was a self-made archaeologist whose love of antiquity had taken him out of a career in business. He had a talent for organization and promotion equal to his dedication and skill as a field archaeologist. In 1927 he was in charge of work at Tell Farah (South) and advocated the choice of Tell el-Ajjul for Petrie's next excavation in 1929. When he decided that the time had come to undertake work in his own name, free of the constraints imposed by Sir Flinders and Lady Petrie, he approached Sir Henry Wellcome with a view to forming an Anglo-

American expedition in collaboration with Dunscombe Colt, to dig either Tell el-Areini (Gath?) in the plain, or Tell ed-Duweir (Lachish?) in the foothills. Financed by Sir Charles Marston and Sir Robert Mond, men long interested in biblical archaeology, he chose Tell ed-Duweir in 1932. 'Petrie's pups', as they were fondly known, followed him, some eagerly, some like Olga Tufnell reluctantly. She was later to rescue the publication of this major excavation after Starkey's murder in January 1938 by armed bandits near Hebron, as he travelled by car to Jerusalem for the opening of the Palestine Archaeological Museum ('the Rockefeller').

Working methods at Tell ed-Duweir were traditional and do not bear comparison with Kenyon's innovative techniques at Samaria (p. 63). As the recent Israeli excavations have shown (p. 160), Starkey's trenches were too restricted in area and time-range to show this mound's full potential, but even so the evidence he retrieved was important for historical understanding of both Canaan and of Judah. Although Starkey gave lectures with such titles as 'Lachish as Illustrating Bible History', he was not preoccupied with this aspect of his work in the way that men like Albright, Glueck and Garstang were at this time.

> He considered that it was his place as a field archaeologist to provide fresh material for interpretation by specialists; he served them ungrudgingly, not only in this way but by so creating and stimulating interest among the general public for matters which were often very technical, that their results received full recognition.[10]

The evidence he retrieved, and published in 1934, for the destruction of the final Canaanite city 'towards the close of the XIXth dynasty' rapidly became a fixed point in contemporary debates over the dating of the Conquest, even if others at the time queried its precision. This crucial information was matched by the discovery in 1935 and 1938 of some twenty-one, ink-written inscriptions on pottery sherds found in the debris of the city-gate destroyed at the time of Nebuchadnezzar II's invasion (level II). These renowned 'Lachish Letters' were rapidly acclaimed for the witness they bore to the language and script used in Judah at the time of Jeremiah, in essentials identical to the Hebrew of the Old Testament. Whether or not they also confirm the identification of the site with ancient Lachish, through internal reference to it, remains an issue, though few now doubt the overall case for it. Starkey had assumed a very short lapse of time between the destruction of level III and that of level II, dating both to the first fifteen years of the sixth century BC. In preparing the final publication after his death Olga Tufnell argued the case for dating the end of level III on the basis of ceramic typologies to the time of Sennacherib's capture of Lachish in 701 BC. Until the renewed excavations at Tell ed-Duweir, from 1973, this remained very much a minority view (p. 160).

Following publication in 1924 of Reisner's monumental report on the Samaria excavations undertaken before the First World War (p. 35), Père Vincent sought to promote fresh work there. In 1931 Crowfoot, Director of the British School of Archaeology in Jerusalem, advised by Fisher who had worked with Reisner, returned to Samaria with an Anglo-American/Hebrew University Expedition. He began where Reisner had left off, but with the advantage of much more precise pottery dating, following Albright's work in the previous decade (p. 71), and the refined techniques of stratigraphical excavation developed in England by Mortimer Wheeler and his wife, now brought to Palestine by his young colleague Kathleen Kenyon, whose precocious skills Crowfoot fully appreciated.

If her contemporary excavation of the north-west gate of the Roman town of Verulamium (St. Albans) in England is compared with her stratigraphical cut through the *tell* at Samaria, the parallels in technique are striking. At St Albans, under Wheeler's direction, the plan of the city gate had been meticulously recovered by Kathleen Kenyon through excavation of the trenches used to rob out its stone foundations when it was dismantled. This work and her experience at Samaria under-pin her later, somewhat extravagant, contention that 'almost identical methods can be applied in the East, though the difficulties are undoubtedly much greater, both from the succession of strata and the difficulty of getting enough intelligent workmen.'[11] The stratigraphy of Samaria was complex and difficult to unravel, rigorously testing the excavators' ability to proceed along bedlines of debris correlating architecture and small finds as they went. But, by doing so, they were able to correct some of Reisner's conclusions. They redated the impressive stone round towers of the acropolis from the Israelite to the Hellenistic period and the 'Herodian' street of columns well into Roman Imperial times. They added a remarkable collection of carved 'Phoenician' ivories of the time of the Divided Monarchy to Reisner's famous discovery of ostraca, though the close dating of both groups remained problematic since neither was recovered from a primary archaeological context. Although the ivories (1938) and the architectural remains (1942) were soon published, the volume on the pottery and other small finds did not appear until 1957, when its publication provoked an important debate on the 'Wheeler-Kenyon' Method of excavation (p. 96).

Jericho was another site first tested by the pioneer excavators to which the next generation now returned. Indeed, no single archaeological site in Palestine, with the obvious exception of Jerusalem, has evoked as much debate among biblical archaeologists. Warren's excavations at Jericho in 1868 were aborted by his lack of every technique necessary to make sense of the *tell*. The German excavators a generation later (p. 35) had been more successful, but their fine report was compromised by misguided pottery analysis. Then in 1926, in the light of more recent research, Watzinger wrote an important article about the archaeology of the final Canaanite occupation at Jericho. His conclusion came remarkably close to the view accepted today: 'in the time of Joshua Jericho was a heap of ruins on which stood perhaps a few isolated huts.'[12]

This summing up provoked sharp controversy. Garstang responded in 1930 by re-opening excavations at Jericho, after undertaking test cuttings into the mounds at Ai (et-Tell) and Hazor (Tell el-Qedah), two other sites important in the Conquest narratives. A year later, in his publication *Joshua and Judges*, Garstang was using the results to argue that all three places still had vigorous settlements as late as 1400 BC. At the time, Garstang's Jericho excavations (1930-36) enjoyed wide public attention; but they were compromised by his inadequate field techniques, which took account neither of Reisner's insights into *tell* excavation nor of Albright's refinements of ceramic typology (p. 71). Glueck was subsequently to describe them as 'an ideal example of how not to proceed.'[13] Poor stratigraphical control was compounded in both popular and scholarly publications of the latest Canaanite levels by a very literal reading of the Old Testament.

Garstang began by concentrating on the lines of mud-brick city wall revealed along the crest of the mound by the earlier German excavations. He cut a number of trenches through them in an attempt to establish a dated sequence. He assigned them all to various phases of the Bronze Age, attributing the most recent, which he believed had been destroyed by earthquake and fire, to the Israelite attack. This he dated on the basis of Egyptian royal scarabs, none later than Amenophis III, found in graves off the mound, to about 1400 BC. 'Our excavations, logically interpreted, point to the fall of the city in the reign of Amenhotep III, possibly late in his reign (which is well represented), but before that of his successor Akhenaten, of whose period there is no trace.'[14] This conclusion immediately became central to discussions of the date of the Exodus and Conquest and remained so until the Kenyon excavations at Jericho (1952-58). Except for the 'Middle Building', which he dated to the time of Seti I and tentatively identified as the palace of Eglon of

Moab (Judges 3:13-14), Garstang argued that the site had been a ruin until restored by Hiel (1 Kings 16:34) in the ninth century BC. Although pottery specialists like Albright and Père Vincent sought to modify Garstang's dating for the Conquest on the basis of his finds at Jericho, they did not question that there had been such an event at sometime in the Late Bronze Age.

When Garstang cut a trial trench into et-Tell (Ai) in 1929, both Albright and he had concluded on the basis of the pottery he recovered that there had been a settlement on this site in the Late Bronze Age; but, as it happened, the pottery was much older. This became evident when the site was more fully excavated from 1933-35 by Judith Marquet-Krause, a locally born archaeologist, on behalf of the Rothschild Foundation. Earlier she had dug briefly with Garstang. Her death brought this project to a premature end in 1936, but not before she had demonstrated a long break in the occupation of et-Tell (Ai) between the end of the Early Bronze Age, about 2200 BC, and an early stage in the Iron Age over a thousand years later. Evidence that seemed to run so directly against other archaeological information for the authenticity of the Conquest narratives inevitably evoked a whole variety of explanations in following decades. Those who wished to sustain the integrity of the given text (Joshua 8:28) have either denied that et-Tell is indeed ancient Ai, or argued that there was a confusion between Ai and nearby Bethel (p. 71), or claimed that et-Tell was a temporary stronghold at the time, so not necessarily recognizable to excavators. In their turn the sceptics had either denied the historicity of this episode or suggested that much earlier or much later events had been attributed to Joshua. Rowley, in an encyclopaedic synthesis in the Schweich Lectures for 1948, was evasive: 'since the case of Ai is an equal embarrassment to every view of Exodus, and cannot be integrated at present into any synthesis of Biblical and non-Biblical material, it must be left out of account.'[15] Thus it stood until renewed excavations at et-Tell from 1964 to 1972 (p. 128).

Although the French were not conspicuous among field archaeologists at this time, two manuals by French scholars were of considerable importance. Père Abel, of the Ecole Biblique, published a two-volume *Géographie de la Palestine* from the standpoint of a moderate conservative in matters of biblical topography. The first volume presented the region's physical geography, the second offered first a review of historical geography and then a gazetteer of biblical sites, which holds an enduring place between the pioneer works on topography from the previous century and Aharoni's contributions a generation later (p. 110). In 1939 Barrois published the first volume of his *Manuel d'archéologie biblique*, which aimed to pick up where Vincent's *Canaan* had left off a generation earlier. The magnitude of the task delayed the appearance of the second volume until 1953. In contrast to the German handbook tradition, Barrois started from the material culture as Vincent had, treating it by categories, and then relating each, whether it be an aspect of architecture or a cult object, to their place in daily life, with appropriate biblical citations. 'Ce qu'il importe de savoir en effet, c'est la connexion même du monument et du document dans le fait humain. C'est pratiquement la que doit porter l'effort de l'archéologie.'[16]

In the 1930s Watzinger crowned his contribution to the archaeology of Palestine with his still useful *Denkmäler Palastinas* in two parts (Leipzig, 1933-35), fairly described at the time by Albright as 'by far the best systematic account of the development of civilization in ancient Palestine.'[17] Watzinger emancipated the subject from the restrictive traditional categories of the conventional German manual or handbook by writing general accounts of specific periods - Prehistoric, Canaanite, Exodus and Conquest, etc. - that were to provide the pattern for all ensuing accounts of the archaeology of Palestine, including Albright's. Alt's collaboration with Watzinger ensured an up-to-date treatment of history and topography.

Between the two World Wars German archaeologists only made a limited contribution to fieldwork. In 1926 Sellin returned to Tell Balatah (Shechem), where he had excavated briefly in 1913-14, working until 1934 with Welter, who had been trained in Greek archaeology, and with an architect, Steckeweh; but this excavation team was riven by differences of personality. Trenching was ill-judged, recording was deficient and, as no account was taken of Albright's improvements in ceramic analysis and dating, an unusable archaeological chronology was produced for this important site. Although Steckeweh began in 1934 to get to grips with the stratigraphy, the absence of any proper publication by Sellin (whose records were destroyed by bombing in Berlin in 1943) left everything to be resolved by new excavations from 1956 (p. 100).

It would be easy to overlook perhaps the most remarkable German contribution of this period since its relevance to archaeology is only now coming to be fully appreciated at a time when ethno-archaeology has finally entered the mainstream of the subject. It was Dalman (1854-1941), director of the German Institute in Jerusalem from 1902-17, who first integrated systematic ethnography into Biblical Studies in years of research which culminated in his multi-volumed, but uncompleted, *Arbeit und Sitte in Palästina* (1928-42). It developed from field studies first undertaken in 1899-1900 and initially published as a series of articles. Through direct personal experience and inquiry they documented many aspects of the daily life of the people of Palestine. As he proceeded Dalman formed an ethnological collection including originals and models for the German Institute. Each of his descriptions records first the modern techniques, tools and terminology, illustrated with drawings and photographs, then the relevant comparative information to be found in the Bible and other ancient written sources. Even now, well over half a century later and with an ever increasing flow of appropriate information from excavations, the third part remains to be undertaken: that in which the ancient material culture is brought forward for integration with Dalman's documentation.

Biblical Archaeology redefined: Albright, Glueck and Wright

Albright was by training an Assyriologist and a biblical scholar, grounded in the Germanic tradition, fluent in German and thoroughly at home with German culture. Initially he brought the post-Wellhausen Old Testament scholarship of Germany to an America ignorant of it, but in his own terms, not in those of its creators. As an archaeologist he was largely self-taught. From the moment he arrived for the first time in Jerusalem in 1919 he initiated a new career in archaeology and historical topography. In time the two were fused to the point where Albright is best described as a cultural historian rather than just as a biblical archaeologist, though he preferred the broad term 'Orientalist'. Although he was to transform biblical archaeology, it was part of a far wider ambition. 'Albright's great aim was the synthesis of the history of the Eastern Mediterranean, within which biblical literature could be understood as belonging to an environment of cultures, instead of being 'a monstrous fossil' having no connection with or illumination from a living position within the newly recovered past.'[18] At every stage he was wary of syntheses based upon internal biblical data alone, subjecting everything to the controls of external information or argument based upon 'typical occurrence' within a specific cultural context. Whatever he studied, be it potsherds or scripts, texts or comparative religion, typology was the key to his methods. In most of what he wrote as a mature scholar there is a unity of aim and method, even if his restless intellect, for ever appraising new data, held him back from the major history of ancient Israel towards which everything he wrote seemed to be directed.

Albright (1891-1971) was raised in a family of self-supporting Protestant missionaries settled in Chile, where his imagination was stimulated and his mind nurtured not so much by the world about him as by his father's small library. He was barely out of his first decade before he was adding Roger's *History of Babylonia and Assyria* to it. He took a degree in Classics at Upper Iowa University in 1912, cultivating a love of ancient Greek philosophy recurrently evident in his more discursive books. Meanwhile, privately, he studied Akkadian and Hebrew. After his first degree he moved to the Johns Hopkins University in Baltimore to pursue ancient Near Eastern studies under Haupt, a distinguished Assyriologist, who supervised his unpublished doctoral thesis on *The Assyrian Deluge Epic* (1916). In the first years of his professional academic career Albright was primarily concerned with Assyriology, accepting his teacher's sceptical attitude to the historical value of biblical traditions.

In 1919 Albright went as Thayer Fellow to the American School in Jerusalem. Almost immediately he became its director, serving from 1920 to 1929 and again from 1933 to 1936, after he had succeeded Haupt as W.W. Spence Professor of Semitic Languages at Johns Hopkins in 1929. He was Vice-President, and a trustee of the American Schools of Oriental Research, for over thirty years. From 1931 to 1968 he edited their bulletin. This played a role in his career that it would be hard to overestimate, since it provided both the means and the encouragement for his almost hyperactive assessment and communication of every new discovery relevant to the interaction of archaeology and biblical studies. It was through the *Bulletin (B.A.S.O.R.)* as much as through his books, that he defined biblical archaeology for his generation.

Two aspects of his personal life during his early years in Palestine are pertinent to an understanding of his career. Soon after his marriage in 1921 his wife converted to Roman Catholicism. Consequently Père Vincent was to serve both as his wife's father confessor and as his master in Palestinian archaeology. His childhood experiences as a Protestant missionary's son in Catholic Chile, the tensions of belief in his own marriage, and his initial identification with the Magnes Movement for a binational Arab-Jewish State left him particularly sensitive to the complexities of religious belief and political life. In the event he was to champion the new state of Israel from its foundation; one of the few archaeologists or biblical scholars in the English-speaking world to do so at the time. Thereafter he exerted a particularly powerful influence on the first generation of Israeli archaeologists.[19]

For someone often referred to in the United States as the greatest archaeologist to work in Palestine this century, Albright's firsthand experience of excavation was relatively restricted, falling largely in a single decade of his long life. As director of the American School in the 1920s, in the Robinson tradition, he laid great emphasis on field trips as the only proper basis for the study of historical topography. It was during such trips that he developed his renowned understanding of ceramic typology as a means for dating archaeological sites from surface collections of pottery sherds, whilst combining his archaeological expertise with his linguistic skills in the identification of biblical sites. In his archaeological studies he drew much upon the vast knowledge and experience of Père Vincent, whose local experience covered the whole of the previous generation. His geographical studies brought him into contact with Dalman, first director of the German Evangelical Church's Institut für Altertumswissenschaft des Heiligen Landes, and his successor, Alt, who arrived in Jerusalem in 1922. They pioneered the famous annual study courses which have done so much to stimulate biblical archaeology in Germany.

It was on the advice of Dalman that Albright finally selected the accessible small site of Tell el-Ful, only three miles north of Jerusalem, for his first excavation in 1922, followed by seasons in 1923 and 1933. In retrospect this dig remains memorable as the first discovery of a settlement of the earliest Iron Age at which the types of pottery later to play so important a part in the study of early Israel were distinguished. Whether or not this is indeed the site of Saul's citadel (Gibeah), as Albright (following Robinson) believed, remains debatable. The site was reinvestigated by Lapp in 1964 (p. 130). He showed that Albright's inexperience of excavation was to some extent counteracted by his acute observation and powers of analysis. Thus his chronological conclusions largely stand, even if architectural and topographical details are in need of revision.

It is, however, his reports on the excavations at Tell Beit Mirsim from 1926 to 1932 that sustain Albright's considerable reputation as a field archaeologist. This work became more widely known through the first and only popular account he ever published of it, in *The Archaeology of Palestine and the Bible* (the Richmond Lectures of the University of Virginia for 1931).

By any standard, one must judge this expedition a very small, inexpensive one with no glamour at all. Yet Albright's archaeological chronology developed from the site . . . made it the type site for the country. The vast difference this made is clearly illustrated, for example, by the work of Alan Rowe and Ernest Sellin at Beth-shean and Shechem, on the one hand, and by the work of the excavators of Megiddo on the other. The former produced unusable archaeological chronologies which were most difficult to correct from the evidence presented, while the Megiddo excavations not only followed the Tell Beit Mirsim chronology, but also elaborated Albright's system of publication so that one had the data to judge and revise for himself.[20]

Albright directed four seasons of excavation at Tell Beit Mirsim assisted by Kyle, a biblical scholar of conservative persuasion, closer to the attitudes of men like Sayce (p. 41) than to any position ever assumed by Albright himself, though such differences never appear to have affected their mutual regard. This mound, no longer generally identified with Debir as it was by Albright, provided a sequence of occupation levels across the Bronze and Iron Ages. In his own mind Albright

> followed the principles worked out by Fisher . . . The main points are: systematic and careful planning, surveying and levelling; excavation of areas rather than trenches; full and exact drawing of pottery forms . . . systematic recording and card-indexing, with the use of a large record-book for the detailed entry of all objects recovered.[21]

The failure to say anything here of stratigraphy or context is striking and significant. Many years later, when his method of excavation was being unfavourably compared to Kenyon's, Albright was moved to comment that, 'of course, we do not claim to have anticipated the Wheeler-Kenyon technique, but merely to have employed stratigraphic evidence in a similar but cruder way.'[22]

To judge from his reports the unifying elements in the excavation were gross architectural units, not carefully distinguished levels of debris, whose correlation and dating owed everything to Albright's analysis of the pottery sherds retrieved from them. The sharpest criticism of this procedure was to come from one of the liveliest archaeologists of the post-war generation, when Lapp noted that

> of the Palestinian pottery published, for example, as from Stratum x of the early twelfth century BC, very little comes from an empirically observed and excavated layer (or group of contemporary layers) delimited by plan and located in section. Much of such pottery cannot be so precisely located on a three-dimensional basis because recording was not that thoroughgoing and excavation did not proceed layer by layer. Often what appears as Stratum x pottery is no more than pottery from arbitrary levels of an excavation that fit accepted typological canons for the date assigned to the stratum.[23]

Albright's priorities are immediately apparent from his manner of publication: two specialist monographs on the pottery in 1932-33, preceding two general reports, one on the Bronze Age (1938), one on the Iron Age (1943), which both treat the site chronologically by 'strata'.

The Bronze Age monograph assumes knowledge of the appropriate pottery volume; but that on the Iron Age is comprehensive in its treatment, including most notably a pioneer study of the pottery technology by a potter, Thorley. It remains the best example of Albright's technique as an archaeologist, demonstrating that there is no substitute for the combination of all aspects of an excavation within a single volume devoted to a particular period of time. Albright's excavations at Tell Beit Mirsim and his rapid publication of them show how, in the long run, it is not so much the sensational aspects of an excavation, for here there were none, but the quality of observation, description and analysis revealed by its publication that ensure its status and enduring legacy.

In 1931 Albright was involved with Sellers in excavations at the citadel of Beth-zur (Khirbet el-Tubeiqa), work extended by a second expedition in 1957, when Albright was not involved, though his influence is apparent in the final publication of 1968. In 1933 he undertook soundings at Ader, his only such enterprise east of the Jordan. Of considerably greater importance for Albright's central role in the realignment of the relationship between Palestinian field archaeology and the Biblical tradition was his direction of excavations in 1934 at Bethel (Beitin), a town mentioned more often in the Bible than all save Jerusalem. He was assisted by Kelso, from the Pittsburgh-Xenia Theological Seminary, which co-sponsored the dig with the American School. They were joined by Bright (p. 104), Pritchard (p. 128) and Wright (p. 77) at the start of their careers.

Kelso resumed work at Bethel in three subsequent campaigns between 1954 and 1960. He was also primarily responsible for the final report on the excavations published in the same year as *Beth-zur* (1968). A new generation[24] did not treat them with much respect, focusing their criticisms on the absence of proper stratigraphical controls in excavation, for which Albright's mastery of pottery dating did not wholly compensate, and on Kelso's inextricable mixture of description and interpretation in reporting work at Bethel; too often his biblical preconceptions became confirmation of a particular biblical interpretation of the material evidence.

Although Albright was not the first critic to bring the evidence of archaeology to bear upon the Wellhausen hypothesis, he achieved unique authority in his time by assembling the results of archaeological investigation, both in Palestine and in adjoining countries, to demonstrate the historicity of many controversial parts of the Old Testament through firsthand knowledge of the land and its archaeology, gained particularly in the 1920s and 1930s. This enabled him to control and critically assess the work of archaeologists in a way other biblical scholars, without this experience, could not. Such experience alone would not have sufficed. The nature of the evidence through which the ancient Near East had been, and continued to be, opened up was such that it also required Albright's mastery of the relevant ancient languages and his encyclopaedic knowledge both of the Bible and of ancient history to give full force to the case he always sought to demonstrate. For him the study of all the relevant extra-biblical sources 'established the accuracy of innumerable details, and has brought increased recognition of the Bible as a source of history.'[25] It was a view welcome to theological conservatives who, at least initially, sometimes made the mistake of taking him for a fundamentalist. Positive as his view of biblical traditions was, it rested not on dogmatic assumptions, but on restless critical inquiry, particularly of every fresh piece of information. If time would show his methods to be faulty and his solutions sometimes simplistic (p. 153), his intellectual vigour and integrity have never been doubted.

Although his contribution to biblical archaeology rested upon the belief that both archaeology and the Bible are substantially trustworthy sources of historical information, Albright was well aware that archaeological evidence is at times equivocal and biblical narratives not all they seem. Even accepting the historicity of the text, it may often be the case that archaeological evidence is also required, if the historical meaning of the text is to be fully understood today. Two biblical themes, in particular, were a lifelong preoccupation for Albright in this respect. For the better part of half a century he tirelessly integrated textual and non-textual evidence recovered by archaeology (in this case largely outside Palestine [p. 81]), to sustain the hypothesis that the Patriarchal narratives were an authentic picture of the migrations of the ancestral Hebrews sometime in the Middle Bronze Age and that the Israelite occupation of Palestine had been achieved through violent conquest, for which the Joshua narratives were an authentic source, towards the end of the Late Bronze Age.

In any attempt to describe Albright's role in the development of biblical archaeology there is always the danger that the result will either artificially isolate this aspect of his work or else submerge it in accounts of his greater enterprise, the comparative history of the religions of the Near East with a particular focus on Canaan and Israel. 'What we have in mind is nothing less than the ultimate reconstruction, as far as possible, of the route which our cultural ancestors travelled in order to reach Judaeo-Christian heights of spiritual insight and ethical monotheism.'[26] The thread in his publications which leads directly from *The Archaeology of Palestine and the Bible* (1932; 3rd edition 1935), his first nontechnical study of the theme he made very much his own, to *The Archaeology of Palestine* (1949; final revised reprint 1960) is sufficient guide through the labyrinth of his innumerable smaller publications progressively bringing system and clarity, where previously there had been chaos, to the mainstream of biblical archaeology; but it is only part of the matter.

The central intellectual achievement of Albright's working life was *From Stone Age to Christianity: Monotheism and the Historical Process*, published in 1940, successively revised and then re-issued in 1957 with a new introduction. It is not what most people would describe as a work of biblical archaeology, yet without Albright's special combination of archaeological expertise and biblical scholarship it is inconceivable. In this panoramic survey of the rediscovery of the ancient Near East from remote prehistory to the time of Christ, Albright concentrated attention on monotheistic religion, which he identified as the uniquely significant feature of the development of human civilization in the region. He traced the roots of monotheism to the primitive cosmologies of Babylonia and Egypt, whilst finding its full emergence as an historical phenomenon in the solar theism of the 'heretic' pharaoh of Egypt, Amenophis IV (Akhenaten), in the fourteenth century BC. This, however, was only a prelude to an exposition of classic monotheism as expressed for him in the career of Moses: 'it is absurd to deny that Moses was actually the founder of the Israelite commonwealth and the framer of Israel's religious system. The fact is emphasized so unaminously by tradition that it may be regarded as absolutely certain';[27] tradition, of course, that for him had been confirmed by archaeology. Albright saw classic monotheism thereafter evolving in the subsequent pronouncements of the great prophets and culminating in the ministry of Christ. It was his fullest challenge to Wellhausen's evolutionary view of Israel's religion, buttressed by his positive attitude to Israel's early traditions as illuminated by a century of archaeological research.

There are some among biblical students and archaeologists who, finding *From the Stone Age to Christianity* a difficult book, have come to regard his Ayer Lectures of 1941, published as *Archaeology and the Religion of Israel*, as their favourite among those of his books which speak more directly to biblical scholars and historians of religion than to archaeologists. It has a flow and clarity, indeed an excitement in discovery and exposition, absent from the more ambitious and complex earlier volume, perhaps through its origins in the lecture hall. The opening chapter on 'Archaeology and the Ancient Near Eastern Mind' may now read as a period piece, but it serves to remind the reader that Albright saw archaeology as a guide as much to the history of ideas as to the writing of history. In the core of the book, on the archaeological evidence for the religion of Canaan and Israel, a theme to which he returned in the more technical *Yahweh and the Gods of Canaan* (1968), his mastery of the sources is as evident as ever, but so increasingly are explicit value judgements.

Albright, having summarized the significance of Israel's borrowings from Canaanite religion as revealed by archaeology, declared that:

> These adaptations lay almost entirely in the domain of religious architecture, cult symbolism and sacrificial practice, poetic language and temple music. But the God of Israel was so far superior to the gods of the pagans, both conceptually and ethically, that theological borrowing from Canaanite sources was scarcely thinkable - at least until much later times, when the elements in question had become dissociated from their crude polytheistic background.[28]

The 'Postcript' takes the matter even further, re-emphasizing his view that with archaeology allowing interpretation of 'each religious phenomenon and movement of the Old Testament in the light of its true background and real sources' it was possible 'to emphasize the fact that the Israelite faith was much closer to Christianity and to rabbinic Judaism than to the basically prelogical religions of the ancient Near East'.

Preoccupied as he was with the massive intellectual project these two books represent, Albright remained at the same time fully involved with highly technical aspects of the structuring of archaeology and history in Mesopotamia, as may be seen in his advocacy of the 'low chronology' for the First Dynasty of Babylon (from about 1830-1530 BC) with which his name is still linked. Although this is now an option favoured only by a few, it has not yet been decisively eliminated. Although Albright had initially accepted the 'middle chronology' (c. 1894-1594 BC), argued primarily by Sidney Smith in 1940 and subsequently adopted for the revised *Cambridge Ancient History* (by all save Albright), he modified this estimate downwards a few years later. After further study of the primary Mesopotamian sources, he confidently concluded in 1945 that 'this latest reduced chronology fits the archaeological and historical picture so exactly that it cannot be appreciably wrong, so far as I can see'.[29]

No survey of Albright's achievements in his prime would be complete without a final glance at what may prove to have been his most enduring achievement in these years, for it gave structure and coherence to the archaeology of Palestine, where previously there had been anarchy and chaos as each man went his own way. Handcock's *The Archaeology of the Holy Land* (1916), illustrates the chaos of chronological terms at the end of the pioneering phase of fieldwork. Even Garstang's attempt in 1922 to establish a classification system, with the assistance of Phythian-Adams, Vincent and Albright himself, though it brought Palestinian terminology within the mainstream of Old World archaeology at the time, was necessarily an interim measure before new excavations were undertaken. It was on the basis of these, not least his own work at Tell Beit Mirsim (p. 70), that Albright, and later Wright, established the system that still has widest currency, using the traditional European 'Three Ages' nomenclature of Stone, Bronze and Iron, with suitable subdivisions and abandoning subsidiary ethnic terminology proposed in 1922: Early, Middle and Late Canaanite (for the Bronze Age); Early, Middle and Late Palestinian (with internal divisions labelled 'Philistine', 'Israelite', 'Jewish' and 'Hellenistic') for the Iron Age. The call for politico-ethnic terms is recurrent, but, as Albright and his colleagues with their wide perspectives appreciated, it is the old technological designations, inexact though they often are, which alone permit the wide-ranging cross-cultural correlations which keep the archaeology of Palestine in touch with the mainstream of world archaeology.

Albright's authority was to be so great and the range of his writings so diverse that criticism of his approach to biblical archaeology rarely emerged in his lifetime in the English-speaking world. Glueck, his first pupil and a leading colleague was not to be so fortunate. His rather narrower contribution to biblical archaeology was as fundamental and, in its own way, as provocative as anything argued by Albright in whose shadow he always seemed to fall. Glueck (1901-71) was the most important Jewish scholar to involve himself with biblical archaeology before 1948. He was born in Cincinnati, studied at the Hebrew Union College there, and was ordained as a rabbi in 1923. At the College Glueck had come under the influence of its president, Morgenstern, whose allegiance to the Wellhausen School in biblical exegesis was modified by his appreciation of the importance of wider cultural and theological factors for elucidating textual histories. Glueck, whilst not adopting Morgenstern's methods, was thereafter forever aware of the complexities of the Bible's documentary history. In 1923 he went to

Germany to study with Gressmann in Berlin and Staerk in Jena, as preparation for a thesis on the concept of *hesed* in the Bible (1927), designed as the first part of a systematic study of major biblical ideas.

From Gressmann, the pioneer of the analysis of tradition in biblical study, Glueck learnt the relevance of archaeological evidence for research on the culture and history of ancient Israel. But it was through working with Albright in Palestine, notably on his excavations at Tell Beit Mirsim, that he discovered his true vocation as an archaeological explorer.

> Nelson Glueck was the first of my students to master the then obscure art of dating Palestinian pottery by use of its many typological differences as well as by careful analysis of changes in form in each type from first introduction to vestigial remains - which often last through several cultural phases.[30]

Between 1932 and 1947, interrupted by the Second World War, Glueck undertook single-handed a remarkable series of surveys in Ammon, Edom and Moab, travelling mostly on foot or on horseback, mapping, photographing and recording. His growing mastery of ceramic dating allowed him to pioneer a method of research now commonplace but then new to the regions he investigated. He constructed maps of settlement distribution, period by period, through the distinctive types of pottery collected from the surface of settlement sites. Glueck's combination of archaeological skills with the drive, endurance and tenacity of an explorer, fired by a deep sense of the history of the region, has not been matched, though modern methods of team survey have modified his conclusions, often radically (p. 167).

Glueck's technical studies were published in volumes of the Annual of the American Schools of Oriental Research between 1934 and 1951; but his ideas became widely known through two popular books *The Other Side of the Jordan* (1940) and *The River Jordan* (1946). It was through them that his approach came to epitomize the aims and methods of biblical archaeology in the eyes of many people. He argued, on the basis of his surveys in Transjordan, that a steep decline of settlement there had followed dense occupation in the later third millennium BC. He associated this phenomenon with the Sodom and Gomorrah traditions in Genesis 13-19. For the next seven hundred years, through the mature Bronze Age, most of Jordan, Glueck argued, had been exclusively inhabited by nomadic or semi-nomadic peoples in total contrast to the pattern of settlement west of the river in Canaan. He saw settlement returning in the thirteenth century BC. He attributed sites of the earliest Iron Age to the emerging Ammonites, Edomites, Israelites and Moabites. It was at this time, not earlier, that he dated the Exodus and Conquest narratives. 'Had the Exodus through southern Transjordan taken place before the thirteenth century BC, the Israelites would have found neither Edomites and Moabites who would have given or withheld permission to traverse their territories.'[31]

It was such statements as this, and the assumption upon which they were so clearly based, that helped to create the pejorative popular view of the Biblical archaeologist as a man working with a Bible in hand, declaring it to be the most reliable guide to the antiquities of the region. It was to make Glueck a particular target for criticism twenty years later (p. 102). In these early years Glueck conducted two excavations, one on the Nabatean Temple at Khirbet et-Tannur (1937), the other at Tell el-Kheleifeh, roughly equidistant between modern Eilat and Aqaba.

In 1932-34 the German engineer and explorer Frank undertook extensive travels in the Arabah, mostly on foot with Bedouin guides, recognizing for the first time many of the ancient copper mines in this area. He found Tell el-Kheleifeh and suggested that it was Ezion-Geber. Glueck, excavating there from 1938-40, accepted this identification and dated the settlement between the tenth and the fifth centuries BC. A large building, heavily scorched and fire blackened, was identified as a sophisticated copper smelting installation, which Glueck magnified into a Solomonic 'Pittsburgh of Palestine'. Subsequent research has dated the earliest occupation here to the eighth century BC, wholly dissociating it from Solomon's enterprises, and eliminated Glueck's metalworking centre as wishful thinking.[32]

By the end of the 1930s, Wright (1909-74), the student who above all others carried Albright's ideas forward into a new generation, had established himself as the heir apparent. Wright had been trained in the Presbyterian tradition. He gained archaeological field experience on the excavations at Bethel and publication experience in preparing a report on Beth-Shemesh; all the time absorbing and developing his skills as a ceramic typologist under Albright's experienced eye. His thesis for the Johns Hopkins University, prepared between 1934 and 1937, was on *The Pottery of Palestine from the Earliest Times to the End of the Early Bronze Age* (1937). Like Albright he had combined a training in biblical scholarship with a very practical apprenticeship in archaeology in Palestine, but a greater interest in theology was to distinguish much of what he later wrote. In Wright's career it was biblical theology specifically that converged with biblical archaeology. For him, much more than for Albright, archaeology's role was to expose the historical basis of the Judaeo-Christian faith, to demonstrate how revelation had come through history.

In 1938, whilst involved with fundraising for the American Schools of Oriental Research, Wright founded a periodical, *The Biblical Archaeologist*, to raise popular consciousness of the Schools and their work in the Near East. What began as little more than a magazine for young people and Sunday school teachers has become in the following half century the primary source for current information, no less than the arena for topical debate, in all areas where the Bible and archaeology interact. The academic integrity established by Wright has ensured its enduring value to layman and scholar alike.

Excavations in Mesopotamia and Syria: Ur 'of the Chaldees' and Nuzi; Mari and Ugarit (Ras Shamra)

It was not only in Palestine that the collapse of the Ottoman Empire in 1917 and the establishment of the British Mandate opened the way for an unprecedented surge of archaeological fieldwork. In the Lebanon, in Syria and in Mesopotamia, also under mandate administrations, the years between the two World Wars produced much of the evidence around which their archaeology is currently structured. In contrast to Palestine, most of the scholars involved there were neither preoccupied with biblical problems nor in religious orders. When not professional field archaeologists, like Woolley, they were most commonly students of Akkadian or Sumerian. Yet all of them were operating within an academic world and reporting to a public, whence came much of their funding, for whom Christianity or Judaism, if not necessarily biblical scholarship, was vital. Although their research programmes might not be primarily conditioned by biblical concerns, they were nonetheless sensitive to the relevance their finds might have for Biblical Studies, if only for the greater publicity that still ensured. Funds for their excavations from sources in Europe or North America still flowed more readily for projects of potential biblical concern than they did for those remote from it and, as the pioneers of biblical archaeology had discovered, it was from Mesopotamia rather than from Palestine that the most immediately illuminating documents were likely to come.

The first major excavation of the mandate years in Mesopotamia was the joint British Museum and University Museum (Philadelphia) Expedition to excavate Tell el-Mukayyar, ancient Ur, about six miles from Nasiriyyah in southern Iraq, directed by Woolley (1880-1960), from 1922-34. This renowned excavation, and its no less remarkable multi-volumed report with the famous 'Royal Cemetery' as its crowning achievement, remains fundamental to modern knowledge of ancient Iraq both through the artefacts and the texts recovered.[33] Woolley was the son of a clergyman and when young considered becoming one himself. He always turned instinctively to the Bible for analogies and comparisons, particularly in his widely read books for the general reader. He had a natural talent for writing and a flair for giving life to the past. Although he had no formal training in oriental languages nor in Biblical Studies, he had a deep knowledge of the Old Testament, which he treated almost without question as an historical source, accepting the arguments of Sayce rather than those of Driver, who were both leading figures in Oxford University when he studied there.

Tell el-Mukayyar had been identified as Ur (Sumerian: *Urim*) from inscriptions found in 1854 in the ruined ziggurat which dominates the site. Thereafter it had been rapidly associated with Ur 'of the Chaldees', home of Abraham, in Genesis 11:31. Although this equation remains uncertain, Woolley never questioned it. From the first he assigned a group of houses in the town outside the ziggurat enclosure and the temple platform dating to the earlier second millennium BC to the 'age of Abraham'. This begged many questions, not the least whether this was indeed biblical Ur and whether Abraham and the biblical traditions about him could be accepted as historical and, if so, at what period. A decade later, in 1936, Woolley published a book for the general public entitled *Abraham: recent Discoveries and Hebrew Origins*, dedicated to Rudyard Kipling 'to whom archaeologists and historians owe much'. It was, indeed, a book for a teller of tales rather than for a critical historian. Written with all Woolley's facility, clarity and conviction, every crucial issue of chronology, history and topography was prejudged in favour of the biblical tradition.

The 'Flood Legend' of Mesopotamia had become well-known and much studied in the decades following Smith's sensational discovery of the first tablet of it recognized in modern times (p. 11). Publication in 1923 of the best surviving copy of the Sumerian King-List (The Weld-Blundell Prism),[34] revealing kings listed before and after 'the Flood', revived interest. But it took Woolley's characteristic interpretation of the prehistoric sequence at Ur to introduce the biblical Flood into field archaeology. Following his discovery of a substantial deposit of water-laid silt separating stages in the earliest fifth-millennium BC village settlement at Ur, Woolley announced in 1929 that he had evidence of the Flood of Sumerian tradition, which had then passed into Genesis. He interpreted this break in occupation as clear indication of a catastrophic flood overwhelming all of southern Mesopotamia. Memories of this natural disaster, he argued, had been handed down orally for many centuries to take the form in which it had survived in the Assyro-Babylonian written tradition and in the Bible. He was never convinced by arguments that his silt deposit was more persuasively explained as evidence for a change in the bed of the river Euphrates or as a local flood in a region where they have always been the most recurrent of natural hazards.

The ensuing debate, both archaeological and scientific, academic and popular, was immediately complicated by claims for comparable flood deposits revealed by excavations at Kish and Tell Farah (ancient Shuruppak) in Iraq. In particular Langdon, an Assyriologist in Oxford who was director of the contemporary Anglo-American expedition excavating at Kish, a few miles to the east of Babylon, swiftly and sharply contested Woolley's claims in favour of finds made at Kish by Watelin, the French field director of excavations there. Although Langdon presented his challenge in letters to leading London newspapers, his real bid for wide public attention was an article entitled 'The Biblical Deluge an Ascertained Fact' in the *Illustrated London News* for February 8th, 1930. This argued that flood deposits at Kish, dating to the early historic period, c. 2800 BC, were much closer in time to the reign of Gilgamesh, king of Uruk, who subsequently became hero of the epic named after him, into which the Flood legend was incorporated. Meanwhile American excavations at Shuruppak (Tell Farah) had revealed another flood deposit of the early historic period with an even stronger claim to be that enshrined in the Sumerian dynastic tradition as revealed in their later King List, since later Assyro-Babylonian sources tell of the 'Flood that was in Shuruppak' and the hero of the Flood in the *Epic of Gilgamesh* is Ziusudra, king of Shuruppak.

Whether or not the Shuruppak flood level is indeed surviving witness to an actual flood in the early third millennium BC, which found its way into the local literary tradition, and thence perhaps into Genesis, it is now generally agreed that Ur's 'flood deposit' is too remote in time to be a candidate. The controversy over the Flood among archaeologists active in Mesopotamia had relatively little impact upon contemporary debates about the character of the Pentateuch and the authenticity of the Patriarchal narratives. The protagonists in that dispute were far more interested in tablets from contemporary excavations at ancient Nuzi, a relatively small site, south-west of Kirkuk, well to the east of the river Tigris in Iraq.

The particular type of cuneiform tablet for which the site of Nuzi was to become renowned had been emerging through clandestine excavations for at least thirty years before the American Schools of Oriental Research excavated Yorghan Tepe, ancient Nuzi, from 1925 to 1931 under the direction of Chiera, Pfeiffer and Starr. From the town at Nuzi, destroyed about 1350 BC, or soon after, the excavators recovered at least four thousand cuneiform tablets mainly from private archives extending back some four or five generations. The family customs, particularly of birth-right and inheritance, among the town's Hurrian-speaking inhabitants were immediately claimed to be remarkably similar to those described in Genesis, the more enigmatic of which, it was argued, could not be fully explained by later biblical practice. Such social and legal parallels became a key ingredient in arguments proposed by Albright and others for dating the 'patriarchal period' to the second millennium BC, though it was accepted that dating within it was flexible, since family custom represented longstanding local patterns of behaviour. However, it was not sufficiently appreciated at the time, nor perhaps often enough thereafter, that the kind of private archives found at Nuzi are rare in the archaeological record in Mesopotamia. Thus it was, and to an extent still is, difficult to establish whether or not any specific sociological practice encountered in them is or is not particularly distinctive of the fifteenth and earlier fourteenth centuries BC or of Nuzi's Hurrian-speaking population. In the first phase of study it was too readily assumed that they were (see p. 153).[35]

An equally important role came to be played in Albright's case for the historicity of the patriarchal narratives by the royal archives from ancient Mari. Albright had identified Tell Hariri, on the middle Euphrates just north of the modern border between Iraq and Syria, as ancient Mari some nine years before French excavations early in the 1930s, under Parrot's direction, confirmed his suggestion. This ancient city had two major periods of activity, the first in the middle of the third millennium BC (p. 152) and the second half a millennium later, when a powerful local dynasty was eventually overthrown by Hammurabi of Babylon, whose destruction of the royal palace in the eighteenth century BC had preserved its archives.

At this time Mari was the home of people speaking three main languages: Akkadian, the language of Assyro-Babylonia; Hurrian, a language also used later at Nuzi; and Amorite, a precursor of biblical Hebrew, which immediately attracted the attention of biblical scholars to the Mari archives. The Amorite-speaking people were predominant on the middle Euphrates and through into what is now western Syria. The

Mari texts are of particular importance for the information they provide about the semi-nomadic communities of sheep-breeding pastoralists, whose tribesmen commonly had Amorite names. Sometimes they were encamped in tents in the desert periphery, sometimes on the outskirts of towns. They served as mercenaries or as casual labour in the royal army and workshops, or made a living from banditry.

From their first publication, Albright's enthusiasm for the information provided by the archives from the royal palace at Mari remained undimmed, since it came to occupy a place at the centre of his arguments for the authenticity of the patriarchal narratives as records of the earlier second millennium BC:

> ... the extraordinary discoveries at Mari ... are in process of yielding authentic information about the Patriarchal Age ... the tablets from Mari are illuminating all corners of the age in question ... Abraham, Isaac and Jacob no longer seem isolated figures, much less reflections of later Israelite history; they now appear as true children of their age, bearing the same names, moving about the same territory, visiting the same towns (especially Harran and Nahar), practising the same customs as their contemporaries. In other words, the patriarchal narratives have a historical nucleus throughout, though it is likely that long oral transmission of the original poems and later prose sagas which underlie the present text of Genesis has considerably refracted the original events.[36]

It would be wrong, however, to credit Albright alone with the conspicuous role Mari occupied in biblical archaeology at this time, since the director of excavations there was himself deeply involved with the subject. Parrot (1901-80), the son of a Lutheran clergyman, had initially wished to be ordained as a priest and his religious faith remained central to his concerns as a scholar. His teachers, both in Paris and at the Ecole Biblique in Jerusalem, had steered him towards field archaeology in which he gained his first experience as a member of Dunand's excavation team at Byblos in the Lebanon. In 1930 he was transferred to Mesopotamia to work briefly at Telloh (Girsu) and Larsa before being entrusted with the Mari expedition, which he was to direct, with a break for and after the Second World War, until 1974 in combination with curatorial duties at the Louvre.

Parrot shared with Woolley his clerical background and his skills as a writer for the general reader, though he lacked Woolley's flair in archaeological fieldwork and publication. In his numerous articles and books on Mari he was ever ready to establish contacts between his finds and the Old Testament. At the same time in books such as *De Babylone à Jericho (L'archéologie contemporaine et la bible)* in the 1930s and from 1952 in a series of *Cahiers d'archéologie biblique*, inaugurated by *Deluge et arche de Noë*, he revitalised biblical archaeology for the French-speaking public. In these short books, some of which were translated into English, Parrot was conservative in his interpretation of the Old Testament and optimistic, at times even more so than Albright, in the confidence he placed in archaeological information as witness to the authenticity of biblical tradition.

Remarkable as the archives of Nuzi and Mari each were in their own way, they were almost wholly eclipsed for students of the Old Testament by the new and unexpected range of tablets recovered by French excavations at Ras Shamra, ancient Ugarit, in Syria under the direction of Schaeffer. This site was discovered by a local farmer in 1928 and has been excavated, with interruptions for the Second World War, ever since. In the very first season of excavation in 1929 clay tablets were discovered with texts in a previously unknown language written alphabetically in cuneiform signs. Some of these texts were speedily published in copies by Virolleaud allowing the script to be deciphered by Bauer and Dhorme, working independently, in a remarkably short time. Within a year or two 'Ugaritic', as it was called, had become among the most famous of rediscovered ancient Near Eastern languages. Although texts written in it are now known from other sites in Syria, the Lebanon and Palestine, they are numerically insignificant in comparison with those from Ras Shamra (Ugarit). There many other languages, notably Akkadian, the diplomatic language of the Late Bronze Age, were soon recognized among a succession of archives from the major secular and religious buildings of the city in the fourteenth and thirteenth centuries BC. The types of text were as various as the languages, embracing administration and commerce, law and diplomacy, school-texts and dictionaries, above all a large body of religious documents, including rituals, lists of deities and sacrifices, and poetry. By 1940 Virolleaud had published most of the literary material found in the 1930s, whilst Gordon had compiled the first of a series of fundamental studies of the Ugaritic language.

The impact of these documents on biblical studies was immediate, profound and enduring. Not only were the new texts in Ugaritic, a relative of ancient Hebrew, of outstanding importance for linguistic study of the text of the Old Testament, but they appeared to offer the first direct evidence for the religion of Canaan, otherwise known only from prejudiced Old Testament accounts and much later, secondary sources. Whether or not it is indeed 'Canaanite', and there has always been a degree of pan-Ugariticism to match the pan-Babylonianism of an earlier generation (p. 46), the literature of Ugarit is more closely related in linguistic terms, in cultural affinity and in time to the earliest Hebrew literature than is that of Assyro-Babylonia or of Egypt. Even if the extreme view that the earliest portions of the Old Testament should be seen as a phase in the development of Canaanite literature is discounted, the texts from Ugarit remain central to Old Testament Studies. They are as important for assessing Hebrew indebtedness to Canaan in language as in culture.

Albright always emphasized, in particular, the importance of these texts for sustaining his argument for the antiquity of the early biblical narratives.

> Here was something undreamed of before 1931 ... a North-west Semitic dialect that is essentially pre-Phoenician Canaanite, which was very closely related to the Hebrew of the time of Moses . . . The poetic structure, style, and even the phraseology of the epics, are closely related to the same features of the oldest poetic texts of the Bible, not to mention the close correspondence of grammar and vocabulary.[37]

He also highlighted the relevance of the material culture of Ugarit, its religious and secular architecture, cult furniture, funerary practices, luxury goods and objects of daily use for a better understanding of Canaanite culture in general.

With the outbreak of the Second World War in 1939 there was virtually a decade of inaction in the archaeology of the Near East. To a degree work went on in universities and seminaries and publications were prepared that might otherwise have been even longer delayed; but fieldwork largely lapsed. When work in the field was again possible, the region had been politically transformed and Biblical Studies were suddenly invigorated by the most remarkable discovery of ancient documents yet made in Palestine.

1 R.E. Mortimer Wheeler, *Archaeology from the Earth*, Oxford, 1954, p. 16.

2 W.F. Albright, *New Horizons in Biblical Research* (Whidden Lectures, 1961), London, 1966, p. 1.

3 Cited in P.J. King, op. cit., n. 13, p. 77.

4 H.G. May and R.M. Engberg, *Material Remains of the Megiddo Cult*, Oriental Institute Publication XXXII, Chicago, 1935, pp. 4ff.; cf. D. Ussishkin, 'Schumacher's Shrine in Building 338 at Megiddo', *I.E.J.* 39 (1989), pp. 149-172.

5 *B.A.S.O.R.* 9, 1923, p. 11.

6 *B.A.S.O.R.* 48, 1932, p. 15.

7 M-L. Buhl and S. Holm Nielsen, *Shiloh*, The National Museum of Denmark, Copenhagen, 1969; cf. D. Schley, *Shiloh* (J.S.O.T. Supplements 1989).

8 R.E. Mortimer Wheeler, op. cit., p. 16.

9 W.F. Albright, *The Archaeology of Palestine* (1956), p. 22.

10 O. Tufnell, 'James Leslie Starkey: an appreciation', *Palestine Exploration Quarterly* 1938, p. 82.

11 K.M. Kenyon, 'Excavation Methods in Palestine', *Palestine Exploration Quarterly* 1939, p. 10.

12 C. Watzinger, 'Zur Chronologie der Schichten von Jericho', *Zeitschrift der Deutschen Morgenländischen Gesellschaft* 80, 1926, pp. 131ff.

13 Cited by P.J. King, *American Archaeology in the Mideast* ... (1983), p. 91.

14 *American Journal of Semitic Languages and Literature LVIII* (1941), p. 370.

15 H.H. Rowley, *From Joseph to Joshua: Biblical Traditions in the Light of Archaeology* (The Schweich Lectures 1948), British Academy, London, 1950, p. 20; cf. J.R. Bartlett, *Jericho*, Lutterworth Press, 1982; P. Bienkowski, *Jericho in the Late Bronze Age*, Warminster, 1986.

16 A-C. Barrois, *Manuel d'Archéologie Biblique*, Paris I (1939), p. 3.

17 *The Archaeology of Palestine and the Bible* (1935), p. 189.

18 Forword to the memorial edition of *The Archaeology of Palestine and the Bible*, Cambridge, Mass., 1974; see now G. van Beek (ed.) *The Scholarship of W.F. Albright*, Scholars Press, 1989.

19 Cf. Y. Yadin, 'William Foxwell Albright', *Eretz Israel* 9, 1969, foreword.

20 G.E. Wright, op. cit. n. 18.

21 W.F. Albright, *The Archaeology of Palestine and the Bible* (1935), p. 66.

22 W.F. Albright, *Bibliotheca Orientalis* 1964, p. 69, in a review of H.J. Franken and C.A. Franken-Battershill, *A Primer of Old Testament Archaeology* (1963).

23 P. Lapp, *Vetus Testamentum* XX, 1970, p. 245 in a review of H.J. Franken, *Excavations at Tell Deir 'Alla* I (1969).

24 Cf. W.G. Dever, 'Archaeological Methods and Results: a review of two recent publications', *Orientalia* 40, (1971), pp. 459ff.

25 W.F. Albright, *The Archaeology of Palestine and the Bible* (1935), p. 128.

26 W.F. Albright, *Archaeology and the Religion of Israel* Baltimore, 1942, p. 4.

27 W.F. Albright, *From Stone Age to Christianity*, Anchor Book A 100, 1957, p. 258.

28 W.F. Albright, *The Archaeology of the Religion of Israel*, 3rd edition, 1953, p. 94.

29 W.F. Albright, 'An indirect synchronism between Egypt and Mesopotamia circa 1739 B.C.', *B.A.S.O.R.* 99, (1945), p. 10.

30 W.F. Albright, 'Nelson Glueck in memoriam', *B.A.S.O.R.* 202 (1971), p. 2.

31 N. Glueck, 'Explorations in eastern Palestine and the Negeb', *B.A.S.O.R.* 55 (1934), p.16; cf. *The Other Side of Jordan* (1940), p. 146.

32 G.D. Practico, 'Nelson Glueck's 1938-1940 Excavations at Tell el-Kheleifeh: a reappraisal', *B.A.S.O.R.* 259 (1985), pp. 1ff.

33 For summary and bibliography see C.L. Woolley, *Ur 'of the Chaldees'*, revised and updated by P.R.S. Moorey, London, 1982.

34 S. Langdon, *Oxford Editions of Cuneiform Texts*, Oxford, 1923; cf. Th. Jacobsen, *The Sumerian King List*, The Oriental Institute, Chicago, Assyriological Studies no. 1, 1939.

35 B.L. Eichler, 'Nuzi and the Bible: a retrospective' in H. Behrens *et al.* (eds.) *DUMU-E₂ DUB-BA-A: Studies in Honor of Åke W. Sjöberg*, Philadelphia, 1989, pp. 107-119.

36 W.F. Albright, *The Archaeology of Palestine*, revised reprint of 1956 edition, Penguin Press 1960, p. 236; cf. now; A. Malamat, *Mari and the Early Israelite Experience*, British Academy, 1989.

37 W.F. Albright, *New Horizons* . . . pp. 6-7; cf. A. Curtis, *Ugarit (Ras Shamra)*, The Lutterworth Press, 1985.

4

New Nations: New Methods
(1948-1959)

> Though archaeology can thus clarify the history and geography of ancient Palestine, it cannot explain the basic miracle of Israel's faith, which remains a unique factor in world history. But archaeology can help enormously in making the miracle rationally plausible to an intelligent person whose vision is not shortened by a materialistic world view (Albright, 1949).[1]

The decade following the end of the British Mandate in Palestine and the creation of the independent states of Israel and Jordan was filled with fresh discoveries and vigorous controversies to compensate for years of inaction in field archaeology. Debate arose over the proper methods of excavation and record in the field, in the light of Kenyon's Jericho excavations (1952-58), and over the appropriate role for archaeological evidence in writing the early history of Israel. The chance find of the Dead Sea Scrolls, and the ensuing excavations at Khirbet Qumran and in the caves whence they had come, transformed study both of the intertestamental period and of the Jewish background to the New Testament. Albright continued to dominate the academic and the popular relationship between archaeology and Biblical Studies, particularly in Israel and in the United States, where the work of his pupils was now increasingly evident. They were almost invariably deferential to the master's views. As America largely replaced Britain and France as the most influential foreign power in the Near East, so the American Protestant tradition remained most obviously the motivating force in biblical archaeology.

The emergence of Israel, however, was set to give the interrelationship of Palestinian archaeology and Old Testament studies a wholly fresh complexion. Trigger has proposed that: 'Israeli archaeology might be classified as being of the colonialist type, were it not that Israelis claim substantial historical roots in the land they are occupying'.[2] Biblical archaeology is so relevant to the nation's sense of identity and legitimacy that its academic status and intellectual integrity have never been questioned in the manner customary elsewhere in recent years among archaeologists. The archaeology of the Biblical and Second Temple periods in Israel not only plays a central role by demonstrating the link of an immigrant people with their remote past, but in so doing focuses directly on an ancestral home. Time and events may have modified the priority given to archaeology in the formative years of the state and tempered the urgency of the people's archaeological curiosity, but they have not, and in all likelihood will not, challenge significantly a discipline so fundamental to the fabric of the nation.

Israel had to create both a museum for archaeology in West Jerusalem and a new antiquities service, dynamically launched by Yeivin, an energetic and strong inaugural director. Israel's archaeologists came, as they continue to come, exclusively from the non-religious sections of her population. Rabbis and Orthodox scholars remain conspicuous by their absence from archaeology in a state where the subject is sustained by a civil religion. Positive Orthodox opposition to archaeology was, however, not to be a significant phenomenon until the 1980s. In the first decade of Israeli archaeology expatriate archaeologists were less common than they were at this time in Jordan and those who worked there tended to concentrate on sites earlier or later than the time-range of the Old Testament. With the creation of the State of Israel the Jewish Palestine Exploration Society became the Israel Exploration Society. Its excavation programme and its scholarly publications, particularly with Aviram as honorary secretary, have been central to the remarkable development of archaeology.

In the Hashemite Kingdom of Jordan the Mandate tradition endured in archaeology for almost a decade, since the British archaeologist, Lankester Harding, a pupil of Petrie's and a colleague of Starkey's at Tell ed-Duweir (p. 62), continued as director of antiquities until 1956, completing twenty years' service. He founded the archaeological museum in Amman, served as curator of the Palestine Archaeological Museum ('the Rockefeller') in Jerusalem, which was still adminstered by international trustees, and encouraged fieldwork by foreign archaeologists. After the partition of Palestine virtually all foreign institutions involved in field archaeology with bases in Jerusalem came within the boundaries of Jordan. Jordan, unlike Israel, did not have a generation of archaeologists in waiting ready to assume responsibility for administration, teaching and research in the newly independent state. The first generation of Jordanian archaeologists were largely young men, trained in the Anglo-American tradition through studies in Britain or America and by participation in excavations under British and American field directors at el-Jib (Pritchard), Jericho (Kenyon) and Shechem (Wright).

Archaeology and the Dead Sea Scrolls: the excavations of Père de Vaux

After a century of research in Palestine it had become almost axiomatic that no ancient documents written on organic materials could have survived there, when suddenly in 1946 a remarkable find of biblical and non-biblical texts was made in caves on the west side of the Dead Sea. Sometime in the winter of 1946-47, in so far as it is now possible to establish the facts, Taᶜamireh Bedouin living in the region between Bethlehem and the Dead Sea became aware of ancient documents of leather and parchment wrapped in linen and placed in pottery jars hidden in local caves. Examples were put onto the antiquities market through a professional cobbler and dealer Kando of Bethlehem. Four leather scrolls went to the head of the Syrian Orthodox Monastery in Jerusalem and three to Sukenik, professor of archaeology in the Hebrew University. Whilst the former was at first advised that they were worthless, Sukenik was discretely convinced of their authenticity through his own expertise. In 1948 the scrolls held by the Syrian Orthodox Monastery were photographed by John Trever, acting director of the American School, and prints were sent to Albright in America. He immediately recognized their importance: 'there is no doubt in my mind that the script is more archaic than that of the Nash Papyrus. I should prefer a date around 100 BC . . . And there can happily not be the slightest doubt in the world about the genuineness of the manuscript'.[3] Vigorous controversy was very soon to surround the date and authenticity of these scrolls. In the event Albright's first impression has proved to be broadly correct.

Meanwhile more manuscripts were coming to light and passing to the Palestine Archaeological Museum in Jerusalem. The worldwide excitement created by the announcement of the discovery of ancient biblical documents was matched at the outset, if not for long, by responsible and effective editorial enthusiasm. In 1948 and in 1950 Sukenik led the way with selective preliminary publication in Hebrew; but it was Millar Burrows, President of the American Schools for Oriental Research (1934-48), who initiated the first full publications. Burrows was a biblical scholar of distinction known at the time among biblical archaeologists for his general study of the subject, *What Mean these Stones* (1941), the best survey since Driver's (p. 43) a generation earlier and like his still of value. His rare combination of the appropriate academic skills with a flair for popular presentation ensured that both worlds were accommodated in early publications. The large Isaiah Scroll, the Habakkuk Commentary and the Manual of Discipline appeared in scholarly editions in 1950-51. Burrows also provided balanced popular appraisals of the Dead Sea Scrolls which found their way on to the bestseller lists in 1955 and 1958.

The admirable standards he set were not to be followed. Many scrolls still remain unpublished and inaccessible, so even the best subsequent studies are correspondingly compromised and the whole issue of academic responsibility for the scrolls remains a contentious question. Four scrolls, which had been taken to the United States by the Syrian Orthodox Archbishop, were subsequently sold to the State of Israel. In 1967, when Israel occupied the West Bank Territories, all the scrolls held in the Palestine Archaeological Museum, already allocated to various scholars for publication, became *de facto* the responsibility of the Israeli Department of Antiquities.

Late in January 1949, some eight miles south of Jericho and over a mile inland from the western shores of the Dead Sea, searches by members of the Arab Legion located the cave whence the first scrolls to appear on the antiquities market had come. It was then properly investigated by Lankester Harding (p. 88) and Père de Vaux, director of the Ecole Biblique (1945-65) and editor of the *Revue Biblique* (1938-53), who had recently opened excavations at Tell el-Farah (North) (p. 93). He was to establish an enduring reputation with his *Ancient Israel: its Life and Institutions* (1961) and his *Early History of Israel*, unfinished at his death in 1971. Their search revealed hundreds of fragments of scrolls, some parts of those already known, associated with pottery and other small objects, wrongly dated at the time to the second century BC; but at least endorsing the view that the scrolls were indeed ancient. At this time Khirbet Qumran, just over half a mile to the south of the cave, was thought to be the ruins of a Roman fort of the third or fourth century AD and its possible relationship to occupation in the adjoining caves was not seriously considered.

It was not until November 1951 that de Vaux began his systematic excavations at Khirbet Qumran completed in 1956. His work revealed a building complex with objects of daily use comparable to those in the caves whence the scrolls had come. The Qumran building once described as a fortress now became a 'monastery' with a 'scriptorium' and a 'refectory'; the world of the Dominican excavators strongly colouring their interpretation of their finds from a time long before such religious communities are known elsewhere. It established an enduring religious context for the buildings which, had it not been for the scrolls and the expectations they aroused, might well have been studied in the light of other contemporary settlements on the shores of the Dead Sea, which were agricultural like that at 'Ain Feshka, to the south, excavated by de Vaux in 1958. The Qumran complex remains unique in scale and layout.

De Vaux based his absolute chronology for the first major phase of occupation at Qumran on the numismatic evidence, arguing that the foundation might be pushed back to the middle of the second century BC. However, as has subsequently been pointed out, a foundation date in the closing years of the century is more convincingly sustained by the coin evidence de Vaux published. The archaeological framework is vital, since this dated sequence has been used both to control the chronology of the scrolls and also to sustain historical reconstructions of events in the history of the community obliquely described in the non-biblical scrolls. In fact, the difficulties of identifying the personalities referred to in the sectarian scrolls and the time of their activity is a problem independent of archaeology and not best controlled from the type of evidence it provided at Qumran. The evidence from de Vaux's excavation offered no compelling independent indication of the identity of the inhabitants of the buildings who still have to be identified on the basis of textual evidence, usually taken to indicate that they were Essenes. Nor does it unequivocally indicate, as has often been assumed, that one and the same community used Qumran from the late second century BC to about AD 68, when the Roman suppression of the First Jewish Revolt ended the settlement.

Throughout the period when Qumran was under excavation the search for caves containing scrolls went on intermittently until a total of eleven containing manuscripts had been recorded among a much larger number yielding only contemporary objects of daily use. The density of occupation in caves, some natural, some artificial, increased in the neighbourhood of the buildings at Qumran. The caves tend to fall into groups, as if the people who had lived in them were likewise subdivided. The many inhabited caves might indicate that the buildings at Qumran were predominantly used by a largely non-resident community for special purposes.

Archaeological investigation of the caves was also important initially for confirming that the scrolls sold by the Bedouin had indeed been concealed in the way and in the places they had claimed. The undisturbed caves (number 3, 5, 7-10), discovered by the archaeologists, yielded manuscripts and fragments (including two copper scrolls), as did caves first discovered by the Bedouin when systematically reinvestigated. None of the non-biblical manuscripts are internally date, though they contain isolated historical references which provide *termini post quem*, nor do the biblical manuscripts from the caves indicate when, or where, the copyist finished his work. They have then to be dated to some extent through the associated objects in the caves, especially pottery, and their links with finds in the buildings at Qumran, though no scroll fragments were found there by de Vaux. On the basis of ink wells and plaster fragments, controversially reconstructed as benches for scribes, he proposed the existence of a 'scriptorium' at Qumran; but there is no compelling archaeological evidence that any of the Dead Sea scrolls came from a 'library' at Qumran or that they were copied there.

The excavations at Qumran offered little or no information on the religious beliefs and practices of the people who had once flourished there, save perhaps in the highly enigmatic clues to extensive use of water and to communal meals in their rituals. But they did provide a range of information on the social and economic life of the residents and might well reveal more if the adjacent cemetery were to be properly excavated. By contrast, the non-biblical scrolls from the caves are rich in information on ideology and ritual with scraps of historical information, but offer a very unbalanced picture of the everyday life of the people who produced them. As continuing debates make clear, neither separately nor in conjunction do texts and artefacts offer self-evident truths. Qumran illustrates particularly well how each aspect of the evidence needs to be recurrently probed in the light of the other to yield something approaching an objective view. Once it had become accepted that excavations in the ruins at Qumran were revealing a building contemporary, and in some way associated, with the occupation levels of the neighbouring caves yielding scrolls, uncritical harmonization of the internal evidence of the scrolls and the archaeological data was a constant danger. In the absence of a definitive excavation report the necessary critical reassessment of the initial conclusions is virtually impossible; a delay as unfortunate as the slow progress in publication of the scrolls.

De Vaux reported regularly on his excavations in the *Revue Biblique*. In an expanded version of his 1959 Schweich Lectures, *Archaeology and the Dead Sea Scrolls* (posthumously published in 1973), he vividly presented his considered view of Qumran which remains that most widely accepted. The only extended critical assessment of de Vaux's work, by Laperrousaz *Qoumran, l' etablissement essenien des bords de la Mer Morte: Histoire et archéologie du site* (1976), is an excellent commentary raising a number of pertinent questions that only a final excavation report may adequately address.

In view of his formidable commitments to teaching, research and writing at the Ecole Biblique, it is not surprising that Père de Vaux never achieved final publications of his excavations, the more so when it is appreciated that since 1946 he had been responsible for another important excavation at Tell el-Farah (North), which would continue intermittently until 1960, after which he joined Kathleen Kenyon as co-director of the Jerusalem (Ophel) excavations. The Farah excavations had been undertaken to elucidate the history of an important *tell* at a cross-roads in a fertile region; to refine knowledge of the archaeology of the centre of ancient Palestine; and to identify, if possible, whether it was indeed ancient Tirzah, Jeroboam's capital, as Albright had argued in 1931, or one of the other towns proposed by scholars.

De Vaux's interpretation of the final Late Bronze Age occupation at Tell el-Farah and the succeeding Iron Age levels is a classic illustration of contemporary methods of interpretation in biblical archaeology, when stratigraphical breaks were explained in terms of Old Testament texts accepted as reliable historical sources without discussion:

> Archaeology confirms this identification [Farah = Tirzah], and it is possible to read in the different levels of the Tell all the history of Tirzah as told by the Bible . . . the destruction of the Late Bronze Age level . . . would mark the capture of the town by the Israelites (Joshua 12:24). They occupied it for a long period in peace - which is our third level. But, at the beginning of the 9th century, this level is overturned; we know from the Bible that . . . Omri laid siege to Tirzah and took it (1 Kings 16:15-18) . . . It was only after he had made his position secure that Omri could think of building at Tirzah: they are the buildings whose foundations reach down into the third level. These same buildings, however, were never finished, for two years later . . . Omri took the decision to leave Tirzah and to found a capital on the hill of Samaria . . . The buildings where we found work suddenly stopped are a vivid illustration of this transfer . . . even possible that Omri . . . took with him all or part of the population of Tirzah. This would explain the poverty of our intermediate level of the 9th century, preceded perhaps by a short period of abandonment . . . [4]

De Vaux believed, on the evidence of pottery typology, that the evidence for dove tailing Tirzah and Samaria was equally convincing at the latter site: 'the first two periods at Samaria . . . have no corresponding period at Tell el-Farah . . . contact begins only during the third period of Samaria and our intermediary level of the 9th century . . . '. The argument is perilously close to being circular: a perfect example of a procedure shrewdly summed up twenty years later by Franken (p. 132) in a penetrating critique of this approach to Biblical topography:

> If an archaeologist accepts uncritically the biblical evidence as a principle of explanation of archaeological finds, dates those finds from the biblical 'evidence', or provides dates for biblical events having first used such 'evidence' for identification and explanation of archaeological features, it becomes utterly impossible after a while to unravel the arguments, to see what is concluded from which evidence, or to find out how much of it is based on circular reasoning.[5]

Significantly, recent full publication of Père de Vaux's Iron Age finds at Tell el-Farah, which he did not complete himself, is very cautious about the stratigraphical interpretation:

> the excavator introduced a break, contemporary with Samaria I-II, and an intermediate level, with little building, corresponding with Samaria III. This sub-division cannot be ruled out, but the observed stratigraphy, as with the development of ceramic typology, is not precise enough to confirm an exact correspondence.[6]

Kenyon at Jericho (1952-58): old problems, new methods

The British School of Archaeology in Jerusalem had been unable to operate during the 1940s. For two decades after 1950 its existence was to be fused with the later career of Kathleen Kenyon (1906-1978).

> The fact that the Jerusalem institution did reopen and forthwith proceeded to carry out on a large scale exploratory work . . . was essentially due not to the modest generosity of Her Majesty's Treasury, but to the fortunate availability of a scholar of first class quality, fortified by a small but useful domestic bank balance and other accessible outside resources . [7]

Apart from her early experience with the Crowfoots, excavating at Samaria (p. 63), Kathleen Kenyon had served her apprenticeship, after graduating in history at Oxford, in British archaeology with 'two in particular . . . Dr. R.E.M. Wheeler, to whom I owe all my training in field archaeology and constant inspiration towards improved methods, and Professor V. Gordon Childe, whose brilliant analyses and syntheses of archaeological subjects are such a stimulus to a broad view'.[8]

In 1951, when she was lecturer in Palestinian Archaeology in the Institute of Archaeology in London University, Kenyon had published a paper in the *Palestine Exploration Quarterly* at Garstang's invitation, reassessing the stratigraphy of Tell es-Sultan (Jericho) as it had been revealed by his excavations there between 1930 and 1936 (p. 64). In considering the Bronze Age remains she agreed with both Watzinger (p. 64) and Garstang that the glacis and related encircling wall belonged to Middle Bronze II, in the second quarter of the second millennium BC; but in her reconstruction of the layer beneath, which she attributed to Early Bronze III (c. 2600-2400 BC) she laid the foundations for the radical revision of Garstang's dating of the 'double wall' on the crest of the mound that was to follow from her excavations. Moreover, she argued, on the basis of improved pottery chronologies, that pottery typical of Late Bronze I (c. 1500-1400 BC) was absent from the upper levels of the mound and from the tombs excavated by Garstang. There was, she pointed out, no evidence of a fifteenth-century town nor of town walls destroyed by earthquake and fire at the end of that century; but there were, in her view, slight traces of occupation in the following century, c. 1400-1300 BC.

No less important for an understanding of the impact Kenyon's methods were to have in the years after 1952 is her textbook, *Beginning in Archaeology* (1952), which clearly expounds them and their origins in her work with Wheeler. In so far as Palestine is concerned she had anticipated this book, which deals only with her British experience, in an essay in the *Palestine Exploration Quarterly* in 1939. It already describes and advocates the essentials of what has subsequently become popularly known as the Wheeler-Kenyon (or debris-layer) Method.

> When the season's work is over, the excavator thus has a complete record of the site. He has plans of walls which he can prove are contemporary by their association with the same floors. He has pottery and objects from the various levels, with measured sections to prove to which of the various building periods they belong.[9]

In other words rather than working to an *a priori* pattern of recording provided by architects and surveyors, as earlier archaeologists in Palestine had largely done, cutting wide trenches with little or no close attention to the interrelation of debris, structures and objects, Kenyon concentrated on smaller trenches. For her the direct observation and proper recording, in drawings and photography, of the different layers of deposit as found and the interpretation of their relationship to one another and any structures or small finds, was paramount.

> It is therefore an absolute principle of excavation, which allows of no exceptions at all, that the whole area must not be cleared simultaneously. Standing sections [or baulks] must be left at frequent intervals from the surface down, and it must be possible to relate all structures or disturbances

to them. The method of doing this will depend on the type of site being dug.[10]

Jericho, as it happened, was almost the perfect site for demonstrating the full potential of the 'Wheeler-Kenyon' Method. The mound had deposits covering eight millennia and important problems outstanding after earlier excavations remained to be resolved. Its biblical associations ensured wide publicity. Within two or three years of the start of work there in 1952 Kenyon had shown through deep trenching, anathema to the older school of excavators, through precise stratigraphic controls and through layer-by-layer recording, the errors of earlier excavations. Her achievement was two fold, first for biblical archaeology, and then for prehistory, revealing one of the oldest settlements in the region.

In her re-examination of the upper levels of this much eroded tell she revealed only a tiny area of occupation in the Late Bronze Age and no traces of this period in archaeological material from the lower slopes. At the end of Kenyon's work in 1958 it was clear to her that archaeology only offered evidence for a small unwalled settlement at Jericho c. 1425-1275 BC, with no indication of fortifications or of the destruction attributed by Garstang to Joshua's assault c. 1400 BC. This site had then been abandoned by the second quarter of the thirteenth century and not reoccupied until the eleventh BC. Kenyon died before her full *Jericho* report was complete. Publication of the raw data in volumes edited by Holland (1981-3) reopened controversy over the date and nature of the occupation of Jericho from the late Middle Bronze Age to the early Iron Age.

In 1954 Wheeler published his own study of archaeological field techniques, *Archaeology from the Earth*, isolating Palestine as a supreme example of malpractice. Kathleen Kenyon, who had provided the ammunition for this now famous denunciation, not least its illustrations, always claimed she had done so unwittingly. Three years later her pioneer work at Samaria (p. 63) was finally published in *Samaria-Sebaste III: the Objects*. This provided reviewers with their first real opportunity to debate the claims made for the 'Wheeler-Kenyon' Method, not least its novelty. Then, and on many subsequent occasions, advocates of this method have tended to over-emphasize its originality, detractors to underplay it, attributing a greater role to Reisner in the definition of stratigraphical excavation than either Kenyon or Wheeler had allowed. Such historical aspects of the debate, not a little affected by chauvinism, are peripheral to the main thrust of the critical attack, which will be considered below. In the event, within a decade or so, the improved field techniques advocated and demonstrated by Kenyon became, to a greater or lesser extent, the norm in Jordan through members of the international teams who had worked with her or the many archaeologists who came to observe her at work. Israeli archaeologists, who were unable to participate or to observe, adhered for much longer to the Fisher-Albright tradition in excavation.

The debate over excavation technique had two primary aspects, the one turning on procedures during excavation, the other on the interpretation of stratigraphy and small finds, particularly pottery, after excavation. American and Israeli archaeologists in particular over the years after 1958 advocated refinements in the handling of pottery, the excavation of much wider horizontal areas, and more co-ordinated teamwork both during excavation and afterwards in the preparation of finds for publication. They argued, above all, that Kenyon's methods 'are so tedious and demanding in application that scarcely ever is a single building completely cleared, let alone a building complex large enough to give us an adequate exposure on which to base our understanding of the material culture of the period'.[11] There was justice in such comments, as the results of excavation at Jericho make clear, but they did not allow sufficiently for Kenyon's pragmatism, clear from a careful reading of *Beginning in Archaeology*, and her conviction that the problems to be resolved at Jericho (as later in Jerusalem) were best tackled in the time and with the resources available by deep trenching and only small area excavations. She believed, as did Wheeler, that there was no single right way to excavate, though there were many wrong ones, particularly exemplified by work in Palestine. By precept and example she sought to show how the wrong ones might best be avoided at a time when such lessons were badly needed. The justice of her case and the general virtue of the method, albeit modified, were witnessed by its subsequent transformation of standards in fieldwork throughout the region. Events were to show that the great weaknesses of the Wheeler-Kenyon procedures were not so much in field practices, which might be continuously refined, but in the ensuing passage to full publication, which was the acid test.

Both American (Albright and Wright) and Israeli (Aharoni and Amiran) reviewers of *Samaria-Sebaste III* drew particular attention to what they saw as a fatal flaw; the absence of any clear distinction in Kenyon's analysis between 'building periods and pottery periods'.[12] Samaria provides what might seem to be a uniquely clear point-of-departure for any chronological analysis of material evidence, since the date of Omri's fortified foundation there is broadly known, c. 870 BC.

However, the Old Testament (1 Kings 16:24) is not as explicit as Kenyon maintained on whether or not Omri had acquired a virgin site, indeed the linguistic relationship between Shemer and the name Shomron suggests that he had not. Her critics pointed out that, although the stone structures of her Building Periods I and II were reasonably identified as the work of masons commissioned by Omri and Ahab, much of the associated pottery of these periods in her presentation, both stratigraphically and typologically, should be dated to the late tenth or early ninth century, indicating the presence of some earlier settlement on the site Omri had acquired.

When she replied, in 1964, Kenyon sidestepped the ceramic issue by resting her case entirely upon stratigraphy:

> the difficulties arise partly from the differences of method and partly from correlations which seem frankly to be erroneous. In the Samaria excavations, the British method was followed, by which the pottery and other finds ascribed to a structural period are those actually associated with the building operation, from the foundation trenches, floor make-up and so on. Admittedly such fills will include earlier, derived material, together with that dropped by the builders, but it is a commonplace of British archaeology that a building is dated by the latest object in its building deposits. The method at Hazor and most other Near Eastern sites is different. The material assigned to a stratum is that above its floors. There are two objections to this. In the absence of any published sections observed and drawn in the field (as distinct from schematic ones built-up from a collection of theodolite levels) at Hazor, there is no means of telling whether the objects come from one or more successive occupation levels, from destruction debris or from subsequent robber destruction.[13]

Even if the general stratigraphic case as presented here is sound, it does not answer the specific question or face the challenge to digging in narrow trenches posed by Albright when he argued that 'archaeology can advance only by putting tentative stratigraphic results to experimental tests, not once but repeatedly'.[14]

Kathleen Kenyon's failure to complete her report on excavations at Jericho have convinced many archaeologists that to apply the 'Wheeler-Kenyon' Method properly and to publish the results on any but the smallest scale is a task for carefully balanced and integrated teams. The raw data set out in the posthumously published *Jericho* volumes III-IV (1981-83) illustrate how necessary the excavator's guiding hand really is, from start to finish. It is only the director of the work who can provide the necessary cohesion and concluding overall interpretation which makes integrated sense of the myriad details of stratigraphy and ceramic typology upon which ultimately the enduring contributions to knowledge rest, particularly when the director alone, as in Kenyon's case, controlled all aspects of field procedures:'It is my firm conviction that no detailed conclusions as to the history of a site, or part of a site, can be reached while the excavations are in progress. In a complex site, such as a tell, everything has to be done in stages',[15] was her own reflection on the matter.

Albright: Bright: Wright - challenges and responses

For at least a decade after the return of archaeological fieldwork to Israel and Jordan the aims and the origins of the American participants were very much what they had been before 1939, as indeed were the leading personalities. Although Albright himself did not again become directly involved in fieldwork, one of his old collaborators did. When Sellers was injured in an aeroplane crash, Kelso (1892-1978), who had returned to Jerusalem in 1949 for a sabbatical year, assumed the Directorship of the American School and, with Baramki, opened excavations from 1949 to 1951 on what was thought to be the site of New Testament Jericho. Pritchard joined them in 1951. Subsequent Israeli excavations, directed by Netzer, were to show that the Americans had in fact discovered the pleasure palace of the Hasmonean Kings embellished by Herod the Great, whilst New Testament Jericho probably underlay the present town there. In 1954, 1957 and 1960 Kelso returned to dig Bethel (p. 71) and in 1964, his last year in the region, he was President of the re-opened excavations at Tell el-Ful (p. 69) directed by Lapp, soon to be the young standard-bearer of American field archaeology in Jordan (p. 130). Valid criticisms of Kelso's simplistic biblical interpretations of his discoveries at Bethel have subsequently eclipsed his very real contribution to reviving American research. No less noteworthy was his personal involvement, rare at this time, with interdisciplinary research on material culture involving natural scientists and technologists.

New sites as well as old were now investigated. But they were all, to a marked degree, biblical choices, since the excavators were still predominantly ordained Protestant clergymen or biblical specialists teaching in theological seminaries or in departments of religion in colleges and universities. Pritchard, who revitalized the great field tradition of the University Museum in Philadelphia, though a professor of Religious Thought from an Episcopalian background, was somewhat removed from the Albright tradition. His excavations at el-Jib (Gibeon).

northwest of Jerusalem, from 1956 to 1962, not only confirmed Robinson's identification of this site by finding the handles of pottery storage jars inscribed *Gibeon*, but revealed an extensive Iron Age water-system and wine-producing centre. Meanwhile, east of the river Jordan, where excavators still rarely penetrated, a sequence of American and Canadian directors from 1950 to 1956 excavated Dibon (ancient Dhiban), source of the renowned Moabite Stone (p. 20). Year by year more and more information was extracted from this complex site as techniques learnt from Kenyon's contemporary dig at Jericho were brought to bear on it.

It was not until 1956, when Wright (p. 77) returned to fieldwork at Shechem, that new ideas and new procedures were generated within the American field tradition and began significantly to modify methods inherited from the pioneers. The impact of this excavation on the rising generation of archaeologists from the United States was as great as Kenyon's at Jericho or, within Israel, Yadin's at Hazor. The senior staff of the later American excavations at Ai, Gezer and Taanach were nearly all trained at Shechem. It was a major part of Wright's purpose, though he had chosen this site for its importance in the Old Testament, to confound the growing view among archaeologists and ancient historians at large that excavations in the Holy Land represented everything that was unscientific in contemporary archaeology. He strove to create a broadly based expertise and a carefully co-ordinated team effort among the experienced and the less experienced, with the master instructing his apprentices in a field workshop.

Although Wright was very much aware of the value of the new techniques Kenyon was pioneering, and had closely observed her in action (as he had Yadin), he cast himself more in the Reisner-Fisher-Albright tradition. He sought to improve this legacy with aims and methods akin to those of Wheeler and Kenyon, yet distinct from them, for Wright did not understand and apply stratigraphical analysis in their sense. He published archaeological section drawings in his preliminary reports, but they are 'schematic', not on-site drawings of the stratigraphy as revealed in trenches. Nor were the small finds individually attributed to natural bedlines, or debris separated in the course of excavation. Although Wright placed day-to-day study of ceramic typology ('pottery-reading') at the centre both of his explanatory procedures and of his teaching of his young team, it was not conceived as the critical complement to observed stratigraphy in the manner which Kenyon demanded; indeed to such an extent that she undertook the daily review of it herself, believing the firsthand study and integration of stratigraphy and ceramic typology was the prime responsibility of an excavation director.

Unfortunately Wright did not live to publish the final reports on Shechem from which his achievements as a field archaeologist might best be assessed. His synthesis of archaeological and biblical evidence in the semi-popular *Shechem: the Biography of a Biblical City* (1965) met with criticism both from professional archaeologists, largely in the English-speaking world, and from biblical scholars, particularly in Germany. In a sense this was predictable, since Wright's career as a field archaeologist at this time cannot be understood without reference on the one hand to his position as Albright's foremost pupil in biblical archaeology and on the other, to his deep involvement with the 'Biblical Theology' movement, as expressed in *God who Acts* (1952). If, as Wright argued there, God's revelation to Israel was through the events of her history not through the Old Testament itself, then establishing the historicity of these acts was of central importance. Although he progressively tempered his statements of this conviction in his archaeological writing across the next twenty years, he was by then compromised in the eyes of many for whom biblical archaeology even without biblical theology was deeply suspect as a rigorous discipline.

Wright had published a popular survey *Biblical Archaeology* in 1957, very soon after initiating the Shechem expedition. It also proved controversial as much in Germany, on account of its complete acceptance of Albright's approach, as in the United States, where Wright's theological position aroused objections to his general writings avoided by Albright who, in this respect, did not share Wright's position. Wright made his approach crystal clear from the outset of this important survey:

> Biblical archaeology is a special 'armchair' variety of general archaeology. The Biblical archaeologist may or may not be an archaeologist himself, but he studies the discoveries of the excavations in order to glean from them every fact that throws a direct, indirect or even diffused light upon the Bible. He must be intelligently concerned with stratigraphy and typology, upon which the methodology of modern archaeology rests . . . Yet his chief concern is not with methods or pots or weapons in themselves alone. His central and absorbing interest is the understanding and exposition of the Scriptures . . . The intensive study of the Biblical archaeologist is thus the fruit of the vital concern for history which the Bible has instilled in us. We cannot, therefore, assume that the knowledge of Biblical history is unessential to the faith. *Biblical theology and Biblical archaeology must go hand in hand, if we are to comprehend the Bible's meaning* [my italics].[16]

Wright placed himself in a particularly exposed position when he appeared to argue that recent archaeological research had established the reliability of the biblical history that was central to his faith. Theologians criticized his use of the category of 'revelation in history', whilst archaeologists doubted his objectivity. Meanwhile the general reader, for whom he was so often writing, was encouraged in the view that biblical archaeology was indeed primarily concerned to prove the truth of the Bible. That such a view was as widely held in the German as it was in the English-speaking world was spectacularly demonstrated by the enormous contemporary success of a popular book on biblical archaeology by a German journalist, Werner Keller, whose title says all: *Und die Bibel hat doch Recht: Forscher beweisen die historische Wahrheit* (1955), succinctly rendered for the English reader as *The Bible as History* (more precisely 'The Bible is indeed correct').

By the later 1950s Wright found himself defending both his own position and that of Nelson Glueck, with apologetic arguments rather than hard facts, when Finkelstein, a distinguished Jewish scholar of ancient Near Eastern Languages, and a professor in the University of California, used a lengthy review of Glueck's non-academic account of his surveys in the Negev, *Rivers of the Desert* (1959), to launch a vigorous attack on the claim that archaeology was capable of proving the historicity of the Bible.[17] Although prepared to be indulgent to religious fundamentalists and to popularizers like Keller, Finkelstein took sharp exception to scholars who, in his view, were uncritical in their use of evidence, particularly if they claimed to be scientific in their procedures. Glueck, who wrote with an uninhibited enthusiasm in a colourful style in his popular books, was a much easier target than either Albright or Wright as Finkelstein's careful selection of quotations mercilessly showed. When Glueck claimed that: 'it may be stated categorically that no archaeological discovery has ever controverted a Biblical reference',[18] Finkelstein simply cited the archaeological problems at Jericho. Although Finkelstein chose to scrutinize a book for the general reader rather than an academic monograph, he was one of the first scholars in America to raise questions from within Biblical and Ancient Near Eastern Studies that were to challenge fundamentally Albright's conception of biblical archaeology.

There was now to be a steadily increasing number of people who believed that Albright and his most prominent pupils had established what Finkelstein termed ' . . . the new trend, which requires that every contradiction between archaeological evidence and the Biblical text be harmonized to uphold the veracity of scripture'. The charge that biblical archaeologists could be neither objective nor properly scientific was one that Wright was thereafter to wrestle with to the end of his life in 1974, whilst Glueck in the revised edition of *The River Jordan* (1968) inserted a fresh section specifically rejecting any idea of 'archaeological proofs' of the Bible;[19] but by then the damage had been done. Even in his most circumspect publications Glueck, more than any other field archaeologist of his stature, epitomized the pejorative view of the biblical archaeologist as the explorer with a Bible in his hand wherever he went declaring it to be the most reliable guide to ancient Palestine. One of his most forthright critics of the younger generation, the Dutch archaeologist Franken, put the point thus:

> One has only to read Glueck's 'Explorations in TransJordan' to find how from ca. 2000 BC his whole interpretation of the history of the country is based on biblical data . . . Glueck has accordingly dated his finds to . . . biblical-historical events which in fact are part of the religious tradition of ancient Israel. One wonders which came first, a biblical date for Chedorlaomer [Genesis 14:5ff.] or an archaeological date for the end of Middle Bronze Age (M.B.) I civilization. Did Glueck find clear evidence for the dates of the two events; (a) the Chedorlaomer raid, and (b) the destruction of the M.B. I civilization so that he would say that they coincided? Or did he just guess that the M.B. I stopped in Transjordan at the same time that it stopped in Palestine and guess simultaneously that this coincided with the time of Abraham and Chedorlaomer, and that this king was able to destroy a whole country in one raid.[20]

Wright's *Biblical Archaeology* is best characterized by comparison with the more famous synthesis of this period, Albright's *The Archaeology of Palestine*, which had first appeared eight years earlier and then in regularly revised editions until 1960. Wright's book was designed to present a summary of 'the archaeological discoveries which directly illumine biblical history, in order that the Bible's setting in the ancient world and its relation to its environment may be more readily comprehended', by the general reader, passing from earliest times to the first spread of Christianity. The framework is that of the Bible and the perspective into which the information provided by archaeology is set is that of the men who wrote the scriptures. Throughout the author writes of himself as a biblical scholar, rather than as an archaeologist and the book is very much a product of Wright's religious thinking and personal pre-occupations. Albright's book is different; but only up to a point.

In the first place it is a contribution to a pioneering and influential series of archaeological books designed in the words of Mallowan, their editor, 'to present a picture of ancient man chiefly from archaeological evidence'. Albright starts with the procedures of *tell* excavation, recounts the early history of archaeology in Palestine, and in five masterly chapters reviews the results phase by phase, in archaeological terms, from remote prehistory to Graeco-Roman times. Two chapters are then assigned to a succinct survey of peoples, languages, literature and daily life as illuminated by excavations. Finally in a chapter devoted to each Testament, Albright interrelates the archaeological record and Biblical Studies now making very clear his own motivation. 'In one's enthusiasm for archaeological research, one is sometimes tempted to disregard the enduring reason for any special interest in Palestine - nearly all the Hebrew Old Testament is a product of Palestinian soil and Israelite writers, while most of the events which underlie the Greek New Testament took place in the same sacred terrain.'[21] But it is only in a final chapter on 'Ancient Palestine in World History' that Albright in explicit value judgements comes close to Wright's perspective: 'to one who believes in the historical mission of Palestine, its archaeology possesses a value which raises it far above the level of the artifacts with which it must constantly deal, into a region where history and theology share a common faith in the eternal realities of existence'.[22]

In these years, as much through the writing of his pupil Bright as in his own name, Albright was again engaged in debate over the relevance of archaeological evidence for historians of early Israel. By the middle of the 1950s in the English-speaking world it might have seemed as if the central place of archaeology in Biblical Studies championed by Albright and his School had carried all before it. But it had never been accepted by his most distinguished German colleagues in biblical scholarship, notably Alt and Noth. They retained Wellhausen's scepticism over the historicity of the Pentateuch. They had little or no confidence in the correlations Albright had long sought to establish between the witness of archaeology, whether text-aided or textless, and the biblical narratives of the Patriarchs, of the Exodus, and of the Conquest. Whilst Albright sought to shift the weight of proof of historicity onto external evidence, they equally vigorously asserted the primacy of internal evidence, of critical analysis of the Old Testament text, without denying that actual historical events lay behind the biblical traditions.

As it has commonly been said, or at least implied, in the English-speaking world that Alt and Noth neglected or ignored archaeological evidence, it is important at the outset to clarify the position. It would be fair to say that Alt in his two major studies of the entry of Israel into Canaan, published respectively in 1925 and 1939, rarely cited archaeo-

104

logical information. However, in the earlier monograph he specifically and justifiably stated that this was on account of the unsatisfactory nature of the evidence then available from excavations in Palestine, with which he was directly familiar (p. 47). Fifteen years later the situation was certainly better and Alt might have been expected then to take more account of the new archaeological data than he did; but already his pupil Noth was engaged in a vigorous debate on this subject with Albright, interrupted by the Second World War. When Alt wrote of excavated evidence 'that not every destruction which happened to a Canaanite place in the time of the Israelite Conquest needs to be the result of conquest; not every conquest the work of Israelites',[23] he was not so much disregarding archaeology as challenging its limitations.

Noth, a decade or so later, was more precise and forceful in his criticism, probing directly the fundamental question of what can and what cannot properly be proved by archaeology about historical events. He never disputed the importance of excavated evidence for modern understanding of the background to the Old Testament, and was fully informed about it; but he did radically challenge its role in the reconstruction of Israel's earliest history:

> The fact that an event can be shown to have been possible is no proof that it actually occurred, and the archaeological illumination of the general situation in any particular period does not in any way enable us to dispense with the study of the nature of the traditions enshrined in the records which have been handed down. On the other hand, however, information attested by the tradition can usually be understood more precisely and concretely, and therefore more positively and comprehensively, and appreciated and visualized more vividly in the setting of a particular period when illuminated by the material remains, than would be the case without them.[24]

The American response was neither so measured nor so temperate. 'Not only is Noth unable to rely on the Hexateuch traditions for the writing of Israel's early history, *he is unable to fill the void thus created by an appeal to archaeological evidence*. Indeed, he exhibits a nihilism regarding archaeology that virtually denies it the right to speak to the point at all.'[25] Bright's tart comment, repeating the charge of 'nihilism' first used by Albright in 1939, and particularly resented by scholars of Noth's persuasion, is characteristic of his polemic in favour of Albright's position. Not only is the accusation gratuitous, but it diverts attention from the true force of Noth's argument in raising the crucial question whether in the instances particularly at issue, the Patriarchal and the

Conquest narratives, archaeological data were being properly or improperly used by the Albright School to establish the case for historicity.

In his *Early Israel in Recent History Writing* (1956) and then four years later in the first edition of his *A History of Israel*, dedicated to Albright as his teacher, Bright attributed substantial historical value to the Old Testament narratives on the grounds that they had been adequately authenticated by ancient Near Eastern texts and the discoveries of textless archaeology in Palestine and adjoining countries. He conceded to the German School that they were not primary historical documents, but argued against Noth that they contained an 'appreciable nucleus of historical fact in the Biblical traditions in the form in which they have come down to us'.[26] He also allowed that 'in spite of all the amazing evidence that archaeology has brought, not one single item in the entire Hexateuch tradition has been proved true in the strict sense of that word. Archaeology cannot bring that sort of proof'.[27] But to establish a continuing role for archaeological evidence in history writing Bright explicitly stated the nature of the arguments implicit in Albright's method:

> The question is not: does archaeology 'prove' the biblical tradition? but: *where is the balance of probability in the matter*? That is, indeed, the area in which the historian usually labours. He weighs the evidence, *and does not brush aside the more probable for the less probable*.[28]

The crux of the matter was, of course, that well-informed scholars radically disagreed as to which was which. As successive editions of Bright's renowned *History* now bear witness, the balance of probability where archaeology is concerned is less easily set than it is for an historian working with written sources, which may more easily be judged and distinguished as primary, secondary, tertiary, etc. By the third edition of his *History*, published in 1980, Bright acknowledged that 'especially where the earliest periods are concerned, almost everything seems once again to have been thrown into question. At many points where one could have spoken a few years ago of something resembling a consensus, one now finds a veritable chaos of conflicting opinions.'[29]

Archaeology in Israel: the first decade

The founding fathers of archaeology in Israel, men like Avigad, Avi-Yonah, Ben-Dor, Biran, Benjamin Mazar, Sukenik and Yeivin, had started their local careers in the years of the Mandate, but often after academic training abroad in ancient Near Eastern Languages, Biblical Studies or Classics. They learnt to excavate by participation or observation. The nature of the times and their familiarity from early childhood with the Hebrew Old Testament, whatever their specialist academic training, meant that it provided their primary frame of reference. The pioneer work of Jewish archaeologists in Palestine had been largely devoted to sites and monuments important for Jewish history (p. 50). Although this trend continued with renewed purpose and vigour after 1948, a number of sites relevant to the cultural history of Canaan and Philistia were excavated in the early years of the new state, as at Affulah and Nahariah (M. Dothan) and Tell Qasile (Benjamin Mazar). But it was only with Yadin's large-scale excavations at Hazor from 1955 that Israeli field archaeology found a major focus in the Old Testament period.

It was no accident that Yadin chose Tell el-Qedah (Hazor). It was a site vital to any investigation of Israel's entry into Canaan at the end of the Bronze Age. No young archaeologist had been more immediately involved with the military establishment of Israel than Yadin had nor was any other Israeli archaeologist to be more eloquent internationally in promoting the new nation's cultural heritage, with which his own research was always pre-occupied. This was as evident in his excavations at Hazor, at Masada and in the caves of Bar Kochba, as it was in his writings on the Dead Sea Scrolls, a field of study pioneered by his father Sukenik, and always for Yadin the most vital and emotive link between the Jewish past and the Jewish present in Israel.

Yadin (1917-84)[30] had a uniquely varied career after training at the Hebrew University, where he took courses in Arabic and Hebrew philology, as well as in Jewish archaeology and history. There have been a number of distinguished soldiers who were also fine archaeologists, and one or two men who have combined archaeology with politics, but Yadin was alone in playing a prominent role for over a generation in the archaeological, military and political life of his country in its formative years. It was above all on Israeli archaeology that he left his most enduring mark as practitioner, publicist and teacher. His scholarship was distinguished by its combination of intellectual adventurousness and a deeply conservative approach to biblical tradition. As with Albright in the United States and Kenyon in the United Kingdom, his influence moulded a whole generation of archaeologists. The intellectual opposition he provoked was as fruitful as the discoveries he made; his legacy as a teacher was as crucial as his unusual skills as an organizer and ambassador at large for Israeli archaeology.

Like Wheeler, whom he much admired, Yadin had an eye for a 'big' site. The excavations at Hazor, like those at Masada in the 1960s, fused the aspirations of a new nation seeking her roots with the need to train a local school of young archaeologists in challenging circumstances. Yadin's military background was evident in proper staffing, integrated teamwork, and a routine blend of instruction and direct experience. His dependence on his 'archaeological architect', Dunayevsky (1906-68), who had been trained as an engineer, for guidance in the principles and processes of excavation was considerable. In the ensuing years Dunayevsky was to be responsible for the development and teaching of field methods in Israel. He and Yadin largely followed the Reisner-Fisher tradition as modified by Albright, exposing large areas carefully chosen to investigate the urban development of Hazor. The large outer town, long misidentified as a chariot park, was as carefully investigated as the *tell* itself.

As the excavation proceeded buildings, floors and small finds were related to one another architecturally rather than through the observed and recorded details of stratigraphy. The published drawings of sections through the mound are reconstructed from the surveyor's plans in a way that reveals nothing of the deposits of debris between the structures nor do they show how much attention was paid to separating them during excavation. As in Albright's excavations, pottery played a crucial role in establishing temporal relationships within buildings and across the site through the skills of the pottery experts Ruth Amiran and Trude Dothan. A new emphasis was laid on the restoration of complete pots and their reassembly into original groups. After his visit to the Hazor excavations Wright (p. 100) noted 'that its staff was composed of forty-five people . . . and its procedure was beautifully organized. I learned much from it, though I found myself wishing that Miss Kenyon's methods were more seriously taken . . . '[31]

Although Yadin was well aware in choosing to excavate at Hazor that 'its importance to biblical scholars lay for many years mainly in the role it played in the history of Ancient Israel',[32] he was no less interested in its much wider role within the ancient Near East, evident from the unusual number of extra-biblical references to the city. His excavations were to offer instructive interrelationships of dirt archaeology and texts. The decisive change in the urban history of Hazor started in the second quarter of the second millennium BC, when the huge lower city was created and a well-fortified acropolis was established on the adjacent mound, which already bore witness to a long history of settlement. Reference to Hazor in the Egyptian Execration texts and in the archives at Mari (p. 8) have to be seen within this archaeological context. When Hazor was mentioned in documents of the New Kingdom, not least the

Amarna Letters, excavation revealed that it was then the largest city in Canaan, with its lower city alternately ravaged and restored. The whole city was destroyed, never to be rebuilt on the same scale, at a date in the thirteenth century BC still debated by experts.

For Yadin this destruction was that described in the Book of Joshua, followed after an interval of uncertain length by a temporary settlement, which he identified as Israelite. This became a fixed point in the continuing controversy over the role of archaeological evidence in establishing more precisely the true historical core in the admittedly confused biblical conquest narratives. Yadin, like Albright, defended the conquest as described, though accepting a degree of editorial interpolation. Yadin was even more explicit about his dependence on biblical support for his interpretation of finds at Hazor when he considered the re-appearance of a well-fortified town in the Iron Age on top of the Bronze Age mound:

> the possibility of identifying the structures and finds from Stratum X with Solomon is not only a good example of how the Old Testament data can play an important role in field archaeology in the Holy Land, but, and this is more important, it enables us now to fix the pottery sequence of the first centuries of the first millennium BC with much greater accuracy.[33]

By an ingenious exercise in comparative archaeology Yadin went on to identify an unrecognized Solomonic city gate (later re-excavated by the Americans) in Macalister's plans of his work at Gezer decades earlier and to pinpoint more firmly its counterpart in the American excavations at Megiddo (cf. 1 Kings 9:15). It must, however, be emphasized that even if a direct association between specific structures in an excavation and a particular biblical passage is accepted, it is still possible to dispute, as Kenyon did (p. 98), whether the methods of excavation, retrieval and record used at Hazor allowed for sufficient accuracy in the isolation of those pottery types certainly contemporary with the building of structures attributed to Solomon's masons. This is the root of a long-standing disjunction of Iron Age ceramic chronologies, uneasily torn between Kenyon's low Samarian one and the high one for Hazor advocated by Aharoni and Amiran.[34] The final biblical reference to Hazor (2 Kings 15:29), its capture by the Assyrian King Tiglath-Pileser III (c. 744-727 BC), with other Galilean towns, was correlated with the destruction of the final fortified town (as distinct from the citadel) on the site.

It was at Hazor that a significantly divisive clash of personality in the formative years of Israeli archaeology, that between Aharoni and Yadin, first became apparent. The excavations at Hazor and Aharoni's survey in Galilee, revealing many unwalled settlements of the earlier phases of the Iron Age, allowed for the combination of two distinct types of evidence in a single region. To Aharoni his results seemed to sustain Alt's understanding of the Israelite settlement, with small rural settlements emerging in relatively inhospitable Upper Galilee, which had been almost uninhabited in the Late Bronze Age, before the destruction of Hazor level XIII. Yadin argued that Israelite settlement began only after the destruction of Hazor as described in Joshua 9:10-14.

Aharoni (1919-76) had joined the Hazor expedition in 1956 as a field supervisor working on the gate attributed to the Solomonic period, as he was the first to argue. His career and achievements have inevitably been compared and contrasted with Yadin's, for their stormy academic relationship and dominant roles as university teachers were to polarize Israeli archaeology for the better part of twenty years. Yadin was the guiding light of the Institute of Archaeology in the Hebrew University in Jerusalem, whilst Aharoni was to be the founder and inspiration of a similar institute in Tel Aviv University. Aharoni was first and foremost an historical-geographer, the man who redefined study of the Land of the Bible for the first generation of Israelis to whom this discipline had assumed a cultural significance inconceivable to the great nineteenth-century expatriate pioneers of historical topography in Palestine.

Aharoni had arrived there in 1933 from Germany, living as a member of a kibbutz from 1938 to 1947. It was as an exercise leader for youth movements and kibbutzim that his talents were nourished, pioneering exploration of caves in the Judaean Desert and joining the first archaeological expedition to Masada in the early days of the new state. He received his doctorate from the Hebrew University for a thesis, supervised by Benjamin Mazar, on *The Settlement of the Israelite Tribes in Upper Galilee* (in Hebrew; 1957), where he served as an archaeological inspector for the Department of Antiquities.

From first to last Aharoni was most concerned with the Iron Age, for him the 'Israelite Period', and with establishing, through surface surveys, which he pioneered in Israel, and selective excavation, the nature of the settlement of the tribes of Israel, first in Upper Galilee and then in the Negev (p. 118). His emotional involvement with the land and its early history was as profound as his first-hand knowledge of the landscape and its biblical topography was deep, qualities fused in his masterpeice *The Land of the Bible* (Hebrew 1962; English 1967; posthumous revised edition). To all his research, archaeological, historical and topographical, his regard for the text of the Old Testament was central, though not necessarily uncritical, and this was to give his choice of sites to excavate, and his interpretation of what he found there, a marked biblical bias. His influence in Israeli archaeology in its formative years, through the able and loyal students who shared his ideals, was to be as persuasive, if not as conspicuous, as Yadin's.

In 1954 Aharoni began excavations at Ramat Rahel, just to the south of Jerusalem, in collaboration with Italian archaeologists, that were to last until 1962. This may be biblical Beth-haccherem. There he revealed remains of a fortified palace of the Kings of Judah in the seventh century BC, though his detailed chronological analysis of his finds is open to debate. A unique line drawing on potsherds, found in 1960-61, representing a seated man, may possibly show a king of Judah.

Petrie had placed the study of pottery at the heart of Palestinian archaeology from the outset. In 1930 Duncan, using his classification and finds from the recent excavations at Tells Jemmeh and Farah (South), published a *Corpus of Palestinian Pottery*. It was, however, rigorously typological in its approach, structured without due regard to chronological distinctions and reductionist in its range. In 1958 the Israel Department of Antiquities published a booklet on the *Ancient Pottery of the Holy Land* by Ruth Amiran, subsequently to establish her reputation as excavator of the Early Bronze Age town at Arad. This essay rapidly evolved into a book of the same title, published in Hebrew in 1963 and in English in 1969, which brought much needed system into an ever increasing body of basic information. For the first time the full range and variety of Palestinian pottery, in chronological sequence, was made clear. It illustrated how the priorities and skills of the Albright School in particular had inspired the pioneer generation of Israeli archaeologists. His thinking about archaeology and history in early Israel was congenial to them and he made himself accessible to them in the first decade of the new state when many of his peers did not.

1 W.F. Albright, *The Archaeology of Palestine*, Pelican Books, 1960 edition, p. 255.

2 B.G. Trigger, 'Alternative archaeologies: nationalist, colonialist, imperialist', *Man* 19 (1984), p. 358.

3 W.F. Albright, *B.A.S.O.R.* 11 (1948), p. 55; cf. P.R. Davies, *Qumran*, Lutterworth Press, 1982.

4 R. de Vaux, 'The excavations at Tell el-Farʿah and the site of ancient Tirzah', *P.E.Q.* 1956, pp. 137-8.

5 H.J. Franken, 'The problem of identification in Biblical Archaeology', *P.E.Q.* 1976, p. 7.

6 A. Chambon, *Tell el-Far'ah I: L'Age du Fer*, Paris, 1984, p. 12 (comment on chart).

7 R.E.M. Wheeler, *The British Academy 1949-1968*, British Academy, London, 1970, p. 21.

8 K.M. Kenyon, *Beginning in Archaeology*, London, 1952, preface.

9 K.M. Kenyon, 'Excavation Methods in Palestine', *P.E.Q.* 1939, p. 35.

10 K.M. Kenyon, op. cit. n. 8, p. 77.

11 W.G. Dever, 'Two approaches to archaeological method - the architectural and the stratigraphic', *Eretz-Israel* XI (1973), p. 1*.

12 See the reviews in *I.E.J.* 8 (1958), pp. 171-184; *B.A.S.O.R.* 150 (1958), pp. 21-25; *B.A.S.O.R.* 155 (1959), pp. 13-29; see now L.E. Stager, 'Shemer's Estate' *B.A.S.O.R.* 277-8 (1990), pp. 93-107.

13 K.M. Kenyon, 'Megiddo, Hazor, Samaria and Chronology', *Bulletin of the Institute of Archaeology, London University*, 4 (1964), pp. 145-6.

14 W.F. Albright, 'Recent progress in Palestinian Archaeology: *Samaria-Sebaste* III and *Hazor* I', *B.A.S.O.R.* 150 (1958), p. 23.

15 K.M. Kenyon, 'An essay on archaeological technique: the publication of results from the excavation of a *tell*', *Harvard Theological Review*, 64 (1971), p. 272.

16 G.E. Wright, *Biblical Archaeology*, London, 1957, p. 17.

17 J.J. Finkelstein, *Commentary*, 27 (4) (April, 1959), pp. 341-50; G.E. Wright, 'Is Glueck's aim to prove that the Bible is true ?', *Biblical Archaeologist* XXII (1959), pp. 101-8.

18 N. Glueck, *Rivers in the Desert*, London, 1959, p. 31.

19 N. Glueck, *The River Jordan*, New York and London, 1968, pp. 6-7: 'the purpose of Biblical Archaeology'.

20 H.J. Franken, 'The other side of the Jordan', *Annual of the Department of Antiquities of Jordan* XV (1970), pp. 7-8.

21 W.F. Albright, *The Archaeology of Palestine*, Pelican Books, 1960 edition, p. 219.

22 Ibid., p. 256.

23 A. Alt, 'Erwägungen über die Landnahme der Israeliten in Palästina', 1939; in *Kleine Schriften* I, Münich; 4th ed, 1968, p. 156; for an early paper by Noth see 'Grundsätzliches zur geschichtlichen Deutung archäologischer Befunde auf dem Boden Palästinas', *P.J.* 34, pp. 7-22.

24 M. Noth, *The History of Israel* (London, 1960), p. 48; cf. 'Der Beitrag der

Archäologie zur Geschichte Israels', *Vetus Testamentum Supplements*, 7 (1960), pp. 262-282.

25 J. Bright, *Early Israel in Recent History Writing*, London, 1956, p. 87.

26 Ibid., p. 83.

27 Ibid., pp. 87-8.

28 Ibid., p. 88.

29. J. Bright, *A History of Israel*, London, 3rd edition, 1980, foreword.

30 For Yadin see various memoirs in *Eretz Israel* 20 (1989).

31 G.E. Wright, *Shechem: the biography of a Biblical City*, London, 1965, p. 52.

32 Y. Yadin, *Hazor* (The Schweich Lectures, 1970), London, 1972, p. 1.

33 Y. Yadin, 'Hazor' in D. Winton Thomas (ed.) *Archaeology and Old Testament Study*, London, 1967, p. 259.

34 For a succinct summary of this dilemma see J.N. Coldstream, *Greek Geometric Pottery*, London, 1968, pp. 305-9.

5

The Passing of the Old Order: Towards an Identity Crisis
(1958-1974)

> The real business of archaeology is to establish factual benchmarks in
> the world of the Bible to guide interpreters (Callaway, 1965).[1]

The years between the publication of Wright's *Biblical Archaeology*
(1957) and Thompson's *The Historicity of the Patriarchal Narratives*
(1974), from which Albright's reputation has never fully recovered, was
a time of transition. It was a period divided by the Arab-Israeli war of
1967, which altered many things on the ground when east Jerusalem and
the West Bank Territories passed under Israeli control. It was marked
towards the end by the death of scholars like Lapp (1970) and Wright
(1974) before their time, and others, like Albright (1971) in the fullness
of their years. Archaeology underwent a transformation in the United
States that reverberated through all aspects of the subject, challenging
basic assumptions as they had not been questioned before and forcing
biblical archaeologists in America particularly to take stock. In Germany a new generation of biblical scholars was no less forceful than their
teachers in scrutinizing the claims of archaeological evidence in the
continuing debate over historicity.

The 'Wheeler-Kenyon' Method, providing better stratigraphic controls in excavations, was now increasingly regarded as the key to proper
procedures, though variously modified by excavators like Aharoni,
Franken and Wright in order to encompass wider horizontal exposures
in the excavation of settlements or to introduce fresh approaches,
typological and technological, to the study of pottery. Excavations, even
on major biblical sites, were now more carefully planned (not least since
costs were escalating), were conceived with specific, not necessarily

biblical, problems in mind and were undertaken with larger supervisory teams, drawing upon an ever wider range of expertise both in the humanities and in the natural sciences. A broader spectrum of evidence was thus sought and recovered from the soil for study. Excavated sites were increasingly seen as part of a landscape, with its own complex history of exploitation by man, not as self-sufficient units. Surface surveys, both those independent of specific excavations and those complementary to them, were more and more effectively conducted. Their results were integrated with material from controlled excavations in which research on single-period sites was now seen as an important alternative to the traditional emphasis on multi-period *tells*.

These were, moreover, the years when the information explosion had its first real impact upon biblical archaeology. The days were rapidly passing when any single individual could possibly hope to master the skills required to control critically, as Albright had done for so long, the flood of new literature on all aspects of ancient Near Eastern studies. The new generation of archaeologists in Palestine, working more often as team members than as individuals, proved quite unable to sustain the regularity of primary publication achieved by the generation of Petrie, Reisner and Watzinger. Nor increasingly were they able to prepare those full, but judicious syntheses of data which every scholarly discipline periodically needs to sustain the momentum of confident development. When specialists faltered, it was hardly likely that those whose training had been primarily in Biblical Studies would be any better placed to direct the growing flood of information. Until the last year of his life Albright moved with apparent ease through Assyriology, Egyptology and related studies, through Hebrew epigraphy and archaeology, in addition to biblical scholarship more narrowly defined, tirelessly and rapidly presenting in print the new information relevant to the scriptures. His students and their contemporaries by contrast were forced increasingly to specialize and were much less likely to be recurrently applying the fruits of one discipline to fertilize another.

With a growing professionalism in archaeology at large and a demand for 'problem-orientated' research, the goals of the new generation of field archaeologists were now more often unrelated to Biblical Studies, even when applied to sites or regions insignificant for Israel's early history. Increasingly archaeological investigations involved natural and social scientists. To an unprecedented degree it was being appreciated that archaeology allowed questions to be posed which the literary tradition did not even suggest. When once they might have dealt with newly deciphered languages, with epigraphy and with philology, those biblical archaeologists who sought to emulate Albright now had to master a range of evidence that went far beyond their traditional training in the humanities. As the range of inquiry widened, the age-old problem of the difference between asking intelligent questions and producing convincing answers increased dramatically.

Archaeology in Israel: Aharoni and Yadin

For almost two decades after the excavations ceased at Hazor the development of archaeology in Israel was much affected by the rivalry of Aharoni and Yadin, with few able to remain wholly indifferent to the partisan spirit that fired their respective institutes in Tel Aviv and Jerusalem. Whereas Yadin was cast as the nation's archaeological spokesman and ambassador, a role for which he was eminently well equipped by character and talent, Aharoni, equally true to his skills and temperament, quietly traced the nation's roots in a landscape whose historical topography fascinated him. Their major research projects were as typical of these two very different scholars as was the manner in which they chose to pursue them.

Unique international attention and local enthusiasm attended Yadin's spectacular excavations at Masada from 1963 to 1965. As he well appreciated, they were calculated to arouse, as no other site would have done, the patriotic aspirations of a new nation of immigrants seeking a unifying symbol of identity, all the more powerful for epitomizing defiant self-sacrifice. This project accentuated the political dimension in Israeli archaeology, whilst stimulating research on the Herodian period which remains a major focus of interest in Israel. Yadin's military background and training allowed him a command of local resources without which excavation at Masada on such a scale would have been inconceivable. His decision to involve international teams of volunteers as diggers brilliantly combined economy with publicity. Regrettably, save for a remarkable popular book, *Masada: Herod's Fortress and the Zealot's Last Stand* (1966), Yadin failed to complete the major publication of this excavation, whose significance Albright justly assessed:

> Masada has driven the fundamental significance of archaeology home to the Israelis to an extent never approached by any past excavation anywhere in the world. The historian may think it more important to find fragments, large and small, of ancient Hebrew manuscripts. Masada has yielded such finds, giving the *coup-de-grâce* to both too early and too late dating of the Qumran Scrolls, since the latest script at Qumran is substantially the same, and in no case later, than the latest written

remains of Masada. But from the standpoint of the impact of archaeology on national life Masada has no historical parallel; it remains unique.[2]

The Masada excavations were notable archaeologically for the light they threw upon Herod's palace and on the buildings of the Jewish defenders against Rome in the final stages of the First Revolt (AD 66-74), which included such necessary installations as two ritual baths, what may have been 'a religious study house', and a synagogue. A remarkable variety of small objects were retrieved from living quarters established within the casemates of the encircling defensive wall by the Jewish occupants. Over two hundred ostraca written in Aramaic and Hebrew usually identify the contents of a vessel and record the owner's name. The fragments of scrolls were more various. The Old Testament was represented by small pieces of Genesis and Leviticus with a rather larger fragment of Psalms; the Apocrypha by over twenty pieces of Ecclesiasticus, perhaps copied within a century of its composition; and the Qumran Canon by the so-called Angelic Liturgy. The presence of this last text at Masada might mean that the Qumran community were Zealots, unlikely on other grounds; or that some Essenes from Qumran took part in the Zealots struggle with Rome, as Josephus implies they did; or that Zealots had brought manuscripts from Qumran to Masada.

Meanwhile Aharoni, who was more inclined to develop extended research programmes and was more innovative in his use of excavation and survey, had begun a thorough investigation of the biblical Negev in the Iron Age. His work was centred on the Beersheba valley to the west, on Arad to the east. At Arad, where he excavated from 1962 to 1967, Aharoni was responsible for work on the Iron Age settlements, whilst Ruth Amiran, a colleague at Hazor and Israel's leading expert on ancient pottery, concentrated on the impressive town site of the Early Bronze Age. The methods of excavation used in the Iron Age citadel at Arad have susequently been much criticized, since they left so many questions of context and stratigraphy open to doubt. As the whole fortress was excavated, they may not be resolved by further excavation. It is now commonly argued that the famous shrine found within this fortress was not, as Aharoni argued, a foundation of the Solomonic Period nor does its subsequent history correlate, as he believed, with the religious reforms of Hezekiah or Josiah. Indeed, it may only have existed from sometime in the seventh to the early sixth century BC, when it was destroyed.[3] Reference to 'House of God' on an ostracon sealed in this destruction level has been variously interpreted as referring to the shrine itself or to the Temple in Jerusalem. Recovery of some two hundred ostraca, some inscribed in Hebrew during the later Iron Age from the citadel, others in Aramaic of the Persian Period from the related settlement, bears tribute to Aharoni's innovative insistence on the dipping of all pottery sherds in water and careful inspection for traces of writing before they were scrubbed. This was not then standard practice elsewhere and many ostraca may well have been lost through over enthusiastic cleaning in earlier (and later) years.

Excavations followed in the years 1969 to 1976 at Tell es-Seba', a site widely but not universally identified with biblical Beersheba. Aharoni and his colleagues, who were responsible for publication of these excavations after his death, associated the earliest settlement with the Patriarchal narratives, seeking to establish an archaeological context for the biblical text through a line of argument based on highly controversial assumptions:

> The way of life of the Patriarchs, as related in the book of Genesis, faithfully describes a form of tribal existence that is very compatible with the archaeological picture of stratum IX at Beer-sheba. If we add to this evidence of the remarkable well that was probably sunk at this time and the role of such wells in the squabbles between the Patriarchs and the rulers of the area ... we can claim that not only the well, but all of Stratum IX, is the first solid archaeological evidence to throw direct light on the patriarchal tradition of Genesis, and that the historical events that form the background to the legends of Abraham and Isaac at Beer-sheba [Genesis 21:26] occurred between the second half of the twelfth century and the first half of the eleventh.[4]

It is ironic that Aharoni, who is one of the very few archaeologists to give a careful, clear justification of his aims and methods as part of his final report, *Beer-sheba* I (1973), has attracted considerable criticism on account of it. As Aharoni stood in the tradition descending from Petrie through Fisher (not Reisner as he supposed), his sharpest critics have been those for whom the 'Wheeler-Kenyon' Method offers the ideal[5] They have focused their attention on the fact that, however innovative and thoughtful Aharoni may have been in supplementary procedures, his digging was compromised by working with *a priori* units rather than with the natural bedlines of debris, isolating and removing each layer with due attention to the associated sequence of structures and artefacts.

The settlement hypothesis of German scholars rather than the conquest hypothesis of Albright is central to Aharoni's posthumously published *The Archaeology of the Land of Israel* (Hebrew 1978; English 1982). As the title indicates the chronological focus is more restricted than in the earlier surveys by Albright (p. 103) and Kenyon (p. 122), with virtually half the book, and that the better part, devoted to the Iron Age

(c. 1200-586 BC), where Aharoni's own research in Galilee and the Negev is very evident. Rainey, who was responsible for the English translation, in his introduction specifically calls attention to the bias: '[it] will give student and specialist alike an awareness of the achievements that resulted from the work of Aharoni and his closest disciples'. Fired by the living tradition of his people as transmitted through the Old Testament Aharoni sought to illuminate the biblical text with the aid of a rapidly growing range of archaeological information. Although he always worked with a biblical agenda, Aharoni was not a fundamentalist either in interpretation or in chronology.

On the question of Israel's entry into Canaan he argued for settlement first, as Alt had. He saw this as a protracted process of peaceful infiltration, starting as early as the fourteenth century, followed by a phase of settlement and expansion which brought intermittent conflict with Canaanite cities. In this, as in much else, Yadin argued against Aharoni preferring Albright's model of 'conquest first'. Across these years, from the late 1950s to the mid 1970s, the two men were often to engage in sharp polemics over aspects of Israel's archaeology and history, usually arising out of Aharoni's interpretation of his fieldwork. However, much as they might differ over details, they were united in the primary role they gave Old Testament narratives in their preferred solutions.

Ancillary to Aharoni's work in the Beersheba valley were Kochavi's excavations at Tel Malhatta (1967, 1971), a site whose biblical identity is debated, and those of a joint Tel Aviv University and University of Mainz Expedition, directed by Kempinski and Fritz, at Tel Masos (1972-75). This German contribution marked the end of her postwar isolation from active participation in field archaeology in the region. The excavation revitalised the debate about the earliest Israelite settlement. Aharoni saw its results as an endorsement of his view that the process had begun in marginal areas uninhabited in the Late Bronze Age. Each of the excavators developed his own theory about it as an Early Iron Age Israelite site, later challenged by Kochavi and others, who preferred to regard it as a settlement of Amalekites or other local peoples. Consequently, biblical identifications have varied, principally concentrating on Hormah or 'the city of Amalek' (1 Samuel 15:5).

Another regional project, although originally independent, came eventually to be associated with the Institute of Archaeology at Tel Aviv. From 1959 to 1964 Rothenberg investigated the traces of ancient copper mining and processing in the Timna Valley on the west side of the Wadi Arabah. It was a multidisciplinary exercise on a scale not undertaken before, involving chemists and geologists, metallurgists and field archaeologists, with experimental archaeology introduced to test theories about ancient smelting practices by recreating them. From 1964 to 1970 Rothenberg directed a series of excavations to check the chronology established by survey, notably at site 200 in Timna, which proved to be a shrine dedicated to the Egyptian goddess Hathor, patron deity of miners here as she was in the more famous mines at Serabit el-Khadim in Sinai. Votive objects placed in the shrine sometimes bore Egyptian royal names indicating that the mines had been exploited by the Egyptians, using local labour, during the thirteenth and twelfth centuries BC. As there was no evidence for mining thereafter until the Roman Period, popular identifications of 'King Solomon's Mines' hereabouts, which owed much to Glueck's supposed discovery of tenth century smelting installations at Tell el-Kheleifeh (p. 77), have to be abandoned.

The rapid proliferation of excavations that was to characterize Israeli archaeology in the 1970s and 1980s was less evident in the previous decade, but even then the activities of Aharoni and Yadin were but the most conspicuous in an already rapidly expanding enterprise, at times on sites earlier than the biblical periods. Research on the Philistines, a favourite subject earlier in the century (p. 31), was promoted by Moshe Dothan's excavations for the Department of Antiquities at Ashdod from 1962 to 1972. This research programme became well-known through his wife Trude's publication of *The Philistines and their Material Culture* (Hebrew 1967; English 1982), one of the few major studies of its kind yet published in Israel. This research was significantly extended by her own subsequent work at Deir el-Balah from 1972 to 1981.

For over twenty years Biran has been digging at Tel Dan (Tell el-Qadi), one of the most important sites in northern Israel, whose occupation extends well back into the third millennium BC and whose biblical identity has been confirmed by the recovery of a bilingual Greek and Aramaic inscription of the second century BC: 'the vow of Zilas to the god of Dan'. The most spectacular of the finds to date have been a fully preserved mudbrick city gate of the Middle Bronze Age and cult installations of the mature Iron Age, perhaps those established by Jeroboam I in the late tenth century, when the kingdoms first divided.

When in 1967 Israel overran Sinai and the West Bank Territories, including the Old City of Jerusalem, her archaeological horizons were significantly extended. Systematic survey and selective excavation in Sinai revealed much about its exploitation by man, but predominantly in the prehistoric and early historic periods. Elsewhere in the occupied areas it was the archaeology of the Second Temple Period which particularly flourished, not least in Jerusalem, now investigated with unparalleled intensity by many archaeologists. In 1968 Benjamin Mazar started excavations south and southwest of the Temple platform where it is estimated he removed some 300,000 cubic metres of debris, largely with the help of earth moving machinery, in the most extensive excavations yet undertaken in the city. He revealed the remains of the royal portico and the major entrances to the Temple on this side with their impressive approach stairways, whilst showing that 'Robinson's Arch' had been part of a massive structure supporting a stairway which led up from the Tyropoeon Valley. From 1967 the Jewish Quarter of the Old City underwent a radical programme of clearance and reconstruction with archaeological work undertaken beforehand, largely under the direction of Avigad. First, he discovered clear evidence that by at least the later eight century BC the western hill ('Upper City') was inhabited and by 700 BC defended by walls with suburbs beyond them. Second, he revealed for the first time a domestic quarter of the Herodian Period distinguished by fine, richly equipped houses with frescoes, stucco decoration and mosaics as well as elaborate water installations, including ritual baths. There was vivid, if grim, evidence hereabouts of the sack of the city in AD 70.

Meanwhile other expeditions were working in the Citadel, on scattered sections of the defensive walls, and on tombs, both of the First and Second Temple Periods. The archaeology of Jerusalem remains unusually preoccupied with historical topography rather than with problems of urban life at various periods. In 1954-56 Vincent's monumental *Jerusalem de l'Ancien Testament* reviewed a century's research on the fortifications, the fortresses of Akra and Antonia, the palaces, the water installations, the cemeteries and the Temple. The following quarter of a century transformed knowledge, demanding a synthesis on an even grander scale. Sadly, though Avigad has produced a masterly semi-popular summary of his work in *Discovering Jerusalem* (1980), remarkably little of this recent work is available in full reports.

Outside Jerusalem the buildings of Herod have been the subject of considerable research independent of the Masada Expedition. At Jericho in 1973 Netzer re-opened excavations of the winter palace of Herod and its Hasmonean predecessor, with spectacular results. This is even truer of his exploration of the Herodium since 1972, both of the fortress-palace on the summit, where an Italian expedition had worked previously, and of the extensive building complex at the foot of the hill. Whilst such research threw particular emphasis on Hellenistic influences in Jewish society in the time of the New Testament, the excavations at Masada and continuing research on the Dead Sea Scrolls, as well as numerous less spectacular Israeli projects, steadily increased knowledge of the more uniquely Jewish characteristics of the period.

Kenyon and the younger generation

Kathleen Kenyon's impact on the archaeology of Palestine through her excavations at Jericho from 1952 to 1958 was complemented in the next decade, when she was engaged in extensive excavations in East Jerusalem, by a series of publications both for the scholar and for the general reader. The popular *Digging up Jericho* (1957), where the drama of discovery was matched by a clear, unadorned style, reached an international public in the original and in a number of translations, effectively disposing of Garstang's interpretation of the Late Bronze Age levels, which had found a prominent place in all books about the historicity of the Old Testament up to that time. *Jerusalem - Excavating 3000 Years of History* (1967) and *Digging Up Jerusalem* (1974) were less successful. In sacrificing her natural directness of treatment for unresolved archaeological and topographical arguments, she too easily bewildered the non-specialist reader. The chapters on Syro-Palestine in the Bronze Age, which she contributed to the revised *Cambridge Ancient History* (1965-6, 1971), suffer by comparison with those written by Albright and Père de Vaux, since Kenyon wrote always as a field archaeologist, reconstructing cultural history from a restricted range of material evidence, lacking their more acute historical sense and skill in judicious generalization on the basis of a wider range of information.

The first edition of her masterpiece, a highly influential and enduring textbook, *Archaeology in the Holy Land*, was published in 1960; a revised fourth edition appeared a year after her death. It may lack the range and historical skills of Albright's *The Archaeology of Palestine*, being primarily organized round her own excavations, and Aharoni's mastery of historical topography. But its clear, plain style and the basic information concisely conveyed have ensured its status as a constant and durable guide for anyone interested in the subject. Indeed, until it is superseded her viewpoint and treatment will remain correspondingly pervasive. Here again she wrote above all as a working archaeologist, the mistress of technique in digging, reading and analyzing stratigraphy and ceramics, reconstructing the cultural history of the region in its bare essentials. When appropriate she correlated her archaeological material with texts, biblical and extra-biblical, but only in the most simplistic

122

way. Pots too easily became peoples and cultural change is almost invariably interpreted as the result of conquest or migration.

Kathleen Kenyon, who had no training in Biblical Studies, treated the biblical narratives in general much as Albright did, but for other reasons. Her historical training as a student at Oxford University had taught her how elsewhere literary criticism had too often denied historical value to old traditions, whilst her devout Anglicanism brought with it a due respect for the scriptures. Although her archaeological data might indicate that Garstang's interpretations were erroneous, she still believed that there was historical information in the Joshua narratives; archaeologists might do no more than challenge biblical scholars to recheck their sources.

Kenyon's Schweich Lectures, *Amorites and Canaanites* (1966), were 'an attempt to assemble the archaeological evidence concerning the inhabitants of Palestine up to the period of the entry of the Israelites', though, in fact, the Late Bronze Age receives little attention and the emphasis falls on the Middle Bronze Age. Of all her books this has dated most rapidly among archaeologists and historians, since she accepted without question that artefacts are indicators of cultural diffusion and signs of ethnic or cultural identity and that the historical accuracy of Joshua and Numbers allowed her to plot accurately Amorite and Canaanite settlements at the end of the Bronze Age. Moreover the material evidence was drawn overwhelmingly from Jericho and Megiddo, Byblos and Ras Shamra (Ugarit), an archaeological perspective as restricting as was the absence of a balancing critical assessment of the historical sources.

Kathleen Kenyon's decision to excavate in Jerusalem after work at Jericho was closed, rather than at a site like Taanach which she also considered, took account of a longstanding British interest in the city's archaeology and the ever more rapid encroachment of urban development on Ophel (the southern hill). Excavations were opened in 1961 (and lasted until 1967) in collaboration with the Ecole Biblique, represented by Père de Vaux, for the first three years, and the Royal Ontario Museum throughout, represented by Tushingham who was associate director as he had been previously at Jericho. It was a distinguished team for the most challenging of all sites in the region and for what was to prove the most controversial of Kenyon's excavations. Again, as at Jericho, a large international team of young site supervisors included a significant number of future professionals, who left deeply versed in the intricacies of the Wheeler-Kenyon techniques of excavation. Her long, deep trench cut down the eastern slopes of Ophel, with ancillary trenches where property rights permitted, determined something of the boundaries of the Jebusite city, particularly in relation to its water supply; of its modification in the Iron Age; and of its destruction by the forces of Nebuchadnezzar II of Babylon early in the sixth century BC. Numerous other cuttings were made inside and outside the Old City in an attempt to resolve long standing controversy about the extent of Jerusalem in the mature Iron Age and later. As a result of this work she was to adopt the most 'minimalist' view of the city's development, which she modified only slightly when the work of Israeli scholars demonstrated the fallibility of her views in the years after her own work had ceased.

Kenyon's Jerusalem excavations illustrate her method at its strongest and at its weakest. It was at its most vulnerable when she concluded that any specific area had or had not been within the walled city at the time in question, on the basis of the presence or absence of building remains or occupation debris in widely separated small cuttings. This approach forced her into the controversial hypothesis that the Pool of Siloam was originally an enclosed cistern cut in the natural rock when, on her reconstruction of the contemporary line of the city walls, it lay outside them. Equally controversial were her views on the lines of the 'second' and 'third' walls in the famous description given by Josephus; but, as with everything to do with the walls of Jerusalem, this is a debate without apparent end. In Jerusalem, as earlier at Samaria and Jericho, her approach was as much a matter of tactics as of techniques. With the resources available to her, and the restricted areas accessible at the time, she believed that deep trenching and strict stratigraphical analysis were the most effective procedures. That they may now be seen not always to be so is as much a lesson for succeeding generations of archaeologists as were her undoubted achievements in Jerusalem.

The limitations of Kenyon's advocacy of 'the straight archaeological evidence' recovered through stratigraphic control in narrow soundings was precisely illustrated in her review of Aharoni's *Beer-Sheba* I, published two years before her death in 1978. Here, accepting the Starkey chronology for the pottery found in Levels III and II at Tell ed-Duweir (Lachish), against Tufnell's critique (p. 160), and her own dating of a single unpublished group of pottery in her Jerusalem excavations, she challenged Aharoni's dating of the destruction of Beersheba II to Sennacherib's campaign of 701 BC by postulating unrecorded enemy action 'neither by Sennacherib nor Nebuchadnezzar but . . . somewhere in the middle of the seventh century BC'.[6] Whatever the merits of the case, arguments aggressively based upon archaeological positivism were not calculated to persuade scholars of biblical history now more vigorously asserting that the processes of evidence evaluation and interpretation were as subjective in field archaeology as in documentary studies, however improved the techniques of digging and recording might be.

Although Kenyon dominated the fieldwork of the British School of Archaeology in Jerusalem in these years, a number of younger archaeologists who had trained with her and served as officials of the School were involved in carrying her legacy across the Jordan to stimulate a more rapid development of field archaeology in Transjordan. Parr, the School's secretary and librarian from 1956-62, undertook a programme of research at Petra (1958-68) with the primary aims of establishing a dated sequence of Nabataean pottery, much needed at the time; of seeking the earliest Nabataean settlement on the site; and of elucidating the architectural development of a particular area of the site, where intermittent clearance and conservation had been going on for some years without much coherent new information emerging. Excavation at Petra had no direct bearing on New Testament Studies, but it was a vital complement to the increasing research on Herodian Palestine and Israeli work on Nabataean sites in the Negev.

Working with Parr at Petra in 1958, Crystal Bennett (1918-87) became interested in the Edomite site high on Umm el-Biyarah, thought by some to be ancient Sela, which she investigated in 1960, 1963, and 1965, thus opening an extended research project which for the first time sought to elucidate the archaeology of Edom in the Iron Age. She uncovered a settlement of the eighth to seventh centuries BC, eventually destroyed by a fire which preserved a sealing of 'Qos-gabri king of Edom', who is mentioned in the records of the Assyrian kings Esarhaddon (c. 680-669 BC) and Ashurbanipal (c. 668-627 BC). From 1968 to 1970 (and again in 1982) she dug at Tawilan, close to Petra, revealing what is perhaps a large agricultural settlement rather than a major town, as had been anticipated by those who believed this was ancient Teman. It was here that she found the first cuneiform tablet, of the Persian Period, to be excavated in Jordan.

As Director of the British School of Archaeology in Jerusalem (1970-78) and then of the newly founded British Institute at Amman (1978-82), Crystal Bennett turned her attention to Buseirah, probably the Edomite capital Bozrah, in 1971-74 and 1980. Here excavations revealed a strongly fortified town with an acropolis of buildings to a design perhaps influenced by Assyrian overlords and a collection of Edomite pottery of Iron Age II, which served as a useful check on conclusions drawn from Glueck's surveys and his excavations at Tell el-Kheleifeh (p. 77). Over a period of twenty years, with Kenyon's vigorous encouragement, Crystal Bennett had opened up the study of peoples east of the Jordan who had played an important peripheral role in biblical narratives.

Meanwhile, from 1965 to 1970, Hennessy, the Australian director of the British School in Jerusalem, returned to problems in the city's topography in the New Testament period with renewed excavations at the Damascus Gate, later much extended by Israeli archaeologists. In 1968 he went briefly to Samaria at Kenyon's suggestion to investigate the possible location of a lower city below the acropolis, where she had excavated a generation before. The results were largely negative and the location of the lower city, if there was one, in the Iron Age went unresolved. In a sense this brief excavation marked the end of an era in the history of the School during which a revolution in field techniques had been applied to resolving questions raised by earlier excavations; all, since they involved sites like Jericho, Jerusalem and Samaria, central to Old Testament studies. The British School of Archaeology did not return to excavating a site of biblical significance until the end of the 1980s, when they undertook excavations at Tel Jezreel in collaboration with Institute of Archaeology of Tel Aviv University.

G.E. Wright and a new American generation

In 1959 Wright became Parkman Professor of Divinity at Harvard University, where for the first time he had responsibility for research students. Seven years later, just before the war of 1967 transformed the political situation, he assumed the Presidency of the American Schools of Oriental Research, a position he held with a dynamic authority until his early death in 1974, a mere three years after Albright's. In these years he took a prominent, far-sighted role in training a new generation of American students in the most modern methods of field research, whilst gradually assuming a more defensive attitude in the continuing debate over the academic status of biblical archaeology. He now took a much less conspicuous role in controversies over Biblical Theology. In his concern for the proper instruction of students he sought to set up problem-orientated research projects serviced by teams of experts in the natural and social sciences as well as in the traditional disciplines of the field archaeologist and the philologist.

The expedition to Gezer (Wright 1964-65; Dever 1966-71, 1984) in personnel and in techniques was a direct development of Wright's earlier Shechem project (p. 100), but now for the first time truly interdisciplinary in conception and execution. A generation earlier Wright had very nearly written his doctoral thesis for Albright on Gezer, recognizing the enduring significance of a site whose potential Macalister had confusingly revealed long ago (p. 32). Now he recommended it to two of his own students, Dever and Lance, who were to carry the project through to publication after his death. Inspired by Yadin's success at Masada (p. 116), they recruited international teams of student diggers to replace increasingly expensive local labour. The expedition became an integral part of student training, with classes supplementing the daily routines of excavation. In future such field schools were to distinguish American and Israeli excavations, often collaborative efforts, from those of their European and Jordanian colleagues. There was certainly a positive educational aspect to their work, but it was neither so highly structured nor usually on so lavish a scale and local labour continued to be used extensively.

Initially it was impossible to return to Gezer except in Macalister's footsteps, if only because in 1958, on the basis of parallels at Hazor and Megiddo, Yadin had reinterpreted part of what Macalister had described as a 'Maccabean Castle' as a tenth century Solomonic gateway; a brilliant deduction, which was confirmed in the course of the new American excavations. As their major goals the expedition sought to unscramble and date Macalister's 'Inner' and 'Outer' city wall; to re-excavate and date remaining monumental structures, notably the famous 'High Place' and the Iron Age defences; to sample a sequence of domestic settlement immediately inside the city walls; and to open large areas not dug by Macalister in order to secure detailed stratification as well as to search for administrative and cultic installations, which might lie in the vicinity of the acropolis.

The excavation procedures at Gezer combined stratigraphic control with a co-ordinated daily recording system involving systematic paper work. These became the techniques favoured by a whole new American generation and also influenced Israeli archaeologists who after 1967 were able to see them in operation. These new methods continued to be applied most effectively to biblical sites dug long before, as in the renewed excavations at Tell el-Hesi (from 1970), again inspired by Wright. Since the excavations of Petrie and Bliss (p. 27), the identity of this site had been much debated, particularly after Tell ed-Duweir was widely accepted to be ancient Lachish. For Wright, Tell el-Hesi, if not particularly important in the political history of the region, remained archaeologically significant and a perfect subject for a field school on the Gezer model, distinguished by the quality of its interdisciplinary research and staff. As earlier excavations had indicated, Hesi provided particularly valuable information on the Early Bronze Age, on the mature Iron Age, when the acropolis had a massive defensive system, and in the Persian Period, when many subterranean pits indicate that the *tell* was a major grain storage area for neighbouring settlements.

Such pits are also an important feature of Tell Jemmeh, which Van Beek re-excavated from 1970-78. He had worked with Kenyon and was now sponsored by the Smithsonian Institution in Washington. Although some twenty miles from Tell el-Hesi, Tell Jemmeh had a complementary history, distinguished in the archaeological record by the finest mudbrick, barrel-vaulted structures of the Assyrian Period so far found in Palestine. They may be part of the residence of an Assyrian governor in the 670s BC, when the Assyrian king Esarhaddon (c. 680-669 BC) launched his invasion of Egypt.

Excavations were also resumed at et-Tell (Ai) by Callaway (1920-88). Trained in Biblical Studies in the Southern Baptist tradition, he had received his first experience of field archaeology with Wright at Shechem and then in Jerusalem with Kenyon, whose courses he also took in her final year as lecturer in Palestinian archaeology in the Institute of Archaeology in London University (1961-62). Whilst there, his attention was directed to unpublished material from the Early Bronze Age tombs at Ai, which he published in 1964, establishing an interest that was to lead to his major re-excavation of this site from 1964 to 1972. He confirmed Marquet-Krause's earlier conclusion (p. 65) that Ai (et-Tell) had been uninhabited from the end of the Early Bronze Age to early in the Iron Age. Initially Callaway favoured a conquest date for Ai in the twelfth century, towards the end of the first Iron I phase; but eventually he concluded that the Iron I settlers at Ai had been Canaanites rather than Hebrews, coming from the west not the east. If there was a conquest, as in Joshua 7-8, then it had occurred in the eleventh century, when the settlement was destroyed and abandoned. Sadly, Callaway's death forestalled the appearance of his full report on these levels. His masterly final reports on the Early Bronze Age at Ai (1972; 1980) indicate how regrettable this loss is, since they set an exemplary standard for excavations conducted both to the rigorous requirements of Kenyon and with Wright's broader perspectives always in mind.

One of the archaeological casualties of the Six Day War in 1967 were Pritchard's excavations at Tell es-Saidiyeh, often identified with biblical Zarethan, in the Jordan Valley, an area little known at the time to archaeologists. This work, begun in 1964, was complementary to that at Deir 'Alla (p. 132), thought by some to be biblical Succoth. In his four seasons of digging Pritchard revealed the great potential of the site, particularly for the late phases of the Bronze Age and the beginning of the Iron Age; a promise confirmed by renewed excavations there since 1985 by a British Museum expedition directed by Tubb. After the 1967 conflict Pritchard moved north into the Lebanon to undertake a rare opportunity to excavate a Phoenician site at Sarafend, between Tyre and Sidon, confirmed as ancient Zarephath (Greek: Sarepta) by an inscription he found. He completed only four seasons of work before political circumstances once again brought his work to a premature end; but not before he had revealed evidence of a vigorous pottery industry and a seventh century BC. Phoenician sanctuary in some ways comparable to the earlier Philistine one on the coast at Tel Qasile in Israel (p. 159).

It was in response to changed political circumstances after 1967 that the Americans undertook their first major team project east of the Jordan, when Horn of Andrews University, with Boraas as chief archaeologist, opened trenches at Tell Hesban, about fifteen miles southwest of Amman. This was to prove a seminal project in the development of modern archaeology in the region, passing in 1974 into the hands of Geraty. Horn initially sought to study the transition from the Bronze Age to the Iron Age, the supposed time of the entry of Israel into Canaan, at the site traditionally said to be the Moabite city that Sihon, king of the Amorites, had conquered and made his capital, before suffering defeat at the hands of the Israelites (Numbers 21:21-31). But, in the absence of finds earlier than Iron I, this association remains as open on archaeological as it does on historical grounds. By the time Geraty, a pupil of Wright's, assumed the directorship, this expedition had become a trendsetter exemplifying many of Wright's aims in his later years, notably in its combination of excavation and field survey, in the creation of a field school for local and expatriate archaeologists, and in the blend of scientific and computer skills increasingly necessary for proper study and record (p. 168).

Pervasive as was Wright's personal influence in the formulation and control of American research strategy in the years from 1959 until his death in 1974 and in a continuing legacy through his associates and students thereafter, the most remarkable American archaeologist in the field at this time was Lapp (1930-70), whose promising early career as a field archaeologist was crowned by his sadly brief period as Director of the American School. Lapp had studied with Albright at the Johns Hopkins University and with Wright at Harvard, writing his archaeological dissertation on *Palestinian Ceramic Chronology 200 B.C. to*

A.D. 70 (1961), after an earlier academic training in theology and education and ordination into the Lutheran Protestant ministry in 1955. In the decade before his tragic early death by drowning off Kyrenia in 1970, Lapp passed like a meteor through the firmament of archaeology in Jordan; hyperactive and intense, dynamic and versatile, few save Petrie have done so much in so brief a time. His bibliography, embracing history, philology and theology, as well as various aspects of archaeology, is but a shadow of what it might have been, since his remarkable excavation programme was left for his widow and colleagues to publish after his sudden death. His most important excavations were on the enigmatic Hellenistic building (Qasr) at Araq el-Amir (1961-62), perhaps a temple; at Tell el-Ful, where he revised, but largely confirmed Albright's pioneering work (1964); in the caves of the Wadi Daliyeh, whence bedouin had recovered a remarkable group of fourth-century BC papyri (1963); at Tell er-Rumeith, an Iron Age II fortress in Gilead (1961, 1967); and at Taanach (1963-68).

Lapp was impressed by Taanach's potential as a site for study of a major Canaanite city through Sellin's achievement in his pioneer excavations there (p. 33), as shown by his 'prompt and in many respects perceptive reports'.[7] This city, moreover, had played a prominent role in Old Testament narratives. This was no small concern for a team principally staffed from the Lutheran Concordia Seminary of St Louis, Missouri, where Lapp had studied theology. His excavations, as with those at Ai, Gezer and Shechem, showed how the new precision of technique in excavation might elucidate the obscurities of earlier excavations whilst extending the range of data. Two cuneiform tablets, one written in the Akkadian language, one in Canaanite, and an ornamental baked-clay cult-stand of the mature Iron Age closely paralleled Sellin's most famous finds. Lapp was also able to date the early occupation of the site back into the third millennium BC and to reveal the fortifications that had eluded earlier investigation.

When in 1968 Lapp was appointed Professor of Old Testament and Archaeology in the Pittsburgh Theological Seminary, he was poised to assume the mantle of Albright and Wright in due course. Death intervened at a time when his drive and critical intelligence were particularly needed. He was not only constructively thoughtful, but said what he thought to audiences not always receptive to his honesty of view:

> My view point here [in 1963] is that such a tiny fraction of the archaeological material has been excavated, and such a small fraction of that satisfactorily published, that even the most assured archaeological conclusions must still be considered far from final . . . specifying

limitations in archaeological reporting is especially crucial. In the social and physical sciences, comparable human or laboratory circumstances may be repeated to test a given hypothesis, but an archaeologist cannot easily make another slice through his mound to test his hypothesis about, let us say, an unusual Late Bronze Age building. An ideal final archaeological report should make it possible for the reader to reconstruct the layers and associated structures and artifacts as they existed before excavation; but up to now this goal has not been approached even by the best archaeological publications. No one is in as advantageous a position as the archaeologist himself to understand the limitations of his evidence, and it is crucial that he report them.[8]

Fate denied Lapp the opportunity, as indeed it has done to so many others who had more time and laboured hard with this intractable problem. The next generation was to see many attempts to grapple with the complexities of publishing archaeological data recovered with the thoroughness now demanded. The 'ideal final report' is as elusive as ever; but here, as in much else, Lapp saw more clearly, or at least chose to state more explicitly in print than any of his contemporaries in America, what the present condition of the subject was.

It is not a co-incidence that some of Lapp's strongest statements are to be read in his perceptive review of Franken's controversial first report on the Deir 'Alla excavations (p. 132); a review published in the year Lapp met his death. In a few sentences he gets closer to the heart of the matter than do many pages soon to be written when biblical archaeology, indeed Palestinian archaeology as a whole, faced the challenge of the so-called 'new' archaeology. Lapp's critique reveals what the subject lost with his premature death on the eve of the subject's greatest crisis of confidence so far:

Too much of the structure of Palestinian archaeology is an inflated fabrication. By that I do not mean to imply any intentional deception but to suggest that the structure of Palestinian archaeology appears much more formidable than its foundations warrant. Too often a subjective interpretation, not based on empirical stratigraphic observation, is used to demonstrate the validity of another subjective interpretation. We assign close dates to a group of pots on subjective typological grounds and go on to cite our opinion as independent evidence for similarly dating a parallel group. Too much of Palestinian archaeology's foundation building has involved chasing *ad hominem* arguments around a circle.[9]

Franken shared his reviewer's radical standpoint to a large extent, bringing it to bear on biblical archaeology in particular.

Franken's excavations at Deir 'Alla: challenges to orthodoxy

In the 1960s there was only one scholar actively engaged as a field archaeologist in Palestine whose research programme and occasional writings challenged orthodoxies both in field technique and in biblical archaeology. The Dutch scholar Franken, a man of firm convictions and marked independence of mind, is unusual in combining the varied skills of an anthropologist, an archaeologist, and a Biblical scholar. His most original contribution has been twofold. In collaboration with professional potters, notably Kalsbeek, he has sought to transform the archaeological study and publication of pottery much as Kenyon, whose stratigraphical methods of analysis he much admires, modernized excavation techniques.

> I have argued in this report for the necessity of giving shape - or 'appearance' - typologies a more scientific basis. This can be done by an analysis of the ancient potter's methods of potmaking, which starts with research into the collecting of raw materials and ends up with the firing and marketing methods. Up to a certain point at least this research can be supported by experiments in which theories are tested ... This report also argues that it is necessary to rethink the validity of comparative studies of individual pieces of pottery as far as they are not based on an analysis of the potter's work in its totality: all the daily activities in the potter's workshop.[10]

No less radical has been his challenge to the whole trend of biblical archaeology as conceived and practised by Albright and his school. 'An important reason that we still know so little is that Palestinian archaeology has built an enormous structure of archaeological "evidence" around the historicity of the Old Testament.'[11] Franken has long argued with considerable cogency that the school of biblical exegesis to which an excavator belongs, if he is a trained biblical scholar or a theologian, has directly affected his interpretation of archaeological finds; a view which anticipated the renewed debate over biblical archaeology in the mid and later 1970s.

After working with Kenyon at Jericho Franken established his own research excavations at Deir 'Alla further up the Jordan Valley in 1960 to train Dutch archaeologists in the techniques of excavation in the Near East and to investigate certain specific problems. He sought to fill gaps in the ceramic typologies of Jericho, with particular reference to cultural developments in the transition from the Late Bronze to the Early Iron Age, and to apply innovative methods in the study of ceramics based on the way they were made as much as on shape and decoration (typology). 'It can now be proved that the Early Iron Age cooking-pot cannot be a straight descendant of the Late Bronze cooking-pot, as is generally assumed. It is made by potters with a different tradition of manufacture, not indigenous to Palestine.'[12]

A Primer of Old Testament Archaeology (1963), written by Franken in collaboration with his wife, was the first systematic attempt by two scholars who combined experience of anthropology, archaeology and biblical study to educate theological students in the ways of archaeologists through a textbook. It was harshly reviewed, if not neglected, at the time and has since received little notice. Some of the proposals deserved to be challenged, as did rather negligent production, but this book is more important historically than its original reception might suggest. The authors' sharp way with their contemporaries not converted to precise stratigraphical digging as they conceived it, their apparent disrespect for the pioneers, and their scepticism of Albright's use of archaeological data for historical reconstruction blinded many to the book's positive challenges. 'It scarcely touches the Old Testament at all - except indirectly . . . Nor is it "a manual of field archaeology" . . . its chief purpose is polemic' was Albright's uncharacteristically dismissive verdict.[13] The subject was soon to experience polemic considerably more forceful than this and not always so well directed.

The Frankens' textbook remains a unique attempt at a difficult task: to show biblical students that there are no archaeological 'facts', only hypotheses or relative explanations, by examining a series of specific examples in a way that was as cautionary as it was didactic. More important in the long run was their demonstration that old reports, the good, the bad and the indifferent, can still yield fresh knowledge when properly reinterrogated in the light of the most recent information. The Frankens used case-histories to show how the Late Bronze to Early Iron Age transition was or was not illuminated by excavations at Megiddo, Bethshan, Tell Farah (South) and Jericho; and how material evidence for architecture, for crafts and industries, and for ideologies, might be extracted from excavation reports and appropriately used by biblical students to avoid that perennial hazard so memorably expressed by Wheeler: 'the archaeologist may find the tub but altogether miss Diogenes.'

In 1963 Franken's continuing excavations at Deir 'Alla in the Jordan Valley were known only from preliminary reports that did not convey the radical nature of his approach in a manner from which it might be fairly assessed. That stage was reached with the publication in 1969 of Excavations at Tell Deir 'Alla I: a stratigraphical and analytical study of the Early Iron Age Pottery. With the sole exception of the penetrating review article by Lapp already noted (p. 131), this report evoked an almost universally negative reaction, largely on account of its neglect of traditional comparative ceramic typologies and its indifference to conventional reconstructions of a cultural framework for material evidence.

Franken, in a procedure new to Palestinian archaeology at the time, had sought not only to emphasize the limitations of existing archaeological procedures, but also to indicate how the deficiences might be remedied by new ways of structuring the subject's basic data in the field, in the laboratory, and in the final published reports. For him, at this stage, the traditional goals, focusing on the sequence of settlement observed through architecture, were secondary to technological and statistical study of pottery. With the pottery he was in quest of an industry and its development rather than a few aspects (and those not necessarily the most significant) of one stage of it. This volume shared with many seminal works a lack of balance. The new, however relevant it might be, did not compensate for a total absence of traditional descriptions by eye. The way forward, as time was to show, was in a blend of typological and technological study, fortified by such scientific techniques as petrographic and trace-element analyses of pottery.

Franken's Deir 'Alla excavations have come to be best known among biblical scholars not for his provocative *critiques* and innovative methods, but for a single major find. In 1967 he excavated fragments of a remarkable inscription written on wall plaster in the late eighth century in a linear script in a dialect whose identity is much debated. Fragmentary as this text is, and controversial as it has proved since publication in 1976, there has been no doubt that the Balaam, son of Beor, who plays an important role in it, is indeed the man, mentioned in the Old Testament as a non-Israelite diviner, who was asked to come and curse the Israelites as they entered the Promised Land (Numbers 22-4).

Franken's own perspective on this inscription illustrates particularly well his general attitude to biblical archaeology:

Digging up the Holy Land does not mean digging up the Bible. Archaeology can provide background information about situations known from the Bible. The nature of this information, however, is inherently different from the biblical information - it does not have a message. The Bible presents historical events in the light of a very specific religious interpretation, which archaeological situations do not possess. These 'frozen' situations reflect a once-existing reality of daily life. Texts like the one found at Tell Deir 'Alla may reveal that archaeology under favourable circumstances can provide evidence which the Bible does not, and which was thought to be irrelevant or which was suppressed on purpose . . . If the archaeological situation is not allowed to tell its own story in its own language, as modern archaeology understands it, then archaeology will become disappointingly sterile.[14]

The passing of the giants: a growing crisis of confidence

The archaeology of Palestine is no exception to the rule that a subject is largely defined by its textbooks and the fewer they are the more pervasive their influence. As the American archaeologist Gitin recently put it:

> In the past, the strength of personality, the force of argument of a particular scholar, and the format of the presentation were paramount. Those scholars who presented their ideas in the format of a textbook exerted a greater influence upon the selection and acceptance process of archaeological terminology and chronology than their colleagues, who published disparate articles scattered throughout numerous journals in a dozen different languages.[15]

Even when Albright, Kenyon and de Vaux ceased to dominate the scene on the ground or in the lecture theatre, *The Archaeology of Palestine, Archaeology in the Holy Land* and the relevant chapters of the revised *Cambridge Ancient History* endured as the basic sources for students and serious amateurs alike, soon to be joined by Aharoni's *The Archaeology of the Land of Israel*. Père de Vaux's contributions to the *Cambridge Ancient History* and the archaeological sections of his *Early History of Israel* have a range and balance which eluded Aharoni, Albright and Kenyon, who structured the archaeology of the region to a marked degree on the results of their own research projects, respectively in Upper Galilee and the Negev, at Tell Beit Mirsim, and at Jericho, Jerusalem and Samaria.

In 1970 Lapp was drowned; in 1971 Albright, Glueck and Père de Vaux died; from 1972 to 1978 Kenyon lived in retirement though much preoccupied to the last with unfinished final reports on her excavations at Jericho and in Jerusalem. Three of the primary traditions that had sustained archaeology in Palestine for almost two generations were passing into eclipse.

The American Protestant legacy, which had allowed archaeological data a pre-eminent role in contemporary controversies over biblical historicity, had passed in almost dynastic succession from Albright to Wright, who died in his early sixties in 1974, and to Lapp, whose promise as a dynamic and innovative archaeologist had been cut off before his prime in which he might well have proved more of a heretic than a new high priest.

The French Catholic tradition in Palestinian archaeology, cautiously liberal both in archaeological and textual analysis and synthesis, had passed directly from Lagrange through Vincent to de Vaux in its home, the Ecole Biblique in Jerusalem. This line was linked to the American tradition, since both Albright and de Vaux, the one informally, the other formally, had been students of Vincent. One of de Vaux's last decisions, early in 1971, was to propose a new French excavation on the imposing Tell Keisan in a plain south of Akko. Here, as excavations from 1971-76 were to demonstrate, a Byzantine church overlay a sequence reaching back to at least the Late Bronze Age. Prignaud, Briend and Humbert were responsible for the work and an admirably prompt report *Tell Keisan (1971-76), une cité phénicienne en Galilee* (1980).

A secular archaeological tradition, which might have descended either from Petrie through Starkey (p.61) had he lived, or from Reisner through Fisher, had in the event emerged most effectively in the work of Kenyon, trained by Wheeler in England, by Crowfoot in Palestine, and her younger colleagues. Not surprisingly it was the American and French archaeologists who also contributed substantially to the writing of the early history of Israel; the British did not, remaining content to write archaeological rather than historical accounts.

The position of Germany has always been different, since on more than one occasion politics have disrupted the development of biblical archaeology there. The First World War (1914-18) cut short an enterprising and successful first generation of field archaeologists. Thereafter dire economic circumstances followed by the anti-semitic ideology and actions of the Nazi regime blighted the subject for decades. When biblical archaeology has developed in Germany it has been most often, as in America, in Protestant academic institutions and church-sponsored societies. Perhaps more than anywhere else, biblical archaeology has been and largely remains an ancillary element within Biblical Studies. If this explains the consistently high level of the critical interaction of archaeological and textual sources in the writing of ancient Israel's early history in the German-speaking world, then the course of modern history explains the long absence of German scholars from fieldwork.

The emergence of a new generation of biblical archaeologists in Germany was marked by publication in 1967 of Weippert's thesis, *Die Landnahme der israelitischen Stämme*. This relatively short monograph served as a catalyst. It was not only 'both learned and original' in

Albright's words,[16] but was also distinguished by the clarity of its analysis and equity of judgement. Weippert, whilst, in the spirit of the German School, dealing a devastating blow to the 'conquest' hypothesis so vigorously defended by Albright, stimulated new ways of interpreting the archaeological evidence. In defending Noth's 'settlement' model his detached critical review exposed its weaknesses to vitalizing scrutiny, particularly Noth's amphictyony hypothesis and his archaic treatment of nomadism. Weippert gave equal critical attention to Mendenhall's 'peasants revolt' model, so far little more than sketched out in a short popular article in 1962. This creative *critique* showed the way out of an exhausted debate, anticipating to some extent how the methods of anthropology and sociology might give it fresh life.

If in their later years Albright and Glueck revealed no decline of confidence in the role of archaeology in Biblical Studies, the same may not be said of Père de Vaux or of Wright. In the *Festschrift* for Glueck, published a year before his death, de Vaux reflected on a lifetime's experience in a memorable essay entitled 'On Right and Wrong Uses of Archaeology':

> Archaeology does not confirm the text, which is what it is, it can only confirm the interpretation which we give it. If the results of archaeology seem to be opposed to the conclusions of text criticism, the reason may perhaps be that not enough archaeological facts are known or that they have not been firmly established; the reason also may be that the text has been wrongly interpreted.[17]

This essay, if it did not actually prompt, certainly fortified Wright's inclination to separate himself even further in print from his old popular image as an advocate of 'archaeology proves the Bible'. In 1971 in a paper whose title, 'What Archaeology Can and Cannot do', echoes Père de Vaux's, he described the opening sentence of de Vaux's conclusion, cited above, as 'axiomatic'. 'Conversely', he went on to argue, 'archaeology, dealing with the wreckage of antiquity, proves nothing in itself. It must be analyzed in a variety of ways, and then with all other data available, its meaning in the overall picture of a cultural continuum is expressed by interpretation.'[18]

It was now, with the limitations of the role of archaeology in establishing the historicity of biblical narratives rising ever higher on the research agenda of the senior generation, that first Dever in the United States and then Thompson, an American trained in Germany (p. 153), generated an enduring crisis of confidence in Albright's legacy. Early in 1972 Dever redefined the debate over biblical archaeology when delivering the William C. Winslow Lectures, at Seabury-Western

Theological Seminary in Evanston, Illinois. They were published two years later as *Archaeology and Biblical Studies: retrospects and prospects.*

Dever had received his doctorate at Harvard University in 1966, under Wright's supervision, with a dissertation on the pottery of the Early Bronze IV/Middle Bronze I period in Palestine. He had been closely involved with the Gezer Expedition (p. 127), after early experience in fieldwork at Shechem, graduating to its Directorship from 1966 and then in 1971 becoming head of the Albright Institute in Jerusalem (formerly the American School of Oriental Research). In this capacity he served until 1975. His close association with Wright in the classroom and in the field, as well as an initial training in theology, whilst giving him particular authority in commenting on the relationship of archaeology and the Bible, inevitably conditioned his initial terms of reference. He stated them clearly from the outset, 'to avoid some of the frequent distortions by which our subject is plagued'. It was evident from the start that this was to be a debate conducted from a much narrower base, and within much more restricted intellectual horizons, than those Birch had recognized a century earlier (p. 3) and Albright had largely endorsed half a century later (p. 54). Dever was 'speaking only about the scene in *America* . . . I also stress that I am speaking only about the Archaeology of *Palestine*, rather than Near Eastern Archaeology in general'.[19] At the heart of his argument at this stage was a highly personal premise that '"Biblical Archaeology" is a peculiarly American phenomenon and that it must be understood as such to be understood at all'.[20] Israeli archaeologists, in particular, were bewildered by such a restrictive claim and not a few were incensed by the presumption of it.

What Dever sought to indicate was that a particular relationship had developed in certain academic circles in America between archaeology and Protestant and Biblical Studies. This had given the term 'biblical archaeology' a distinctive local meaning which it did not necessarily have elsewhere in the English-speaking world, nor for that matter among practitioners in Israel, France or Germany. For Dever the uniqueness of the pioneering American contribution to the archaeology of Palestine was to be found in the almost exclusive participation of Protestant biblical scholars and clergymen sponsored by seminaries and departments of religion in colleges and universities. This was in marked contrast to the role of secular scholars among the prominent field archaeologists, especially from Britain and Israel, actively involved in the study of those periods most relevant to Biblical Studies:

> The tools [with] which we have been equipped are largely Biblical languages and literature . . . our interests have been dominated, not

surprisingly by the Biblical sites ... our focus has been further restricted to sites of the Old Testament Period ... our orientation has been more toward the literary remains, especially the Bible, which for us looms largest as the principal surviving document from the Ancient Near East and undoubtedly as the one document uniquely 'authoritative'. Our objective has been to recover what I would characterize as the "political history" of the sites which we have excavated. This is in striking contrast to the concern elsewhere in the worlds of anthropology or cultural history.[21]

A decade later he was to speculate on whether this 'political history' was 'a product of the Calvinistic mentality of the practitioners of biblical archaeology, or of the general intellectual climate in America in the 1920s-1930s'.[22] The explanation may well be more simple and more general. At a time when archaeology was almost universally regarded as an auxiliary discipline for historical study it tended to be enlisted as evidence in the writing of the type of history most current at the time, that usually termed 'political'. As indeed, until very recently, were all histories of Israel. It is then hardly surprising that the pioneers structured the archaeology of the early historical periods in Palestine in that way, both in America and elsewhere.

Many biblical scholars, Dever argued in 1972, were now sceptical of the role of archaeology in biblical scholarship, obviously so in Germany but increasingly so elsewhere, whilst professional archaeologists in America had come to regard biblical archaeologists as unscientific amateurs. Biblical archaeology had been irredeemably tainted, it seemed to him, by its popularity with fundamentalists and its evidently poor field methods, to the point where responsible and irresponsible claims for its achievements were inextricably confused. This had inevitably lowered the whole subject's reputation among amateurs and professionals alike, ignorant of what Dever distinguished as the separate American secular achievement in 'Palestinian Archaeology'. It is this aspect of the subject which Dever sought to establish as an independent discipline disassociated entirely from what he saw as an anchronistic and hopelessly compromised biblical archaeology. Its aims and methods were to be radically modernized with infusions from the social and natural sciences so that it would accommodate a new school of secular professionals who were trained as archaeologists first, as specialists in Syro-Palestinian archaeology second. Implicitly, if not explicitly at this point, he was arguing that there was no hope that biblical archaeology itself might evolve, developing a new legitimacy in America as a scientific discipline. It simply had to give way, as beyond redemption, if American archaeologists working in the lands of the Bible were not to loose touch with modern archaeology altogether. His apparent assumption that a pre-occupation with Biblical Studies necessarily made one's fieldwork unscientific was to prove particularly contentious. Over the next ten years Dever sustained this pessimistic argument, modifying and varying it, but still with the same ultimate message. His disillusion only increased when appointment to a professorship in the University of Arizona at Tucson took him to one of the centres of the so-called 'new' archaeology, where the challenges of a rapidly changing anthropological archaeology even more severely tested what remained of Albright and Wright's legacy in his thinking.

Archaeology's loss of innocence

The full implications of Dever's arguments and their changing emphasis through the 1970s and early 1980s, may only be properly appreciated in the light of the transformation archaeology had undergone in North America during the 1960s and was still undergoing as he wrote and lectured. This alone would justify a diversion to consider the popularly termed 'new' archaeology; but this phenomenon is also central to any understanding of where archaeology in the Near East has been going in the hands of a younger generation of scholars in the last twenty years. It was no longer a matter of improved excavation techniques, since that battle had been largely won, but of aims and aspirations. The ultimate goal of the most committed idealists among the new archaeologists in the United States was to use archaeological information to establish universal generalizations about human behaviour that might be of practical value in modern society.

The new archaeology was originally preached as a gospel with a fervour and self-righteousness that often alienated non-American audiences. It was a peculiarly American phenomenon combining distaste for historical studies, common among local social scientists, with a marked respect for useful, relevant knowledge, a more deep-seated trait of the North American intellectual tradition. That alone would not, however, have made it as controversial as it proved to be. It was the corollary denigration of studies of regional archaeology through the reconstruction of cultural history that proved particularly unacceptable to what might be broadly termed the European tradition. It was almost inevitable, moreover, that a movement which rejected, as this seemed to do, the importance of relationships between the past and the present in any particular part of the world would not appeal to the mainstream of Israeli archaeologists.

Its most enduring impact, however, was at a more mundane level. The 'new' archaeologists argued with unprecedented intensity that behind practical archaeology there must always be *explicitly* formulated ideas about how to make sense of the past which excavation and survey sought to reveal. It was all very well, they argued, to improve methods of excavations, of record and recovery; but to what purpose, if there were no appropriate methods ('models') to use material culture in an efficient and justifiable way to explain what had happened in the past and why it happened as it did. The terms of the debate might not always be as new as its leading participants believed, but its range and the pertinence of its questions accelerated what has been called archaeology's 'loss of innocence', creating a crisis of confidence in all aspects of the subject.

By the early 1960s among young prehistorians in the United States there was increasing unease with the accepted procedures of archaeology, which were still predominantly those of Gordon Childe, expounded in numerous articles and books in the previous thirty years. He had concentrated on the recognition and classification of objects into categories (typology) and of categories into assemblages or archaeological cultures, plotted in time and space, to write the cultural history of the ancient peoples they were taken to represent. In their seminal study, *Method and Theory in American Archaeology* (1958), Willey and Phillips had used a phrase which more than any other came to be the rallying cry of the reformers, 'archaeology is anthropology or it is nothing', appropriately echoed in 1962 in the title of an article by Binford generally taken to mark the birth of the 'new' archaeology: 'Archaeology as Anthropology'.[23] This inaugural paper, like so much that was to follow, combined considerable originality of thought with an inelegant, at times inpenetrable style and a tone so arrogant that even the sympathetic regretted it. It might not be intellectually persuasive beyond the intellectual *milieu* whence it came; but amongst young archaeologists in the English-speaking world its effect was electric.

'New' archaeologists argued that description had characterized archaeological research for too long without sufficient attention to explanation. Archaeology should no longer concentrate so exclusively on the surviving material evidence. It should aspire more confidently and systematically towards reconstructing ancient ways of life and thought rather than concentrating on the development of ideal typological systems, whether of objects or cultures, which were essentially static. This conception of archaeology as a dynamic social science, studying

141

processes with appropriately tested methods, was intimately linked to a new and emphatic preoccupation with theory in archaeological inquiry. In time this aspect of the movement took many forms, most of them united only by attempts to emulate the procedures of natural scientists, or rather to model their investigations on the methods advocated by contemporary philosophers of science.

This trend in its most developed form promoted the quest for general laws of cultural dynamics, an approach which was to fall victim as much to changing fashions in the philosophy of science as to the triviality of the proposed laws. Its most durable result was a wider acceptance of the idea that archaeologists should be more concerned with posing questions explicitly as the basis for coherent research programmes. A corollary of this is the continuing debate over aims and methods which tends at times to give the subject the dual aspect of 'pure' and 'applied', long familiar in mathematics and physics. Although this distinction should not be pressed too far, there is a much greater diversity within archaeology than there used to be. At opposite extremes are now to be found those who chose to be pre-occupied with every new twist in the theoretical debate and those who go on digging virtually immune from the conceptual strife.

Critical re-examination has continued through the 1970s and 1980s, embracing a bewildering range of intellectual systems (and fashions) with the participants united by little more than a desire to emphasize that, since fruitful ideas about the past are generally neither obvious nor simple, their clear formulation is a vital preliminary to sound research projects. The most recent controversies have increasingly been pre-occupied with the relativity of scholarship, emphasizing the role of the archaeologist's background, locality and personality in determining the kind of archaeology he or she pursues.

If a significant number of field archaeologists remain indifferent, if not positively opposed, to the more extreme theoretical trends which have followed from Binford's challenge a quarter of a century ago, few, if any, have failed to accept the impact of the natural, as distinct from the social, sciences on their professional work. Although this change was launched well before the new processural archaeology emerged, its progress was greatly accelerated by the new thinking which placed so high a premium on scientific procedures, both in the preparation and in the execution of research. As this survey has already made clear, the transformation of field research by the use of interdisciplinary teams combining the traditional archaeological skills with those of scientists and technologists was well in train by the early 1960s. It had been pioneered in the Near East, from the later 1940s, when the Braidwoods, based in the Oriental Institute in Chicago, used such a team to investigate early farming communities in Iraqi Kurdistan.

An important distinction has to be drawn in any history of biblical archaeology in these critical years. The growing impact of the natural sciences on archaeology was readily appreciated by Wright and many of his contemporaries. These developments brought no crisis of confidence in their conception of biblical archaeology, though some remained clear about their priorities. In a posthumously published address Wright made his position clear:

> archaeology is far too restricted when treated as a discipline in and of itself, whether by those who presume to be pure scientists, or by those who belong to other wings of anthropology or fine arts. In my opinion, archaeology must use all of the science that it can, but in the final analysis it is dealing with human beings, and therefore it can never be anything other than one among the several branches of cultural and humanistic history.[24]

It was the impact of ideas drawn from the social sciences and the philosophy of science which were to provoke dissension among the younger generation of Americans actively involved in biblical archaeology, particularly when colleagues like Dever used the new thinking to justify with renewed force the recurrent charge that their procedures were subjective and unscientific. The challenge presented by Binford and his colleagues to his fellow Americans working in Old World archaeology was far more unsettling than anything they had experienced in debates with European colleagues over improved field techniques or applied archaeological science, since it went to the heart of the matter, the nature of archaeology itself, in a way earlier challenges had not. At least they and their European colleagues had been broadly agreed upon the historical thrust of their enterprise. Now they were faced with concepts and procedures drawn from anthropology, many with a distinctly non-historical, if not positively anti-historical, bias. Dever's polemical writings epitomized their dilemma.

1 Cited by the editors in *Benchmarks in Time and Culture: an introduction to Palestinian Archaeology dedicated to Joseph A. Callaway*, Atlanta, Georgia, 1988.

2 W.F. Albright, 'The Phenomenon of Israeli Archaeology' in *Near Eastern Archaeology in the Twentieth Century* (ed. J.A. Sanders), New York, 1970, p. 63; see now Y. Yadin and J. Naveh, *Masada I: The Aramaic and Hebrew*

Ostraca and Jar Inscriptions; H.M. Cotton and J. Geiger, *Masada II: The Latin and Greek Documents*, both Jerusalem, 1989.

3 See D. Ussishkin, 'The Date of the Judaean Shrine at Arad', *I.E.J.* 38 (1988), pp. 142ff.

4 Z. Herzog and others, *Beer-Sheba II*, Tel Aviv, 1984, p. 74.

5 See, for example, R.L. Chapman, III, 'Excavation techniques and recording systems: a theoretical study', *P.E.Q.* 1986, pp. 5-26.

6 K.M. Kenyon, 'The date of the destruction of Iron Age Beer-Sheba', *P.E.Q.* 1976, pp. 63-64.

7 P. Lapp, *A.S.O.R. Newsletter* 11 (1962), p. 3.

8 P. Lapp, 'Palestine Known but mostly unknown', *B.A.* 26 (1963), pp. 131-134.

9 P. Lapp, *Vetus Testamentum* XX (1970), p. 245.

10 H.J. Franken, *In Search of the Jericho Potters: ceramics from the Iron Age and from the Neolithicum*, Amsterdam, 1974, p. 39.

11 H.J. Franken, 'The problem of identification in Biblical Archaeology', *P.E.Q.* 1976, p. 8.

12 H.J. Franken, *Cambridge Ancient History II* (2), Cambridge, 1975, p. 336.

13 W.F. Albright, *Bibliotheca Orientalis* 21 (1964), pp. 66-70.

14 H.J. Franken, *P.E.Q.* 1976, pp. 10-11.

15 S. Gitin, 'Stratigraphy and its application to chronology and terminology', in *Biblical Archaeology Today* (ed. J. Aviram), Jerusalem, 1985, p. 103.

16 W.F. Albright, *Bibliotheca Orientalis*, 27 (1970), p. 57.

17 J.A. Sanders (ed.), *Near Eastern Archaeology in the Twentieth Century*, New York, 1970, p. 78.

18 *The Biblical Archaeologist*, 1871, pp. 70-76.

19 W.G. Dever, *Archaeology and Biblical Studies: retrospects and prospects*, Evanston, 1974, p. 6; see now W.G. Dever, *Recent Archaeological Discoveries and Biblical Research*, University of Washington Press, 1990.

20 Dever, op. cit. n. 19, p. 6.

21 Dever, op. cit. n. 19, p. 13.

22 W.G. Dever, 'Impact of the "New Archaeology"', in *Benchmarks in Time and Culture* (ed. J.F. Drinkard *et al.*), Atlanta, Georgia, 1988, p. 339.

23 G.R. Willey and P. Phillips, *Method and Theory in American Archaeology*, Chicago, 1958, p. 2; L.R. Binford, 'Archaeology as Anthropology', *American*

Antiquity 28 (1962), pp. 217ff. reprinted in L.R. Binford, *An Archaeological Perspective*, New York and London, 1972, pp. 20ff; see also A.E. Glock, 'Tradition and change in two Archaeologies', *American Antiquity* 20 (1985), pp. 464-77.

24 G.E. Wright, 'The "New" Archaeology', *B.A.* 38 (1975), p. 115.

6

The Growing Impact of the Natural and Social Sciences (1974-1990)

> Whether biblical or classical historians, we have also learned that archaeology and epigraphy cannot take the place of the living tradition of a nation as transmitted by its literary texts. At the same time we have been cured of early delusions that the reliability of historical traditions can be easily demonstrated by the spade of the archaeologist (Momigliano, 1982).[1]

In the middle of the 1970s sensational claims for a close relationship between the Old Testament and third-millennium texts found at Tell Mardikh (ancient Ebla) in Syria suddenly restored a wider perspective to biblical archaeology. Since the primary evidence was only available at the time to the official expert with the excavation team, and anyway there were few scholars equipped to assess these tablets authoritatively, hasty judgements had a more devastating impact than comparable assessments of the Mari and Ras Shamra tablets had had a generation earlier (p. 81). The whole episode served to strengthen the position of those who wished to discredit biblical archaeology, whilst at the same time emphasizing to all how little had been learnt in the previous fifty years about the appropriate means for interrelating the evidence of extra-biblical texts, of 'dirt' archaeology, and of the Old Testament. Biblical archaeologists still striving to absorb the new concepts and fresh information now being provided by natural and social scientists involved in the archaeology of Syro-Palestine were sharply reminded of their vulnerability when confronted with new evidence from philology, the oldest of the ancillary disciplines. This academic confusion was further compounded by the endemic political and ideological conflicts of the region.

In the United States the debate over biblical archaeology, re-opened and to some extent redefined by Dever, rumbled on. Many of his colleagues accepted the force of his arguments against a casual combination of biblical expertise and field archaeology, with the complementary demand that in future all excavators in Syro-Palestine must be professionally trained for the purpose; but others thought he was overstating the case. They argued that the radical separation of 'biblical archaeology' from 'Syro-Palestinian archaeology', which Dever then advocated, was neither realistic nor in the long run in the interests either of Biblical Studies or of the archaeology of this region in the Bronze and Iron Ages. It was as bad, they pointed out, for advocates of dirt archaeology to see some kind of virtue in distancing themselves from written evidence, or to use it indiscriminately without proper attention to decades of critical study, as it was for literary fundamentalists to cite or manipulate uncritically the evidence of textless archaeology for their own particular ends. Sooner or later frontiers had to be crossed, so it was more than ever essential at a time of rapidly proliferating information for those who crossed them to respect and seek to appreciate intelligently the procedures of sister disciplines with their strengths and their weaknesses. The Ebla episode again emphasized how important it was to understand what constituted sense and what nonsense questions and answers in both biblical archaeology and in philology.

Amongst both field archaeologists and students of the Bible there were many who were increasingly cautious about the wilder claims of the 'new' archaeologists. As early as 1974, in an address already cited (p. 143), Wright had shrewdly anticipated one of the more common lines of criticism:

> Furthermore, the extensive verbalization of abstract theories and the almost complete disinterest in the improvement of control in dirt archaeology lead one to wonder whether the methodology is as deficient in the dirt as it is in theoretical models of human determinism.[2]

As the new archaeology itself underwent constant modification through the 1980s, and as the concern with improved techniques on the ground in Israel and Jordan grew, so the nature of the debate evolved. Dever, as well as his opponents, gradually moved closer towards a compromise. By the end of the decade the relationship of archaeology to the biblical text no longer seemed such a critical issue as it had in the 1970s.

As this survey has constantly illustrated, implicitly if not always explicitly, it is in the writing of Israel's early history that the special relationship of archaeologists and biblical scholars is most readily apparent. Through the 1980s there were increasing signs that the more radical historians of ancient Israel were moving along lines complementary to the most thoughtful field archaeologists concerned with the archaeology of the second and first millennia BC in Syro-Palestine, especially those who were substituting an anthropological archaeology concerned with processes for an historical archaeology concerned with peoples and events. The distinction should not be drawn too sharply, but as historians of Israel came under the influence of the French social historians of the *Annales* school, particularly the writings of Bloch and Braudel, they were moving ever closer to the current thinking of progressive archaeologists, not least those who were themselves attentive to the 'new' history. Braudel's concern both with everyday material culture and the enduring undercurrents which may explain the continuities and discontinuities of social and economic life allowed for an accommodation between archaeologists and historians unprecedented in earlier history writing. At much the same time both field archaeologists and writers on Israel's protohistory had come to realise that if new perspectives really were to be opened up, then not only the range of the database had to be improved but so did the ways in which it was to be interrogated and processed.

It is also now possible to detect a growing relationship between archaeologists and New Testament scholars, who had for so long tended to ignore archaeology. Archaeologists for their part had remained indifferent to the neglect, happy to operate within classical archaeology. Even discovery of the Dead Sea Scrolls and the associated excavations had not really broken the mould. They were predominantly an aspect of Jewish Studies to which the archaeology of the Herodian period was now making significant independent contributions in the hands of increasingly energetic Israeli archaeologists. It was not until Dead Sea Scrolls studies had demonstrated the necessity for treating early Christianity and contemporary Judaism jointly, within the wider Graeco-Roman context, that archaeology really began to impinge upon New Testament research. In many ways the 'new' archaeological approach facilitated this change as it began to modify traditional classical archaeology in Syro-Palestine.

As the centenary of Petrie's excavation at Tell el-Hesi approached there were probably few who would have wished to dissent from Freedman's comments in introducing a volume of the *Biblical Archaeologist* in 1982 entitled 'Bible, Archaeology and History'; an issue which may now be seen to mark the beginning of the end of the bible archaeology debate in the terms set out by Dever ten years earlier (p. 137):

Whether there is a discipline we call 'biblical archaeology' is almost irrelevant, and whether the area of overlap in both disciplines should be designated by this expression (or another) hardly matters. What does matter is that each practitioner of a particular discipline be as capable as possible, work as diligently as possible, and be steadfast in the application of the principles and methods of that discipline. Inevitably, the serious faithful pursuit of knowledge in both disciplines will be beneficial not only in the individual discipline but also in the areas where they converge and overlap. So long as the participant is faithful to his or her own discipline, that person cannot fail to make contributions of value to a contiguous research area.[3]

Tablets from Ebla (Tell Mardikh): the historicity of the Patriarchs again

In the first two decades after the end of the Second World War, though archaeological activity everywhere expanded in the Near East and in Egypt, outside Israel and Jordan there were few new archaeological finds which secured the attention of biblical scholars. Syria, the country that might have been expected to contribute most, remained archaeologically underexplored. French excavations at Ras Shamra (Ugarit) continued to illuminate its Late Bronze Age culture through newly discovered tablets and works of art, whilst similar discoveries at Mari steadily increased knowledge of the world of the earlier second millennium BC on the middle Euphrates. In the 1940s and 1950s publication of texts from two levels (VII and IV) of Woolley's excavations at Tell Atchana (Alalakh), and a remarkable autobiography inscribed on the statue of Idrimi, a local ruler in the Late Bronze Age, threw isolated shafts of light across the complex political and social structure of Syro-Palestine between about 1750 and 1350 BC.

Iron Age finds of interest to Biblical students remained sparse. It was not until 1971 that the American excavators published in full the eighth-century BC architectural remains at Tell Tayinat, close to Tell Atchana, excavated almost forty years earlier. The palace and adjacent temple there have long been cited as the best known parallel to the biblical description of Solomon's palace and temple in Jerusalem. From Mallowan's excavations at Nimrud in northern Iraq, through the 1950s, came fresh texts to carry forward the researches of nineteenth-century scholars who had done so much through the fledgling study of Assyriology to create public interest in biblical archaeology.

149

After a century and a half the records of the Neo-Assyrian Empire, primarily from excavations at Nimrud and Nineveh, remain the single most significant extra-biblical source for historians of ancient Israel. In recent years there has been a marked revival in their study with a dual thrust. On the one hand, there is the attempt to provide authoritative modern editions and translations of the royal inscriptions of Mesopotamia, sponsored by the University of Toronto and directed by Grayson, which also produces a steady flow of ancillary research; and Parpola's project, based in the University of Helsinki, to revitalize archival study of Neo-Assyrian tablets with the assistance of modern computer technology. Each is likely to revive the traditional connection between Assyriology and Old Testament Studies, but with a greater respect for the individuality of each discipline as they are better understood in the light of an ever broader database. On the other hand, steadily more penetrating attempts are being made to examine the ideological and literary background of the texts, not least editorial procedures which are likely to be equally relevant to textual analysis of the Old Testament.

The situation in field archaeology and epigraphy was dramatically invigorated by the discovery of the Ebla tablets in 1974-75. In those years Matthiae and his team from Italy, which had been excavating Tell Mardikh since 1964, discovered an archive of thousands of complete and fragmentary clay tablets inscribed in the cuneiform script. They were recovered from the debris of a royal palace destroyed sometime in the third quarter of the third millennium BC. The location of Tell Mardikh, 42 miles south of Aleppo on the road to Hama, had allowed it to play a crucial role in contacts between the Syrian coast and Mesopotamia. Earlier, in 1968, an inscription on a torso from a stone votive statue, dedicated to the goddess Ishtar, had indicated by its reference to a king of Ebla that Tell Mardikh was the site of this ancient city, already known from inscriptions of the Akkadian kings of Mesopotamia (c. 2334-2154 BC), but previously located by scholars elsewhere in Syria. It seems most likely that it was one of these Akkadian kings, Sargon or Naram-Sin, whose army had sacked the palace at Ebla thus preserving the tablets which were to reveal a whole new aspect of urban life in Syria. Most of them were written in the local language (Eblaite), under the strong influence of the Sumerian literary tradition, already almost a millennium old. They deal with the administrative routines and foreign relations of the palace. The only texts written wholly in Sumerian are lexical lists, exactly like those composed for centuries in Sumer, probably for use in training scribes.

The significance of the Ebla tablets may hardly be overestimated, since the tablets were centuries earlier than anything comparable from Syria, revealing a totally unexpected degree of literacy in the city-states of the area in the middle of the third millennium BC. From the outset sensational claims, which were both ideologically and politically sensitive, for a direct relationship between these early texts and the Old Testament combined disastrously with an absence of primary publications of the complete texts upon which they were supposedly based to cause an unprecedented academic crisis. The unity of the excavation team was shattered. The embarassed director replaced the expedition's original epigrapher, Pettinato, responsible for some, if not all, of the claims, with a new one, Archi, thus creating a dual flow of publications over the next decade. Acrimonious controversy for some years undermined academic and public confidence, which is only now being restored by proper publications and responsible debate about their contents:

> Polemics, often harsh and always painful for the author [Matthiae], have arisen from individual speculations about presumed connections between the Ebla texts and Biblical characters, stories and episodes. The interest aroused among the public by these unfounded inferences of a relationship between Ebla and the Bible is understandable, but it must clearly be said that documentary evidence of them is effectively non-existent.[4]

Two claims in particular focused attention on Ebla and the Bible.[5] The first was Pettinato's attribution of the local language to the Northwest Semitic family as 'Old Canaanite', with close ties with Ugaritic, Phoenician and Hebrew; a view extended in some quarters to imply a more intimate link between the Ebla texts and parts of the Old Testament than might otherwise have been thought plausible. The problem persists, with more cautious scholars seeking its affinities in Akkadian or Amorite. Considerably more remarkable at the time was the claim that the 'five cities of the plain', including Sodom and Gomorrah, appeared in their biblical sequence in one of the Ebla texts. Freedman, a biblical scholar who had been a student of Albright's, over-enthusiastically used this information to revive Albright's arguments for the historicity of the patriarchal narratives, but now in an even earlier context than that previously proposed. He also enlisted new archaeological evidence of Early Bronze Age occupation at Bab edh-Dhra' and Numeirah, southeast of the Dead Sea, to endorse his proposal.[6] The print was barely dry on the page before the proposed indentification of the cities of the plain was being withdrawn by the Ebla team's philologist. Archaeologists were quick to point out that the Early Bronze III-IV evidence from Transjordan must be interpreted in its own context and was in no way exceptional. It was a critical, perhaps a decisive, moment in the recent history of biblical archaeology. The majority of scholars endorsed the new scepticism about the possibility of authenticating or refuting biblical traditions on the basis of Near Eastern extra-biblical texts or 'dirt' archaeology.

Rapid eclipse has been the fate of a whole series of other biblical connections in Pettinato's earliest reports on the Ebla texts to which he alone initially had access. Not for the first time sound pioneering research on unprecedented texts was compromised by hasty recourse to biblical parallels. Among the most notable claims were: the supposed presence of *ya*, as a form of Yahweh, in Eblaite personal names; the election and anointing of local kings, claimed to be uniquely reminiscent of practices in early Israel; a mythological introduction to a hymn to the creator deity at Ebla, said to be peculiarly akin to the account of creation in Genesis; and the claim that there were many specific geographical and historical identifications in common between texts from Ebla and the Old Testament. The evidence for social structure provided by the Ebla tablets was also at first said by some scholars to reveal a society more akin to that of nomadic shepherds, organized by tribes, than to a city-state structured as were those of Sumer and Akkad in Mesopotamia. Thus they sought to draw Ebla and its inhabitants more squarely into the debate over the patriarchal narratives.

Fortunately, the real value of these exceptional texts was made rapidly evident once copies were accessible to the community of scholars at large. Controversy persists, but now based on primary sources, not upon rumour and speculation. As authentically scholarly publications make the original texts available, their difficulty is apparent but so is their real significance. They have already transformed knowledge of Syrian urban society in the middle of the third millennium BC and its relationships with the major city-states of Mesopotamia down the line of the Euphrates, particularly Mari and Kish. Although the geographical range of the texts has shrunk since the wildly optimistic claims made on their first reading, they still constitute a unique point-of-reference for historical geography. To what extent these texts bear upon life and society in Palestine in the Early Bronze Age has yet to be properly established, since a fully authoritative synthesis is awaited. Whatever the case, their role in biblical archaeology, strictly speaking, is minimal.

Albright's paradigm moves into eclipse

The speed and enthusiasm with which scholars in the Albright tradition welcomed the initial claims of Old Testament links with the Ebla texts owed something to objections raised in a penetrating critique of Albright's method and arguments presented a year or two earlier in Thompson's thesis, *The Historicity of the Patriarchal Narratives: the Quest for the Historical Abraham* (1974). At the heart of this detailed and intricately constructed monograph is a destructive examination of the circularity of Albright's arguments for the historicity of the patriarchal narratives, a case he had continuously developed over a period of some forty years through a complex integration of data drawn variously from Genesis, from extra-biblical texts, and from 'dirt' archaeology, which is far from easy to pin down:

> Because of this it seems necessary to insist on a methodology of writing the history of the ancient Near East which observes a careful distinction between the types of materials at hand, and which allows historical conclusions to be drawn only after each type of material [i.e. from texts and from 'dirt' archaeology] has been independently examined. Thus, archaeological materials should not be dated or evaluated on the basis of written texts which are independent of these materials; so also written documents should not be interpreted on the basis of archaeological hypotheses.[7]

On this basis Thompson proceeded to scrutinize point by point the manner in which Albright had drawn upon evidence from the Execration Texts, and from tablets found at Nuzi and Mari (p. 81) always emphasizing the similarities with the patriarchal narratives and totally neglecting the dissimilarities. At the same time Thompson exposed the fundamental weakness in Albright's model, which combined two distinct hypotheses: the ultimately text-based concept of an incursion of Amorite-speaking peoples from western Mesopotamia into Palestine in the later third millennium BC and the separate archaeological explanation of the contemporary Early Bronze IV/Middle Bronze I material culture of Palestine as an intrusive, non-urban nomadic phenomenon. Debatable as parts of Thompson's critique might be, the effect of its systematic approach was twofold. It virtually destroyed the archaeological case for a history of the Patriarchs in the terms proposed by Albright, regarded at the time in many quarters as the major achievement of biblical archaeology. Then it forcefully challenged the belief that biblical traditions might be historically evaluated in terms of archaeological evidence and archaeological data structured through Biblical narratives. It demonstrated with cogent clarity how hypotheses drawn from each body of evidence were recurrently assumed to be mutually supportive in Albright's writings:

> Largely because of the long established character of this interpretation there has been a tendency not only to see the patriarchal narratives in the light of this historical background, indeed as historical records themselves - but also to interpret the historical and archaeological information in the light of the Biblical narratives, with a resulting harmonization that makes the hypothesis increasingly difficult to analyse; for such an analysis demands not only an investigation of whether the Biblical traditions really do presuppose the type of background that historical studies and archaeology offer, but it demands a new investigation of the historical and archaeological sources as well.[8]

Thompson's monograph, like Weippert's less than a decade earlier (p. 136), was the more significant in its impact upon reflective biblical archaeologists since it offered a powerful challenge to the reconstruction proposed by Albright and Père de Vaux and questioned aspects of the German approach (in which both young scholars had been nurtured). Their books were symptomatic of a growing secularization, for want of a better word, both in Europe and in North America particularly, which, even without the pressures of such special debates as that provoked by Dever from the archaeological side, was gradually separating Syro-Palestinian archaeology from Bible-related archaeology and the writings of the history of Early Israel from theological restraints, especially those associated with the Biblical Theology movement. The intellectual climate in archaeology and in Biblical Studies in the later 1960s and the 1970s was in general much more favourable to such critiques than it had been a decade earlier, when rather than going to the heart of the matter the critics had largely been content to castigate obvious excesses in the popular writings of biblical archaeologists. Franken (p. 134) had then been virtually alone in his more fundamental criticisms of Albright's conception of the relationship between archaeological evidence and biblical narratives, though before his sudden death Lapp appeared to be approaching a comparable critical position (p. 131).

Soon after Thompson's monograph was published, Miller, a biblical scholar with wide archaeological experience, subjected Albright's presentation of the archaeological case for a thirteenth-century Exodus and Conquest to scrutiny in a brief but equally rigorous study. Like Thompson he was as much pre-occupied with the nature of the arguments used by Albright as with the relevant archaeological evidence available in the middle of the 1970s;

> What sort of conclusion is to be reached when carefully excavated

archaeological evidence does not seem to meet the minimum requirements of the historical implications of the biblical texts? When, if ever, is it methodologically proper to deviate from the most natural interpretation of one in order to bring it into line with the other? Is it ever justifiable to take liberties with both the written and the artefactual evidence in order to achieve correlation? If so - and such procedure has been the order of the day in "biblical archaeology" - are there any objections based on circular argumentations.[9]

A year later, in 1978, in *Redating the Exodus and the Conquest*, Bimson, an ultra-conservative biblical scholar not an archaeologist, sought to demolish the case for a thirteenth-century date for the Conquest in favour of an earlier fifteenth-century invasion in line with the author's literal interpretation of internal biblical chronologies. Although the methods are generally close to those used by Albright, Bimson successfully exposed many circular arguments in ceramic-based chronologies, which biblical scholars had generally taken at face value. In this respect it was a significant step in opening up the debate over the use of archaeological data in this particular instance; but the positive case argued by Bimson had its own archaeological weaknesses, even if the chronological system was accepted, and has not subsequently met with agreement either among archaeologists or biblical historians.

Although archaeological evidence played little or no part in the central argument of Gottwald's massive monograph *The Tribes of Yahweh: a Sociology of the Religion of Liberated Israel 1250-1050 B.C.E.* (1979), as he had no expertise in the subject, his book had important implications for biblical archaeology. It raised questions previously ignored and revitalized increasingly ossified research perspectives. By emphasizing the importance of understanding the economic and social setting in which Israel had emerged, Gottwald effectively modified the over-simplified dichotomy of 'conquest' or 'settlement' in which biblical archaeologists had for so long been caught up, opening the way for approaches much more in tune with new archaeological thinking. Lemche's extended commentary on Gottwald's hypothesis is exactly what its sub-title indicates, *Early Israel: Anthropological and Historical Studies on the Israelite Society before the Monarchy* (1985). The role of archaeological evidence receives passing notice in a way that is significantly critical.

Some archaeologists appear to find it more fascinating to hunt for 'proof' of the presence of Israel, since even the most minute changes in architecture, pottery, town lay-out, and so forth, have been taken to show the presence of new (foreign) elements among the existing population at the time. If a destruction layer is uncovered in the towns and cities of the 13th century, it is held to be clear that the Israelites were the cause (indeed, it is possible that the very dates assigned to such destruction layers derive from the wish to find a connection with the Settlement). A description of the transition between the Late Bronze Age and the Iron Age in Palestine - seen in an international perspective - is definitely a desideratum . . . [10]

Lemche's treatment of contemporary American anthropological thinking leads him into the first notice in a history of early Israel of the new archaeology, though only as an extended, critical footnote.[11]

It is hardly surprising that it was to be practising archaeologists like Finkelstein (p. 163) and Stager (p. 165), rather than biblical scholars, who have most effectively pioneered the way forward after the demise of Albright's conquest hypothesis. The vitality of the debate over appropriate approaches to the investigation of Israel's entry into Canaan as the 1980s drew to a close was evident in a challenging paper by London on the ever contentious correlation of ethnicity and material culture, an issue central to this particular problem:

> Ethnographic studies provide evidence that individual ethnic groups comprise people of diverse lifestyles, both sedentary and migratory. If archaeologists understand variation in material culture as evidence of daily life rather than 'ethnicity', the 'inconsistencies' between biblical texts and the archaeological finds become less problematic. To benefit from the information provided in the Bible requires a more precise excavation strategy that compares and contrasts rural communities in all regions of the country if we are to identify the separateness of Israelites and Canaanites.[12]

A new generation of archaeologists at work in Israel

So long as Aharoni and Yadin, from their respective institutes in Tel Aviv and Jerusalem, dominated archaeology in Israel, it was broadly divided into two schools, distinguished to some extent by their aims and methods. Since Aharoni's death in 1971 and Yadin's entry into politics in 1977 (and death in 1984), a much greater pluralism has become evident among the two hundred or more archaeologists now active in Israel. Two new University institutes - at Beersheba and Haifa - have also broadened the teaching base. In field research the most progressive of the new generation, whilst faithful in the main to the local architectural tradition, taught by Dunayevsky, have sought more and more to adopt and develop field procedures of Anglo-American origin. Israeli archaeologists were now able to observe British and American archaeologists in action, notably at Gezer. In ceramic analysis, still the ABC of field studies, there was a significant shift away from the type-series tradition of Kenyon (pioneered by Petrie), and the meticulous chronological typologies of Albright and Wright, both essentially sherd-based, to a new emphasis on the restoration of complete pottery vessels from good archaeological contexts. This procedure sought to minimize misconceptions arising from the large proportion of earlier and later pottery fragments encountered in any one context in a *tell*.

Surface surveys, popular not least for their cost-effectiveness, have proliferated throughout the country and the occupied territories, revealing thousands of sites in previously unexplored regions and transforming knowledge of ancient settlement patterns. But systematic archaeological maps of the area have yet to appear. The appropriate methods of description and analysis of the results drawn from surveys continue to provoke debate locally as well as in the archaeological world at large. Surveys are increasingly integrated with excavations on *tells* and one-period sites to develop many regional studies like that pioneered by Aharoni and his colleagues in the area of Beersheba and Arad (p. 117). Although Aharoni's distinct biblical bias in the interpretation of his results has met with increasing criticism, the technique and its application have proved extremely fertile in ideas and results.

This work has added a fresh dimension to the study of historical topography. During his years in Palestine Alt had developed the study of ancient territorial units, in the light of the evidence for their history provided by texts, to counteract the difficulties of identifying ancient sites on a one-to-one basis. These studies may now be co-ordinated with regional studies, provided by teams of archaeologists and natural scientists, which reveal more precisely how ancient man exploited particular landscapes, where he lived, and where he farmed. This integration of textual data and archaeological information set within the context of a specific landscape continues to establish biblical topography upon a sounder basis of evidence.

Among regional surveys relevant to the archaeology of the Bronze and Iron Ages a few may be singled out: those in the Sharon Plain centred on the Aphek excavations (p. 158); in the Esdraelon Plain from 1975 (Ben-Tor) linked with excavations at Yoqneam, Tel Qiri and Tel Qashish; in the Negev and northern Sinai concentrating on Iron Age forts (Meshel and Cohen); and variously along the coastal plain, exploring Philistia in the south and greater Phoenicia in the north. In every case select excavations have supplemented and cross-checked the results of survey, which depends ultimately on the close dating of pottery sherds found on the surface.

It is only possible in a brief survey to offer a bird's-eye view of the archaeological excavations which have proliferated in recent years, followed by some assessment of the impact this work has had on those problems traditionally held to be at the heart of biblical archaeology. Although the means of publication have multiplied, the pattern of brief descriptive preliminary reports and virtually no final reports has persisted with a few notable exceptions, since some younger archaeologists are keenly aware of this unsatisfactory legacy from the past. Word-of-mouth and brief, ephemeral conference or seminar papers all too often provide the means for communicating fresh information and challenging new ideas. In such a situation, by no means only confined to Israel, the few exceptions, whilst being invaluable, tend to highlight certain sites or problems, which may not necessarily be the most significant.

Much research has concentrated on the coast from Acre ('Akko = Tell el-Fukhkhar), with its fine harbour, in the north to Deir el-Balah in the south. At 'Akko excavations directed by Moshe Dothan since 1973 have been increasingly combined with underwater archaeology, a fast developing aspect of archaeology in Israel as elsewhere. Stern's excavations at Tell Mevorakh (1973-76) and Tel Dor (since 1980) have contributed substantially to understanding an important area, long under Phoenician influence. These excavations usefully supplemented those by Bikai at Tyre and by Pritchard at Sarepta, conducted before civil war closed the Lebanon to serious archaeological investigation. In the Late Bronze Age at Mevorakh a shrine occupied much of the site, yielding a bronze snake like those retrieved from contemporary temples at Hazor and Timna. Southwards in the plain of Sharon excavations by Kochavi and Beck, of Tel Aviv University, at Aphek (from 1972) are but the most spectacular of a series of digs on mounds in this area, as at Tel Michal and Tel Gerisa (Herzog and Muhly; 1977-80, from 1981-). At Aphek the most striking finds were made in the Late Bronze Age citadel, where epigraphic discoveries included a complete letter in Akkadian from the ruler of Ugarit (Ras Shamra) to a high Egyptian official, presumably resident at Aphek. Other tablet fragments illustrate a multilingual community of scribes involved in widespread administrative and diplomatic contacts.

The full implications of a satellite excavation by Kochavi and Finkelstein at the small village settlement of 'Izbet Sartah (1976-78) three kilometres to the east of Aphek, dated to the twelfth century, remain controversial. The excavators believe it to be an early Israelite settlement, in part because of its architecture. The most remarkable single find was a pottery ostracon, apparently inscribed by a semi-literate person, who wrote four lines either of random letters or of a text not yet understood and then the local linear alphabet ('Proto-Canaanite') from left to right.

Interest in Philistia and the Philistines remains undiminished. A number of major excavations within Philistia, broadly defined, have thrown increasing light upon the complex question of Philistine identity over a period of six hundred years and their relationships with Israel and Judah: Trude Dothan's excavations at Deir el-Balah (1972-82) and, in collaboration with the American scholar Gitin, at Tel Miqne (?Ekron) since 1981; the renewed excavations at Tel Qasile (A. Mazar) from 1982; the excavations at Tell el-Hesi (1970-83) (p. 127); and excavations at Tel Batash (?Timnah), on the frontier of Judah and Philistia, since 1977 (Kelm and A. Mazar), at Tel Ser'a (Oren) from 1972-76 and Tel Halif (Lahav Project) from 1976-80.

Since 1975 many forts in the northern Negev attributed to the mature Iron Age have been excavated, but two sites in particular have attracted considerable attention. Tell el-Qudeirat was most recently excavated by Cohen in 1976-78, revealing a series of three superimposed stone-built fortresses. The most recent yielded pottery of the seventh to sixth centuries BC, and may have been destroyed when the army of Nebuchadnezzar ravaged Judah. The earlier had pottery of the eighth to seventh centuries. The earliest pottery recovered was of the tenth to ninth centuries, the time of the United Monarchy, with no clear indication of any earlier occupation in the areas excavated. This is the *tell* most generally identified as Kadesh-Barnea, since Woolley and Lawrence, who dug there briefly, first made the proposal after their 'Wilderness of Zin' expedition (p. 37).

About fifty kilometres further south, on an isolated hill overlooking one of the few wells in the area, Meshel excavated a stone building in 1975-6 which has provided controversial evidence for cult practice in the ninth to eighth centuries BC. This building at Kuntillet 'Ajrud (Horvat Teiman) served both as a wayside shrine and as a caravanserai on an important route through the Negev, where a variety of peoples would be expected. It is distinguished by rough sketches and inscriptions on large storage jars, wall plaster and other objects found within its rooms. Crude sketches of religious motifs drawn both on jars and wall plaster, sometimes in uncertain relationship to inscriptions, embrace themes used in Syro-Phoenician art and others more familiar from local painted pottery attributed to the Midianites. The inscriptions include letters incised on pottery before firing; dedications incised on stone vessels; and texts in red and black ink on wall plaster, often badly preserved.

Although no full report has yet appeared, a flood of publications has been provoked by the phrase *yhwh* . . . . *w' shrh*, on large storage jar A, with its possible indications of a Yahwistic polytheism. Translation and interpretation of this text and accompanying graffiti remain particularly controversial. The biblical *asherah* has been variously identified as the name of a goddess, a sacred tree, a cult object, a grove or a shrine. The Old Testament indicates that Canaanite deities with consorts were still worshipped under the Divided Monarchy, but the idea that Yahweh could have one, as perhaps suggested by this text and isolated inscriptions found earlier, has raised fundamental questions about the history of religion in early Israel.[13]

Within Judah, Lachish and Jerusalem continue to dominate the archaeological record. Ussishkin renewed systematic excavations at Tell ed-Duweir (Lachish) in 1973 with the declared intention of elucidating problems remaining after publication by Tufnell of the earlier excavations there (p. 62). He assembled a large interdisciplinary team, which has also investigated the natural and human history of the surrounding landscape, epitomized in Rosen's pioneering study *Cities of Clay: the Geoarchaeology of Tells* (1986). The most significant new information for Biblical Studies has come from study of the Late Bronze and Iron Age levels. After sparse occupation in the earlier part of the Late Bronze Age, Lachish was densely populated when it met with sudden, violent destruction late in the period (Level VI). In the debris was a bronze fragment bearing a cartouche of Ramses III (c. 1194-63 BC), a valuable *terminus post quem*, which endorses Tufnell's earlier conclusion about the date of the destruction, later than was favoured by Albright and others. Who destroyed it, archaeology does not reveal (cf. Joshua 10:31-2).

The *tell* seems then to have been largely abandoned (Level V) before being replaced by a garrison city round a massive citadel, perhaps in the late tenth century (Level IV; cf. 2 Chronicles 11:9). This appears to have been seriously damaged by earthquake, perhaps in the first half of the eighth century BC (cf. Amos 1:1; Zechariah 14:5) before being reconstructed with densely packed housing (Level III), finally destroyed in a great fire. This is dated by Ussishkin, as by Tufnell before him (p. 62), to 701 BC, when Sennacherib recorded his sack of Lachish, not a century later as many other scholars had argued. Subsequent, much reduced, occupation of the mound (Level II) was destroyed by the Babylonians in their campaign of 588/86 BC to be followed by brief occupation of the acropolis at the time of the achaemenid Persian Empire. Ussishkin's endorsement of Tufnell's minority view of the sequence-dating at Lachish in the mature Iron Age (Iron II) has important implications for the ceramic chronologies of the period which are still being worked out, since it is now appreciated that there was considerable regional diversity at this time. Indeed the ceramic and architectural sequences of the Iron Age remain as controversial in 1990 as they were fifty years ago.

The remains of the Iron Age gateway, virtually a small fort, and the Assyrian siege ramp, with the defences hastily thrown up by the defenders, at Lachish are so impressive that they have been selected for conservation and partial restoration in recent years. This process has not only revealed previously unsuspected stages in the history of the gateway, but clarified thinking on many other issues. Increasingly, public pressures are forcing archaeologists in Israel not to rebury the architectural finds they uncover, as used to be standard practice, but to consolidate them and present them in a readily comprehensible way both for scholars and laymen.

In 1979 Shiloh, whose work was cut sadly short by his premature death in 1988, re-opened excavations on Ophel ('City of David') in Jerusalem, where Kenyon had dug a decade earlier, though on a scale she was unable to contemplate. Large areas along the eastern ridge were laid open revealing a sequence of occupation from the third millennium BC until the Byzantine period, which largely confirmed Kenyon's major conclusions about the Jebusite city hereabouts and its successors. Critical questions, like the chronology of the elaborate water systems of the area, remain controversial; but important epigraphic discoveries included fragments of monumental stone inscriptions, ostraca and a remarkable series of clay bullae (or tags), bearing inscribed Hebrew seal impressions, preserved in the debris of Nebuchadnezzar's sack in 586 BC. These bullae add one, possibly two names to the tiny group of non-royal biblical personalities known from extra-biblical sources found in Israel and Jordan; Gemariahu, son of Shaphan (cf. Jeremiah 36:10) and perhaps also Azariahu, son of Hilkiahu (cf. 1 Chronicles 5:29-41; 9:10-11).[14]

Among the hundreds of seals and seal impressions now recorded with Hebrew names inscribed on them dating from Old Testament times only a handful bear names which may be taken with some confidence to be those of people mentioned in the Bible. In 1978 Avigad[15] published the first two, without known archaeological context, one an impression bearing the inscription 'belonging to Baruch son of Neriyah the scribe', in all probability the scribe of the prophet Jeremiah mentioned many times in the book of that name and possibly the author of much, if not all, of it (cf. Jeremiah 36:32). The other impression bore the inscription 'of Jerahmeel, the King's son' (cf. Jeremiah 36:26). Although a concise survey of this kind may only concentrate on the highlights, it should not be forgotten that the steady accumulation of inscribed seals and ostraca in the last thirty years is providing a major database for the study not only of epigraphy in Israel and Judah, but also of administrative practice, which touches at many points on biblical questions. Not the least of Ussishkin's finds at Lachish was confirmation that a famous series of seal impressions, stamped on the handles of baked clay storage jars, with the phrase *la-melekh* ('(belonging) to the King') and a place-name, were used predominantly in a brief period at the very end of the eighth century BC, probably in connection with Hezekiah's preparations for an anticipated Assyrian attack on Judah.[16] This largely resolved a long and contentious chronological debate, though their exact significance is not revealed by the archaeological evidence at present available.

The nature of the emergence of Israel in Canaan inevitably remains central to archaeological research in Israel in the early historic periods and the relevant research continues to offer a touchstone for any appreciation of the aims and methods of contemporary archaeology there. It was not a coincidence that the initial, and most lively, session of the first International Congress of Biblical Archaeology held in Jerusalem in 1984 was devoted to this subject (p. 166). Surface surveys have transformed archaeological research into the transition from the Late Bronze Age to the Iron Age at a time when traditional conceptions of the nomadic past of the tribes of Israel and their amphictyonic organization have been superseded by fresh models among historians primarily inspired by anthropology. The urban bias of traditional *tell* archaeology has been countered, revealing the critical importance of landscape studies for what, it has long been agreed, was primarily a rural process.

Until the war of 1967 gave Israeli archaeologists access to the West Bank Territories, they had concentrated their research on the appearance of Israel in Canaan to Upper Galilee, a peripheral area, where penetration was probably relatively late (p. 110), and the Negev. Intensive surveys and excavation of early Iron Age sites since 1967 in the central hills, between Beersheba in the south and Jezreel in the north, the heartland of early Israel in the biblical narratives, has opened a new era of research. Callaway's re-excavation of Ai (1964-72) and his dig at Khirbet Raddanah (1969-72) were first complemented by an Israeli survey of the central region directed by Kochavi in 1968. This revealed for the first time the extent of new settlement in the central hills at the outset of the Iron Age. In the early 1970s attention was switched to the Beersheba valley and it was only in the later 1970s that research in the hill country was energetically resumed with excavations by Finkelstein at Shiloh from 1981, by Amihai Mazar at Giloh (1977-81) and by Zertal on Mt Ebal (1982-87). Important as these excavations may have been, it was the comprehensive surveys of these years which created a wholly new database in Manasseh (Zertal), Ephraim (Finkelstein), Judah (Ofer), Western Galilee (Frankel) and Lower Galilee (Gal), now taken for granted in all studies of the transition from the Bronze Age to the Iron Age by Israeli scholars.

These surveys were much more thorough and more attuned to changing environmental conditions than the pioneer work of earlier years. Emphasis was increasingly placed on scientific reconstruction of the ecological factors affecting early settlement. This aspect of the research restored interest in ethnoarchaeology. After a generation or more of neglect there has been a marked revival of confidence in controlled inferences drawn from records of the economic and social life of the region under the Ottoman Empire. This interest owes something to the aspirations of the 'new' archaeology, but draws upon a distinct local tradition epitomized by the work of Dalman (p. 66), no longer neglected on the grounds that its use in the study of antiquity is neither appropriate nor 'scientific'. Whilst anthropologists and natural scientists seek to exploit the archaeological evidence for agrarian technology in the early Iron Age, sociologists from western urban backgrounds have been forced to challenge their alien preconceptions in confrontation with data from the local recent past, particularly in attempts to understand the process of sedentarization in antiquity. Finkelstein particularly has emphasized a need for intimate knowledge of the landscape.

These projects have brought a change in the historical interpretation accepted amongst Israeli archaeologists. Alt's model (see p. 110) is now increasingly preferred to Albright's (p. 72) as the best fit for the new evidence available for the first phase of the emergence of Israel in Canaan. The biblical concept of conquest and settlement is seen as best suited to the second phase. Finkelstein's *The Archaeology of the Israelite Settlement* (1988) is the first major synthesis to appear since the hill country was opened to investigation by the younger generation of Israeli archaeologists. This study, a combination of archaeological report and anthropological analysis, is based directly on the author's fieldwork in the highland region. He largely ignores the role of the lowland urban, or Canaanite, communities and the relevance of the peripheral regions, which, following the Old Testament narratives, had played a significant role in the traditional archaeological approach to the Israelites as intruders. His hypothesis, that the Israelites were pastoralists of local origin infiltrating the hill country late in the Bronze Age, is compromised by some special pleading and contentious assumptions about the direct relationship of material culture and ethnic identity. He accepts the biblical distribution of peoples as the basis for his analysis, even if seeming to reject entry from the east of the Jordan. Finkelstein's emphasis on the isolation and separation of the Israelites from the outset, and their indigenous origin, is in tune with the thinking of those 'new' archaeologists who reject any idea of diffusion or migration as a means of cultural change. Some critics have also seen in it an explicit political statement. The narrowness of the focus does not do full justice either to the biblical tradition of intrusion nor to the variety and range of the data now available and the socio-anthropological means for explaining it.

In this period increased archaeological investigation has also significantly modified the relative absolute chronologies for major sites, whilst highlighting the regional diversity of material culture, at the time of the Divided Monarchy. The consensus which had followed from Albright's analysis of mature Iron Age pottery at Tell Beit Mirsim in 1932 (p. 70) and the subsequent majority view that Lachish III had been destroyed in 597 BC (p. 160), II in 586 BC, endured through to the 1970s. It was then that opinion began to change in the light of excavations at Beersheba and renewed work at Lachish, accepting Tufnell's minority view that the correct date for the end of III was Sennacherib's campaign of 701 BC. The primary benchmarks round which the majority of scholars evaluate the ceramic chronologies of Iron Age II remain the well established four: the Solomonic building levels at Megiddo, Gezer and Hazor; the building enterprise of Omri and Ahab at Samaria; the destructions of Sennacherib in 701 BC; and of Nebuchadnezzar II just over a century later. A delicate interrelationship of biblical history, extra-biblical Assyro-Babylonian texts, stratigraphy, and ceramic typology currently sustains this framework, which is constantly under review.

In any retrospective view of archaeology in Israel in the last forty years it comes as something of a surprise to find how little archaeological research has been brought to bear upon the cult practices of Canaan and Israel. The traditional school of biblical archaeology as exemplified by the early German handbooks (p. 22) had paid considerable attention to religion and *realia*, despite the restricted information available at the time. More recently Père de Vaux in his *Ancient Israel* (1965) had assembled what comparative data there was, but in an illustrative rather than in a definitive way. Archaeology has much to offer for the elucidation of popular religious practices, helping to balance the information on orthodox cult most often described in the Old Testament. It may show, particularly, the continuities and discontinuities in cult furniture between Canaan and Israel-Judah and their similarities and dissimilarities with religious equipment in adjacent regions. The archaeology of cult is a topic fraught with problems, procedural and explanatory, but excavations continue to reveal relevant sites, as in Amihai Mazar's excavation of the so-called 'bull shrine', north-east of Shechem; Zertal's site on Mt Ebal, controversially described as an early Israelite sanctuary; Beit Arieh's seventh century Edomite shrine at Qitmit; and earlier, Meshel's work at Kuntillet 'Ajrud (p. 159). At the same time cult furniture of all kinds steadily accumulates without any sign of a comprehensive analysis and synthesis of the primary implications for Biblical Studies.

American archaeologists remain active in a number of projects in Israel, notably Stager, holder of the recently created Dorot Professorship of the Archaeology of Israel at Harvard University. He is a pupil of Wright's with wide experience of excavation, at Carthage, in Cyprus and in Israel. Currently engaged on a major excavation at Ashkelon, one of the most important sites on the east Mediterranean coast, he has been one of the more innovative students of the early Israelite period as he prepares Callaway's Iron I material from Ai and Khirbet Raddanah for publication (p. 163). As thoroughly as anyone he has brought concepts drawn from anthropology and sociology, as well as ecology and ethnoarchaeology, to bear upon the traditional source materials provided by the Old Testament and 'dirt' archaeology. In doing so he has urged wider research perspectives, more comprehensive explanations, and a less obsessive concern with 'the idol of origins'. He made his general position clear in a brief response at a Conference:

> So long as the Late Bronze Age markets and exchange networks were still operating, the sheep-goat pastoralists would have found specialization in animal husbandry a worthwhile occupation. However, with the decline of these economic systems in many parts of Canaan . . . the 'pastoralist' sector, engaged in herding and huckstering, may also have found it advantageous to shift towards different subsistence strategies, such as farming with some stock-raising. This group undoubtedly formed part of the village population that emerged quite visibly in the highlands ca. 1200 B.C.E.

The trend was toward decentralization and ruralization especially in marginal 'frontier' zones, brought about by the decline of the Late Bronze Age city-state and, in certain areas, of Egyptian imperial control. It is in this broader framework that we must then try to locate the more specific causes which led to the emergence of early Israel . . . [17]

The First International Congress of Biblical Archaeology, at which this comment was made, was convened in Jerusalem in 1984 to mark the seventieth anniversary of the Israel Exploration Society (formerly the Jewish Palestine Exploration Society). Political tensions were never very far away from the academic issues debated, since this congress was in no small measure Israel's response to a conference on 'Palestinian Archaeology' sponsored by the Syrians in Aleppo in 1981. On that occasion contemporary political messages were equally implied, if not explicit. The Jerusalem proceedings were published in 1985 as *Biblical Archaeology Today*.

The whole academic thrust of the occasion was to sustain the view that a biblical perspective was not only unavoidable, but essential, for any archaeologist working on sites in Syro-Palestine within the chronological and geographical range of the Old Testament. Current intellectual and overtly political criticisms of the idea of biblical archaeology were acknowledged by some speakers in passing; but the perspective throughout was retrospective rather than prospective: Biblical archaeology yesterday rather than tomorrow. This left little room for critical examination of alternative programmes of archaeological research conceived in the spirit of the 'new' archaeology's programme: 'archaeology today, biblical or otherwise, aims at testing hypotheses, not at demonstrating the verity of preconceived "axioms",' was how one local critic later put the point.[18]

The agenda was the traditional one, with a marked emphasis on archaeology's role in the writing of Israel's cultural history from about 1250 BC and on the support it increasingly offered for the widespread local use of reading and writing, not just for administrative purposes but also for the composition and copying of literary texts, even if the existence of a literate society in Judah before the late seventh century remained an open question. Significantly, the emphasis on periods after, rather than before, the thirteenth century BC implicitly marked a departure from the Albright/Bright/Wright reconstruction of Israel's earliest history with its roots in a patriarchal period fixed through archaeological evidence in the early second millennium BC.

The challenge offered by progressive thinking on aims and methods, (p. 140), which this Congress did not confront, has yet to become the subject of widespread debate within archaeological circles in Israel, though isolated local voices are now heard advocating such a discussion. These critics regret that Israeli archaeology is so firmly bound by traditional concepts, even when field methods are progressive, through too close a concentration on material culture studies and a pervasive nationalism, which is especially apparent, it is argued, in any comparison with the internationalism of the 'new' archaeology.[19] If this debate evolves through the 1990s, it will have important implications for the development of the relationship between archaeology and the Old Testament in Israel.

Archaeology in Jordan: The revision of Glueck's synthesis

Until the 1970s the archaeology of Transjordan was relatively neglected. Pioneering surveys and isolated excavations had thrown random shafts of light across the prehistory and early history of the region, but the data obtained was then almost invariably construed as if the cultural and ecological situation was no different from that in regions to the west of the river Jordan. Time and time again it was assumed that what was true for the better known must be equally true for the lesser known, just as the biblical writers (save for the author of Job) had viewed Transjordan from outside, from the west, from a common point of ignorance. The situation is now radically different after two decades in which the pace of research has increased and the framework within which it is done has become ever more systematic and intellectually rigorous. The accelerating pace of agricultural, industrial and urban development in Jordan stimulated royal concern for the proper administration of the antiquities service and for international involvement in the development of field archaeology of all kinds. Archaeology there is now regularly monitored, and to some extent regulated, by biennial international conferences with published proceedings.[20]

Although excavations have played a significant role in this sharp advance of knowledge, surveys may be judged to have been even more immediately effective. They have established broad patterns of settlement in time and space, which may then be cross-checked by regular resurveying of smaller areas and by select excavations.[21] As in Israel modern research surveys have ranged from detailed study of the environment of a particular *tell*, as at Tell Hesban, to area coverage independent of any focal archaeological site. Salvage or rescue surveys, as in the East Jordan Valley Survey (Ibrahim, Sauer, Yassine 1976), seek to retrieve as much information as possible where agricultural and industrial development is transforming the landscape. More and more attention is paid to improving not only the methods of survey, but also the processing of the evidence they recover. Here again the Hesban Expedition (p. 129) has been a pioneer:

> over the two decades since the first strata were excavated at Tell Hesban . . . the goals of the excavators have expanded from an initial concern with the nature and date of a biblical event, namely the settlement of the Hebrews in this vicinity, to its present broader concern with cultural processes . . . The integrative concept which has offered the best solution to the problem of understanding the various data from Tell Hesban and its vicinity is the ancient food system.[22]

The anticipated evidence for an urban occupation in the earliest phase of the Iron Age was absent; some minor occupation at this time may be witnessed by pottery scattered on bedrock or infills. But the idea that Tell Hesban is ancient Heshbon remains open; whether or not it is neighbouring Jalul remains to be seen. The expanded horizon may downgrade the specific biblical perspective, but the new concentration on integrating patterns of human settlement, land use and diet to understand the processes of sedentarization and nomadization focuses on matters of fundamental, if more general, significance for biblical scholars. This expedition's work, reported to involve 'the most complete computerized database of field information ever assembled in ancient Near Eastern archaeology',[23] epitomizes the changing face of archaeology in the area; changes which emphasize the interconnections of social, economic and cultural systems to focus research programmes on the ways in which such systems are developed, maintained and modified.

Glueck had lived to see a number of revisions enter his pioneering synthesis of the archaeology of Transjordan, but in the twenty years since his death his whole model has been radically reconsidered in the light of numerous surveys, many by expatriate archaeologists, in northern, central and southern Jordan.[24] Glueck's view of the Early Bronze Age and its aftermath in the area has been largely sustained, though now wholly divorced from attempts to establish its final phase as the setting for the Abraham narratives. But his conclusion that there was a virtual absence of settlement for much of the second millennium BC has been radically revised, at least for northern and central Jordan, where settlement sites have histories comparable with those in Canaan to the west. Southwards the situation remains rather less clear, but a steadily increasing body of information on settlement patterns looks equally detrimental to Glueck's conception. This may no longer be used to sustain arguments for a late or thirteenth-century BC, rather than an earlier, date for the entry of Israel into Canaan from the east, as Glueck and many of his contemporaries believed. Although the population of Transjordan in the Late Bronze Age is commonly referred to as 'Canaanite-Amorite', there are so far neither inscriptions nor elements of material culture which permit archaeologists to elucidate the problem of ethnicity at this time with confidence. Whether there were or were not Israelites there, remains an open question.

It is now generally thought that Glueck was probably right to see the earliest evidence of an Ammonite, Edomite and Moabite presence in the remains of Iron Age IA (c. 1200-1000 BC), though he dated some of the painted pottery styles of Transjordan too early. In northern and central Transjordan many small settlements were similar to those in the highland region west of the Jordan so intensively surveyed by Israeli archaeologists (p. 163), whilst in the south they were more substantial, with different types of pottery and perhaps slightly later in date. A distinctive urban culture is only attested in the north Jordan valley at sites like Deir 'Alla (Franken), Tell el-Mazar (Yassine), Tell es-Saidiyeh (Pritchard, Tubb) and Pella (Hennessy and others), where enduring Canaanite traditions were modified by contacts with the so-called 'Sea Peoples', including the Philistines, in a manner not yet fully elucidated.

The time of the United Monarchy, when biblical tradition (cf. 2 Samuel 8-12) indicates Israelite domination east of the Jordan, remains archaeologically less well known, though pottery styles indicate growing western contacts. Glueck's view of the mature Iron Age in Transjordan has also been subject to major reconsideration in the light of a rich variety of new evidence. Although the northern part may have suffered when Assyria destroyed the kingdom of Israel in the third quarter of the eighth century BC, settlements in Ammon, Edom and Moab flourished as they continued to do down through the Persian period, contrary to Glueck's negative view of this phase. The archaeological evidence from Ammon, in particular, in recent years shows that she did not suffer from the impact of the Neo-Babylonian campaigns in Judah, indeed she entered upon a period of marked prosperity (cf. 2 Kings 24-5; Jeremiah 39-41). In fact this corresponds, better than Glueck's conclusions, with the biblical indications that when the Jews returned from the Exile to Jerusalem, Ammonites, Idumaeans and possibly Moabites were numbered amongst their successful opponents (cf. Nehemiah 2-13).

In Transjordan, as west of the River, epigraphic evidence from the Iron Age is distinguished more by the steady accumulation of minor finds, primarily inscribed seals and ostraca, than by spectacular objects like the seventh century inscribed bronze bottle from Tell Siran (Amman) listing Kings of Ammon.[25] A clay bulla found in excavations at Tell 'Umeiri bears the inscription, 'Belonging to Milkom-or, the servant of Baalyasha', the Baalis, King of the Ammonites mentioned in Jeremiah 40:14.[26] But such direct points of reference remain very rare; the Moabite Stone (p. 20) is still the major extra-biblical text of the Iron Age recovered from Transjordan.

Current research in Jordan, even more perhaps than in Israel, suggests that it is anthropological archaeology which is yielding the best new evidence and insights for understanding the biblical record of culture and history. Considerable attention is now being paid to investigating how far the process of sedentarization in antiquity resembled the same process as observed first by travellers and more recently by Ottoman and Mandate administrators, whose insights have proved particularly fruitful in elucidating the archaeological data increasingly available. Such information on the reverse process of nomadization is rare, since it is less common phenomenon in the modern Near East, but no less relevant for students of the transience of sedentary occupation east of the Jordan in biblical times. The archaeology of Transjordan has come a long way in a short time, perhaps because it has been less inhibited by axiomatic views and has been able to benefit from the trial of new methods elsewhere.

Towards a New Testament Archaeology?

It is widely acknowledged that New Testament scholars have paid, and largely continue to pay, relatively little attention to archaeology. Students of early Christianity and Jewish Studies place almost exclusive emphasis on the written word, although recent excavations in major cities like Caesarea and Jerusalem within ancient Palestine, and at numerous sites relevant to the dispersion of Christians and Jews outside Palestine from the later first century AD, have revealed a wealth of fresh information relevant to the New Testament period. When Albright[27] treated the relationship between archaeology and New Testament studies in his time he observed that archaeology's potential contribution is much more circumscribed than for the Old Testament, since the events the New Testament recounts involve private persons rather than public figures (with rare exceptions) active over less than a third of a century. However, archaeology's contribution to the manuscript tradition of the New Testament, largely through discoveries of documents in Egypt, had undermined critical views of the dating and authenticity of the New Testament books argued in the previous century. Textless archaeology

Albright cited little, save for its role in showing the devastating impact on Palestine of Rome's defeat of the First Jewish Revolt and in elucidating the historical geography of Palestine in the first century AD. Nor was Wright much more expansive in *Biblical Archaeology* (1956).

A decade later Finegan's comprehensive *The Archaeology of the New Testament: the life of Jesus and of the Early Church* (1969), which virtually confines itself to Palestine, illustrates the persistence of the traditional pattern of the subject. His approach is not far removed in method from that found in books on archaeology and the Old Testament written half a century earlier. It is primarily a topographical study of Christ's ministry, through descriptions of swift visits to the Holy Places, illustrated from the monuments. It is therefore to a marked degree concerned with the material culture of periods later than the first century AD, since that is what is most accessible at the relevant sites. It concerns itself throughout more with received opinion than with critical inquiry: 'with this book in hand one may go, it is hoped, either in actuality or in imagination and study, "to the East . . . to the place where these things were preached and done"'. There is no sign here of the methodological convulsions evident elsewhere at the time in biblical archaeology. Indeed, some twenty years later it is still hard to find literature seriously concerned with the role of modern archaeology in study of the New Testament world.[28]

The terms in which such research might be pursued were briefly, but forcefully, set out in a lecture given over a decade ago by Koester, a New Testament professor at Harvard who has continued to pursue a quest for relevant archaeological information.[29] Arguing that strictly speaking there was no such thing as 'New Testament Archaeology', he proposed a programme of research firmly set within the broad cultural and geographical context of the late Hellenistic and early Imperial Roman Worlds. New Testament archaeology had to avoid being a mere postscript to Old Testament archaeology, whilst being something much more than an Early Christian Archaeology which ran the risk of being reduced to what has irreverently been called the 'archaeology of the empty tomb'. Indeed, if it is the urge to prove the Bible right that has done so much to compromise Old Testament archaeology for generations, then it is a naive archaeology of the Holy Places that has left New Testament archeology in an academic limbo, whence the work of distinguished pioneer scholars like Ramsay failed to release it long ago (p. 21).

As Koester sharply pointed out, 'it is in no way possible to define such archaeological scholarship in terms of geographical or cultural limitations of the history of a particular people, since the early Christian churches did not have such identity'. This is the problem in a nutshell. Students of Old Testament archeology need to a greater or lesser extent to operate within the entire ancient Near East, but Palestine remains central to their concerns at all times. New Testament archaeology belongs to a much wider and even more culturally varied world, where Palestine is peripheral. At a time of increasing academic specialization, when centres of learning are still too often divided by traditional distinctions between study of one cultural area or another in antiquity, any interdisciplinary study which crosses so many frontiers of ideology, language and history, is all too likely not to establish itself on either side of the line, despite energetic advocates.

In recent years an increasing number of trends have improved the situation, potentially at least, for the greater integration of archaeology and New Testament studies. Although the impact of the Dead Sea Scrolls on modern understanding of early Christianity has been less radical than some of the initial studies had anticipated, their study has raised new questions and opened fresh perspectives by illuminating so unexpectedly the socio-religious *milieu* within Palestinian Jewry whence the new creed had come. Archaeology, though evidence for the first century is sparse, increasingly suggests that there was no wholesale emigration from Palestine of Christians and Jews after the First Jewish Revolt was suppressed, as had long been assumed. Significant populations of both groups remained, creating widespread cultural and religious pluralism, with Christian and Jewish places-of-worship closely associated. It is this apparently harmonious relationship that makes the archaeological investigation complex and fascinating.

The remarkable range of research now underway on major sites of the Herodian period and the first century AD has already been noted, not least in Jerusalem (p. 121). It is here also that modern team archaeology increasingly plays a part, though not always with the degree of co-ordination that might seem most effective. At Caesarea, the capital after the fall of Jerusalem in AD 70, varieties of method, nationality and purpose are perhaps to be seen at their greatest. The theatre was dug by the Italians, the Crusader city and the Jewish quarter with its synagogue by the Israelis, the harbour by teams from universities in Haifa, Colorado and Maryland, with other North American teams variously engaged on other parts of this extensive site. The Joint Expedition to Caesarea Maritima, inaugurated by Bull in 1971, alone has embraced some twenty sponsoring institutions. Here, as in the intensive research on other sites of the Roman Imperial period in Palestine, the emphasis is either on

Graeco-Roman or on Jewish aspects of their culture over an extended period of time; but there is an ever growing body of information relevant to the study of the New Testament in its homeland.

The larger part of the New Testament, however, is set outside Palestine, within the wider Graeco-Roman world. Mobility within that frame is at the heart of the matter, as Ramsay appreciated over a century ago when he began a lifetime's research into Paul's journeys through Asia Minor and Greece, attempting to corroborate the biblical account through detailed archaeological investigation (p. 21). The purpose endures, but the focus has changed, since attempts to prove New Testament narratives have been discredited in favour of sharpening modern understanding of the complex and varied social and cultural settings of the Christian congregations addressed in Paul's Letters. Here, as in the relationship between archaeology and the Old Testament text, the case for authenticity has been superseded by the quest for context, broadly defined.

Archaeology and Biblical Studies in 1990: divorce or reconciliation?

As the 1980s came to a close it was apparent that the debate over biblical archaeology as pursued in North America had lost much of its vibrance, whilst a change of emphasis in Old Testament studies lessened tension at the point where Syro-Palestinian archaeology and Biblical Studies meet. The prime focus of progressive biblical scholarship, at least for the Old Testament, had changed from history to literature. The pursuit of those events in history which had formed the biblical traditions, whether through the methods advocated by American, French, German or Israeli scholars, had slipped to a lower place on many academic agendas. At the same time radical biblical scholars, no less than advocates of the new archaeology within Syro-Palestinian studies, were calling for a sharper separation of disciplines:

> No less than Syro-Palestinian archaeology, Israelite history must proceed as a discipline independent of biblical exegesis. So too, biblical exegesis needs to be understood as an historical-critical discipline with its own autonomy apart from historical and archaeological research.[30]

The younger historians of ancient Israel were now also beginning to respond to the challenge provided by anthropology and sociology, as modern historians had been doing for two generations and archaeologists for the past thirty years.[31] The impact of the social sciences has brought to history as much as it did to archaeology a greater concentration on the general and the long term (*longue durée*), as distinct from the specific and the short term (*l'histoire evenementielle*). This change of perspective, particularly associated in history writing with scholars who have contributed to the French journal *Annales* since its foundation in 1929, has long been maturing, as Braudel pointed out:

> This search for a history outside the confines of the event was imposed imperiously by contact with the other human sciences. . . From that time [1929] on, history busied itself in dealing with recurrent events as well as individual occurrences, conscious and unconscious realities alike. From that time on, the historian has wanted to be, and has become, an economist, sociologist, anthropologist, demographer, psychologist, linguist.[32]

The more such a programme is emulated by writers of Israel's early history, the closer they will come to archaeologists thinking as social scientists in the manner championed by the American archaeological reformers of the 1960s (p. 140), the pioneer 'new' archaeologists who seek to reconstruct the social world of antiquity in the widest sense.[33]

So long as paraphrases of the Old Testament, to a greater or lesser extent correlated with information obtained through excavation, served as the framework for histories of ancient Israel the tension between biblical scholars and progressive archaeologists was likely to endure. With the emergence of a broader conception of such histories the data being sought and interpreted by the best of contemporary archaeologists are likely to be more easily accommodated by biblical scholarship. Indeed, it becomes a vital part of the database from which such histories will be written. Archaeological evidence, no longer invoked simply to control political narratives, will not necessarily be less controversial, but it is likely to be more obviously relevant to biblical scholars concerned with the economic and social history of ancient Israel.

The problem of communication between disciplines remains fundamental, much more complex than it was a century ago, when it was already inhibiting enough. Full or 'final' reports on excavations and surveys have always been rare. They become rarer as the intensity of research increases and the range and variety of the evidence to be processed steadily grows. These changes have conspired to make the reports which do appear less readable and less cohesive than was the convention a generation ago. Neither the pioneers of improved field techniques in the 1950s and 1960s nor the advocates of anthropological archaeology in the 1970s and 1980s resolved the basic problem of the effective and relatively rapid publication of their key data: that challenge remains. It is only very slowly being realized that the requirements of the final report should be in the excavator's mind from day one, evolving as he proceeds, and that each dig season should ideally be complemented by a study or preparation for publication season on site before a new round of digging. Time remorselessly modifies excavation teams; people come and go, their commitments change with equal speed and unpredictability.

Even as carefully considered a publication programme as that for Gezer[34] has left all attempts at synthesis to a final volume likely to appear decades after the first. Meanwhile a succession of highly technical volumes make few concessions to professional archaeologists, none to a wider readership. In 1989 the twenty-fifth anniversary of the first season at Gezeer was celebrated at an international conference, where one speaker noted that 'it is now 18 years after the completion of Gezer Phase I and we have a long way to go . . . .' He was also painfully aware that his own projected study of the small finds 'will probably now have to be done by another generation'.[35]

It may now be seen that biblical archaeology in the decades between 1920 and 1970 was too often distinguished by reliance on the pronouncements *ex cathedra* of a few dominant archaeologists who had grown up with the subject. Where relatively little was known, and even less widely available in print, simplistic explanations easily gained the status of axioms. The increasing number of scholars now involved and the information explosion of the last thirty years, combined with a wholly new conception of archaeology, have largely dethroned such authorities and shattered consensus. In the next decade those who seek what archaeology has to offer towards elucidation of biblical problems will have to relocate the areas of interdependence. With the wisdom of a broad separation of archaeological and textual evidence for purposes of study and research now widely accepted, so that they may be structured through the concepts and models thought most appropriate to them, the contentious issues are increasingly likely to lie elsewhere. There will need, above all, to be no less vigilance in ensuring that the anthropological and sociological models of today do not come to prejudice explanation in biblical archaeology in the way the historical hypotheses of yesterday may now be seen to have done.

An American scholar recently defined the purpose of biblical archaeology in a resoundingly traditional way as: 'the clarification and illumination of the biblical text and content through archaeological investigation of the biblical world':[36] a definition Birch and Albright would have endorsed. It is, in short, an aspect of Biblical Studies rather than a branch of archaeology; misunderstandings and tensions in the past have usually arisen when the reverse was taken for granted.

1 A. Momigliano, 'Biblical Studies and Classical Studies: simple reflections about historical method', *B.A.* 45 (1982), p. 224.

2 G.E. Wright, 'The "New Archaeology"', *B.A.* 38 (1975), p. 112.

3 D.N. Freedman, 'From the Editor's Desk', *B.A.* 45 (1982), p. 196.

4 P. Matthiae, *Ebla: an Empire Rediscovered*, London, 1980, p. 11; see also P. Matthiae, *Ebla. Un impero ritrovato: Dai primi scavi ultime scoperte*, Rome, 1988, pp. xix-xxi.

5 G. Pettinato, 'Ebla and the Bible', *B.A.* 43 (1980), pp. 203-206; cf. A. Archi, 'Further concerning Ebla and the Bible', *B.A.* 44 (1981), pp. 145-154.

6 D.N. Freedman, 'The real story of the Ebla Tablets: Ebla and the Cities of the Plain', *B.A.* 41 (1978), p. 143.

7 T.L. Thompson, *The Historicity of the Patriarchal Narratives: the Quest for the Historical Abraham*, Berlin, 1974, pp. 3-4.

8 Ibid., p. 3; J. van Seters, *Abraham in History and Tradition*, New Haven, 1975, covers much the same ground from a different perspective, but fundamentally in agreement with Thompson's critique of Albright's procedures.

9 J.M. Miller, 'Archaeology and the Israelite Conquest of Canaan: some methodological observations', *P.E.Q.* 109 (1977), p. 88.

10 N. Lemche, *Early Israel: Anthropological and Historical Studies on the Israelite Society before the Monarchy*, Leiden, 1985, p. 216.

11 Ibid., pp. 216-219.

12 G. London, 'A comparison of two contemporaneous life styles of the Late Second Millennium B.C.', *B.A.S.O.R.* 273 (1989), pp. 51-52.

13 See Z. Meshel, *Kuntillet 'Ajrud: A Religious Centre from the Time of the Judaean Monarchy on the Border of Sinai*, Israel Museum, Jerusalem, 1978; P. Beck, 'The drawings from Horvat Teiman (Kuntillet 'Ajrud)', *Tel Aviv* 9 (1982), pp. 3-68; for bibliography to 1990 see: B. Margalit, 'The meaning and significance of Asherah', *Vetus Testamentum* XL (1990), pp. 264-297.

14 Y. Shiloh, 'A group of Hebrew bullae from the City of David', *I.E.J.* 36 (1986), pp. 16-38; cf. T. Schneider, 'Azariahu, Son of Hilkiahu (High Priest?) on a City of David bulla', *I.E.J.* 38 (1988), pp. 139-141.

15 N. Avigad, 'Baruch the scribe and Jerahmeel the King's son', *I.E.J.* 28 (1978), pp. 52-56.

16 N. Na'aman, 'Hezekiah's fortified sites and the LMLK stamps', *B.A.S.O.R.* 261 (1986), pp. 5-21.

17 J. Aviram (ed.), *Biblical Archaeology Today*, Jerusalem, 1985, p. 85.

18 A. Rainey, *Review of Biblical Archaeology Today* in *B.A.S.O.R.* 273 (1989), p. 88.

19 For a traditional survey see: O. Bar Yosef and Amihai Mazar 'Israeli Archaeology', *World Archaeology* 13 (1982), pp. 310-323, with a concentration on the periods of Biblical significance; for a radical view: T. Shay, 'Israeli archaeology - ideology and practice', *Antiquity* 241 (1989), pp. 768-772; see also W.G. Dever, 'Yigael Yadin: prototypical Biblical archaeologist', *Eretz Israel* 20 (1989), pp. 44*-51*.

20 *Studies in the History and Archaeology of Jordan* (ed. A. Hadidi), Department of Antiquities, Amman I (1982), II (1985), III (1987).

21 G.L. Mattingly, 'Settlement patterns and sociocultural reconstruction', in J.F. Drinkard and others (eds.) *Benchmarks in Time and Culture*, Atlanta, Georgia, 1988, pp. 389-415.

22 O.S. La Bianca, 'Sociocultural anthropology and Syro-Palestinian Archaeology', in *Benchmarks* (note 21), pp. 374-375.

23 J.F. Strange, 'Computers and archaeological research' in *Benchmarks* (note 21), p. 311.

24 Cf. J. Sauer, 'Transjordan in the Bronze and Iron Ages: a critique of Glueck's synthesis', *B.A.S.O.R.* 263 (1986), pp. 1ff; R.G. Boling, *The Early Biblical Community in Transjordan* (1988).

25 H.O. Thompson, 'The Tell Siran bottle: an additional note', *B.A.S.O.R.* 249 (1983), pp. 87-89.

26 L.G. Herr, 'The servant of Baalis', *B.A.* 48 (1985), pp. 169ff.

27 *The Archaeology of Palestine* (1960), chapter 11.

28 Or Judaic studies at the time: E.M. Meyers, 'Judaic studies and archaeology, the legacy of Avi-Yona', *Eretz Israel* 19 (1987): 21*-27*; cf. E.M. Meyers and J.F. Strange, *Archaeology, the Rabbis and Early Christianity* (1981).

29 H. Koester, 'New Testament and Archaeology', *A.S.O.R. Newsletter*, March 1978.

30 T.L. Thompson, *The Origin Tradition of Ancient Israel I: The Literary Formation of Genesis and Exodus 1-23*, Sheffield, 1987, p. 40.

31 This new integration of the social sciences, including the evidence of archaeology, with the writing of ancient Israel's history is well illustrated by the work of a younger generation of scholars appearing in the series: *Social World of Biblical Antiquity*, published by the Almond Press (University of Sheffield, England and Columbia Theological Seminary in Decatur, Georgia, U.S.A.).

32 F. Braudel, *On History*, London, 1980, p. 68.

33   See recently C. and E. Meyers, 'Expanding the frontiers of Biblical Archaeology', *Eretz Israel* 20 (1989), pp. 140*-147*.

34 W.G. Dever (editor), *Gezer* I (1970), II (1974), III (forthcoming), IV (1986), Annual of the Hebrew Union College/Nelson Glueck School of Biblical Archaeology, Jerusalem.

35 *Biblical Archaeology Review XVI* (2) (1990), p. 28.

36 J.K. Eakins in J.E. Drinkard and others (editors), *Benchmarks in Time and Culture*, Atlanta, Georgia, 1988, p. 441.

Brief Glossary

Baulk: an unexcavated strip in an excavation left to provide visual evidence for the sequence of debris when surrounding areas have been removed by digging (see also *stratigraphy*).

Baulk/debris-layer method: the basic assumptions of this excavation procedure are: that baulks (or sections) will separate the excavation areas to act as regular controls; that digging will proceed stratigraphically following the bedlines of the levels of debris; and that measured drawings will be made *on site* of the sections.

Documentary hypothesis: in its classic form, particularly associated with the German biblical scholar Julius Wellhausen (1844-1918), this hypothesis proposed four literary sources as the primary elements in the Pentateuch or Hexateuch which, in chronological order, are J (Jehovist or Yahwist), E (Elohist), D (Deuteronomist) and P (Priestly Code). J, the oldest, has been assigned to the tenth or ninth century BC.

Fill: rubbish or soil brought in to level uneven ground.

Form criticism: the type of biblical criticism pioneered by the German scholar Hermann Gunkel (1862-1932) which investigated the history of different forms of literature and their relationships to their social settings (*Sitz im Leben*).

Glacis: a sloping bank, usually plastered, at the external foot of a fortification wall to make attack more difficult.

Higher Criticism: a term introduced into Biblical Studies in the late eighteenth century. It does not describe an exaggerated form of ordinary criticism rather a particular type, distinct from *lower* (see below) criticism. Its purpose is to determine the date, literary structure (if composite) and origin of the books of the Old Testament with the assistance of all relevant evidence. Strictly speaking, though much obscured in fact, historical problems fall outside its traditional range.

Khirbet: Arabic for 'ruin'; used to describe an ancient site with remains visible on the surface.

Layer: a level of build-up in a mound (see also *level* and *stratum*, under *stratigraphy*).

Levels: the various layers of debris recognized in an excavation are conventionally called *levels* or *strata* (see also stratigraphy).

Locus (plural: *loci*): unit(s) distinguished within an area of excavation.

Lower Criticism: the study of manuscripts and variant readings (see also *Higher Criticism*).

Ostracon (plural: *ostraca*): Greek for 'potsherd'; used by archaeologists to describe any fragment of pottery, bone or wood used to write on. As papyrus was expensive, ostraca were commonly used in Egypt and Palestine for every day purposes to write in the local cursive scripts, but not for the cuneiform script.

Phase: a stage within an occupational level defined by excavation.

Section: a vertical cut, normally the side of an excavation trench which reveals the structure (or *stratigraphy*) of a mound. It is recorded in drawings, properly made on site, confusingly also referred to as 'sections' (i.e. section drawings).

Sounding: a trial excavation, usually to establish an outline stratigraphy before further excavation.

Stratigraphy: is one of the major interpretative principles of field archaeology borrowed from geology. It depends on the fact that where one deposit of debris overlies another, the upper must have accumulated after the lower, since the latter could not have been inserted beneath it. In practice there are numerous modifications to this general rule, for many acts of nature, from earth quakes to burrowing animals, will disturb any orderly sequence of deposits as will interference by man (pits, graves, fills, foundation trenches, etc.). It is the modern archaeologist's main purpose to distinguish one deposit from another by its texture, colour or contents (which may of course include intruders from other levels), and to draw diagrams (*sections*) of a site's stratigraphy so that others may check the interpretation. The various layers of debris so recognized are conventionally called either *levels* or *strata*. (See E. Harris, *Principles of Archaeological Stratigraphy*, Academic Press, 2nd edition, London, 1989).

Tel (Hebrew); *Tell* (Arabic): artificial mounds which commonly represent the debris of ancient towns and villages in the Near East.

Typology: the study and classification of man-made objects (which may include texts) through shared characteristics.

Select Bibliography

This section is simply intended to sign-post the reader into the enormous bibliography of the relationship between archaeology and Biblical Studies. Titles marked with an asterisk will be found especially useful for their range of bibliographical reference. Much specific bibliographical information will be found in the text and footnotes of this book.

Aharoni, Y. *The Archaeology of the Land of Israel*, London, 1982.

Albright, W.F. *The Archaeology of Palestine and the Bible*, reprinted by the American Schools of Oriental Research, 1974 (original edition: University of Virginia, 1931).

Albright, W.F. *The Archaeology of Palestine*, revised edition, Pelican Books, 1963.

Aviram, J. (ed.) *Biblical Archaeology Today: Proceedings of the International Congress of Biblical Archaeology, Jerusalem, April 1984*, Jerusalem, 1985.

* Avi-Yonah, M. and Stern, E. (eds.) *Encyclopaedia of Archaeological Excavations in the Holy Land*, 1-4, Oxford and Tel Aviv, 1975-8.

Ben-Arieh, Y. *The Rediscovery of the Holy Land in the Nineteenth Century*, Magnes Press, Jerusalem; Detroit: Wayne State University, 1989.

Bernal, M. *Black Athena: the Afroasiatic Roots of Classical Civilization I: The Fabrication of Ancient Greece 1785-1985*, Free Association Books, London, 1987 (for its review of Phoenician studies, pp. 337ff.).

Besant, W. *Twenty-One Years' Work in the Holy Land*, P.E.F., London, 1886.

Besant, W. *Thirty Years' Work in the Holy Land*, P.E.F., London, 1895.

Bliss, F.J. *The Development of Palestine Exploration*, London, 1906.

Daniel, G. and Renfrew, C. *A Hundred and Fifty Years of Archaeology*, London, 1975.

Dever, W.G. *Recent Archaeological Discoveries and Biblical Research*, Seattle and London, 1990.

*Drinkard, J.F. and others (eds.) *Benchmarks in Time and Culture: an introduction to Palestine Archaeology dedicated to Joseph A. Callaway*, Atlanta, Georgia, 1988. (This volume contains five historical essays on the contribution of American, British, French, German and Israeli archaeologists which, together with a variety of other papers on aims and methods, constitute a 'state of the art' review).

Driver, S.R. *Modern Research as illustrating the Bible* (Schweich Lectures 1908), London, 1909.

Franken, H.J. and Franken-Battershill, C.A. *A Primer of Old Testament Archaeology*, Leiden, 1963.

Freedman D.N. and others *The Published Works of William Foxwell Albright: a comprehensive bibliography*, A.S.O.R., Cambridge, Mass., 1975.

Hilprecht, H.V. *Explorations in Bible Lands during the 19th Century*, Edinburgh, 1903.

*Homès-Fredericq, D. and Hennessy, J.B. (eds.) *Archaeology of Jordan I: Bibliography of surveys and sites*, Leuven, 1986; I(1): *books and articles (1986-8)*, Leuven, forthcoming; II: *Field Reports: survey and sites*, Leuven, 1989.

James, T.G.H. (ed.) *Excavating in Egypt: the Egypt Exploration Society 1882-1982*, British Museum, London, 1982.

*Kenyon, K.M. *Archaeology in the Holy Land* (4th edition), London, 1979 (includes a concise site bibliography).

*King, P.J. *American Archaeology in the Mideast: a History of the American Schools of Oriental Research*, A.S.O.R., Philadelphia, 1983.

Kuhnen, H-P. *Palästina in Griechisch-Romischer Zeit*, Münich, 1990.

Macalister, R.A.S. *A Century of Excavation in Palestine*, London, 1925.

Perdue, L.G., Toombs, L.E., Johnson, G.L. (eds.) *Archaeology and Biblical Interpretation*, Atlanta, 1987.

Saggs, H.W.F. *Assyriology and the Study of the Old Testament*, University of Wales Press, 1969.

Shepherd, N. *The Zealous Intruders: The Western Rediscovery of Palestine*, London, 1987; San Francisco, 1988.

Silbermann, N.A. *Digging for God and Country: Exploration, Archaeology and the Secret Struggle for the Holy Land 1799-1917*, New York, 1982.

Winton Thomas, D. (ed.) *Archaeology and Old Testament Study*, Oxford, 1967.

Trigger, B.G.   *A History of Archaeological Thought*, Cambridge, 1989.

Van Beek, G.W. (ed.)   *The Scholarship of William Foxwell Albright: an appraisal*   Harvard Semitic Studies, Scholars Press, 1989.

*Vogel, E.K. and Holtzclaw, B.   *Bibliography of Holy Land Sites* I-II; originally published in the *Hebrew Union College Annual* (Cincinnati) XLII (1971), pp. 1-96 and LII (1981), pp. 1-92; then printed separately: I (1974); II (1982).

Watson, C.M.   *Fifty Years of Work in the Holy Land*, P.E.F., London, 1915.

*Weippert, H.   *Palästina in vorhellenistischer Zeit* (Handbuch der Archäologie Vorderasien II (Band I), München, 1988.

Willey, G.R. and Sabloff, J.A.   *A History of American Archaeology* (revised edition), San Francisco, 1980.

INDEX OF PERSONAL NAMES

184

186

INDEX OF PLACES

187

189